T0361147

Unemployment and Social Exclusion

Regional Policy and Development Series

Series Editor: Ron Martin, Department of Geography, University of Cambridge

Throughout the industrialised world, widespread economic restructuring, rapid technological change, the reconfiguration of State intervention, and increasing globalisation are giving greater prominence to the nature and performance of individual regional and local economies within nations. The old patterns and processes of regional development that characterised the post-war period are being fundamentally redrawn, creating new problems of uneven development and new theoretical and policy challenges. Whatever interpretation of this contemporary transformation is adopted, regions and localities are back on the academic and political agenda. *Regional Policy and Development* is an international series which aims to provide authoritative analyses of this new regional political economy. It seeks to combine fresh theoretical insights with detailed empirical enquiry and constructive policy debate to produce a comprehensive set of conceptual, practical and topical studies in this field. The series is not intended as a collection of synthetic reviews, but rather as original contributions to understanding the processes, problems and policies of regional and local economic development in today's changing world.

Unemployment and Social Exclusion

Landscapes of Labour Inequality

Edited by Paul Lawless, Ron Martin and Sally Hardy

Regional Policy and Development 13

LONDON AND NEW YORK

Regional Studies Association
London

All rights reserved. No paragraph of this publication may be reproduced, copied or transmitted save with written permission or in accordance with the provisions of the Copyright Act 1956 (as amended), or under the terms of any licence permitting limited copying issued by the Copyright Licensing Agency, 33–34 Alfred Place, London WC1E 7DP. Any person who does any unauthorised act in relation to this publication may be liable to criminal prosecution and civil claims for damages.

The right of the contributors to be identified as authors of this work has been asserted by them in accordance with the Copyright, Designs and Patents Act 1988.

First published in the United Kingdom in 1998 by
Jessica Kingsley Publishers Ltd

Published 2004 by Routledge
2 Park Square, Milton Park, Abingdon, Oxon OX14 4RN
711 Third Avenue, New York, NY 10017, USA

First issued in hardback 2017

Routledge is an imprint of the Taylor & Francis Group, an informa business

with
the Regional Studies Association
Registered Charity 252269

Copyright © 1998 Jessica Kingsley Publishers

Library of Congress Cataloguing in Publication Data
A CIP catalogue record for this book is available from the Library of Congress

British Library Cataloguing in Publication Data
A CIP catalogue record for this book is available from the British Library

ISBN 13: 978-1-138-46496-4 (hbk)
ISBN 13: 978-0-11-702375-8 (pbk)

Contents

List of Figures

List of Tables

Preface

The past two decades have been a period of intense change and upheaval in the labour markets of the industrialised countries. In contrast to the full employment conditions of the long post-war boom, the 1980s and 1990s have witnessed the return of high and relentless unemployment. Whereas in the early 1970s some 10 million people were officially recorded as jobless in the OECD countries, by the early 1990s this had escalated to more than 30 million. As the OECD commented in its recent *Jobs Study: Labour Market Trends and Underlying Forces of Change* (1994), unemployment on this scale, 'represents an enormous waste of resources … It reflects both economic inefficiency and human distress. Its persistence is bound to undermine social cohesion and confidence in democratic institutions and market economies' (p.2). At the same time, the nature of employment has also been changing in dramatic ways, involving substantial shifts away from male to female labour, from full-time to part-time work and from unskilled to skilled occupations. Together with unemployment, these shifts have had profound implications for the earning structure, and in some countries – especially the United States and the United Kingdom – income inequalities have widened markedly. As a result of these intersecting developments in the labour market, certain social groups have become increasingly excluded from the mainstream of social and economic life. Furthermore, the incidence of unemployment, low incomes and social exclusion has been distinctly uneven as between different regions and localities within individual nations. In many countries geographical disparities in unemployment and incomes have widened substantially: location has been a key factor in shaping the social incidence of labour market exclusion. These geographical inequalities are the focus of this book.

Many of the contributions are substantially revised versions of papers originally given at recent conferences held by the Regional Studies Association. They cover various aspects of the contemporary landscape of unemployment and associated social exclusion across the European Union as a whole and the United Kingdom more particularly. They also focus on a variety of spatial scales, from the broad regional level down to the urban and local scale. Three themes weave their way through these papers. The first is that the processes of unemployment and social exclusion have an important local level of operation: labour market dynamics are, in part, locally constituted. The second is that official definitions and counts of unemployment are becoming increasingly unreliable as guides to the true scale of joblessness and its spatial incidence, and that wider measures of 'non-employment' are needed to give a complete picture of the landscape of labour market inequality. The third is that locally focused policy interventions and innovations have a vital role to play in helping to reduce the problems of high rates of unemployment, employment insecurity and low incomes that have become entrenched in many of the advanced economies.

Editing a volume such as this necessarily depends on the efforts and patience of the individual contributors, and we are grateful to them all. We also wish to thank Jessica Kingsley for her encouragement. No attempt was made to force the contributions into any single overarching theoretical or conceptual framework, and the reader will be aware of significant differences in orientation and emphasis. But we hope that the collection as a whole will be of interest and value not only to geographers and regional economists, but to all of those concerned with the contemporary unemployment problem.

Paul Lawless
Ron Martin
Sally Hardy

CHAPTER I

Regional Dimensions
of Europe's Unemployment Crisis

Ron Martin

Introduction

During the period from 1945 to the early 1970s, the OECD countries enjoyed what, in retrospect, appears as a 'golden age' in terms of their labour market performance, an era of full employment, job security, rising real incomes and increasing social equality in economic welfare and opportunity. Although there were recurring recessions when employment fell, these were essentially minor interruptions to an otherwise unprecedently buoyant labour market, and for the most part the unemployment that existed was short term and frictional. Many of the advanced countries seemed to have achieved a workable blend of economic efficiency and social equity. Western Europe in particular appeared to be successful in applying the Keynesian-welfarist economic policy model, a form of state intervention in which macroeconomic demand management was used to maintain full employment and a redistributive-tax-and-benefit transfer-based welfare system was used to limit the extremes of wealth and poverty.[1]

In stark contrast to that period, the past two decades have been a period of intense change and upheaval in the OECD economies. Most, if not all, of the labour market certainties and verities of the long post-war boom have been undermined. In contrast to those boom years, since the beginning of the 1980s the labour market has become characterised by increasing uncertainty, insecurity, risk and inequality. One of the most traumatic develop-

---

1. Of course, the precise form of Keynesian-welfarism varied between individual countries (see Esping-Andersen 1990; Hall 1989), as did the scale of welfare spending. But in most cases the basic aim was the same, namely to minimise the extent of unemployment via fiscal and monetary policies and to provide some form of basic social wage in terms of income support and various welfare benefits.

ments, without doubt, has been the dramatic rise in joblessness: the spectre of mass unemployment has once again been haunting much of the industrialised world. In the 1950s and 1960s, OECD unemployment averaged less than 10 million. During the early 1970s, however, it began to rise, and in the recession of the mid 1970s peaked at 18 million. In the next downturn of the early 1980s it rose again, very sharply, to 30 million. Strong economic expansion in the second half of the 1980s did bring some reprieve, but failed to drive the jobless total back down to the levels of the 1970s, let alone the 1950s and 1960s, and in the early 1990s recession it increased once more to reach 35 million, the highest on record. Thus in the space of two decades, between 1972 and 1992, the number of unemployed in the OECD had tripled.

At a very aggregate scale, there is a distinctive international geography to the OECD 'jobs problem', in that the growth of unemployment has been much more pronounced in the European Union than in the United States, the EFTA economies, Japan or the Oceania countries. These international differences have been the focus of a formidable corpus of analytical scrutiny, both by economists (for example, Burgess 1994; Freeman 1994; Glyn 1995; Jackman 1995; Krugman 1994a; Rowthorn and Glyn 1990) and by leading international organisations (European Commission 1993; International Labour Organisation (ILO) 1995; OECD 1994a,b,c). But, equally, there are marked regional and local disparities in the incidence of unemployment and labour market exclusion within individual countries. These regional and sub-regional geographies of unemployment and labour market exclusion are the focus of this book. The following chapters highlight the importance of these sub-national geographies. Although the theory of spatial labour markets and their functioning, adjustment and regulation has received increasing attention over the past few years (see, for example, Blanchard and Katz 1992; Campbell and Duffy 1992; Fischer and Nijkamp 1987; Hanson and Pratt 1992; Marston 1985; Martin 1981, 1986; Martin, Sunley and Wills 1996; Peck 1996; Topel 1986), the development of this field of enquiry is still in its infancy.[2] The papers collected here not only make a valuable contribution towards this endeavour, they also provide a much-needed corrective to the characteristically aspatial approach adopted by

2. An arbitrary and simplistic typology of labour market models might distinguish four main categories: (1) the labour market viewed as a straightforward extension of more general market theories; (2) the labour market seen as a special case, subject to special adjustment processes and deviations from the orthodox market concept, but nevertheless explicable by conventional market behaviour analysis; (3) the labour market as an atypical form entailing the introduction of sociological and cultural factors as causes and constraints; and (4) more general socio-institutional models. All four types could be given different degrees of spatial disaggregation and expression.

economists to the current unemployment crisis. In both senses, the essays help to push the labour market issue into the mainstream of regional theory and policy. My aim in this chapter is to set the context for the discussions that follow by examining, in a deliberately discursive manner, some of the key regional dimensions of Europe's unemployment problem.

The Scale of Regional Unemployment Disparities Across the European Union

As has already been noted, the unemployment crisis is far more severe in Europe than in other parts of the advanced industrial world (see, for example, Adnett 1996; Blanchard and Summers 1986; Dreze and Bean 1990; Michie and Grieve Smith 1994; OECD 1994a,b,c; Symes 1995). Throughout the 1950s and 1960s unemployment rates tended to be much higher in the United States than in Europe. However, during the 1970s unemployment rose rapidly in Western Europe, and by the early 1980s it had overtaken the US as a high unemployment area (Figure 1.1). In 1973 the unemployment rate in the European Union was less than 3 per cent, but by 1994 it had increased to more than 11 per cent, nearly double the rate in the US and almost four times that in Japan. Moreover, neither the US nor Japan have

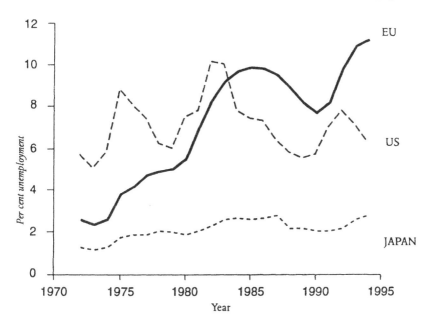

Figure 1.1: Unemployment Rates in the European Union, United States and Japan, 1972–94
Source: OECD (1994a,b,c)

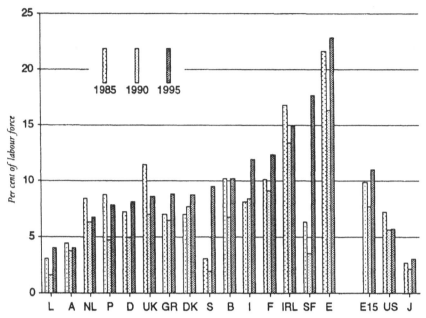

Key: A – Austria; B – Belgium; D– Germany; DK – Denmark; E – Spain; F – France; GR– Greece; I – Italy;
IRL – Ireland; J – Japan; L – Luxembourg; NL – Netherlands; P – Portugal; S – Sweden; SF – Finland;
UK – United Kingdom; US – United States; E15 – European Union 15

Figure 1.2: Unemployment Rates in European Union Countries, the United States and Japan, 1985, 1990 and 1995
Source: European Commission (1995a)

experienced the strong upward trend that has characterised the EU since the
mid 1970s, where the aggregate unemployment rate has tended to rise
further, and fall less, over each successive economic cycle. Unemployment in
the EU increased dramatically during the deep recession of the early 1980s
and continued to increase well after the recession, up to 1985. Although
unemployment fell between 1985 and 1990, when the net addition to jobs
in the Union was greater that at any time over the preceding 30 years, even
at its cyclical trough in 1990 it still remained well above the rate of the late
1970s. The recession of the early 1990s then saw record job losses in the
EU: almost 60 per cent of the extra 10 million jobs created between 1985
and 1990 were lost between 1991 and 1994. As a result, officially recorded
unemployment climbed to its record post-war level of over 18 million.[3]

3. This is the estimate based on the ILO definition of unemployment, that is, those who, during
    any reference week: (1) had no employment, (2) were available to start work within the next
    two weeks, and (3) had actively sought employment at some time during the previous four
    weeks. If a 'broader' definition is used, as is possible using the European Labour Force
    Survey, namely the conventional ILO definition plus those inactive members of the working
    age population who would like to work or are seeking work or who are available for work,
    the estimate of unemployment in the EU increases to nearly 29.5 million.

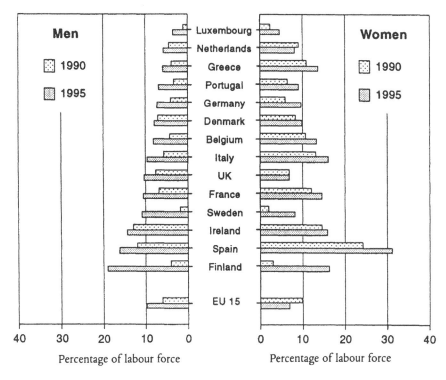

Note: Excludes A, GR June 1994, NL, SF April 1995, all other countries May 1995.

Figure 1.3: Unemployment Rates of Men and Women in European Union Countries, 1990 and 1995
Source: European Commission (1995)

Although the EU-wide unemployment rate stabilised at around 11 per cent during 1995 and 1996, the problem seems unlikely to decline very rapidly in the near future. As the European Commission (1995a, p.7) itself has acknowledged:

> Unemployment remains the major economic – and social problem confronting the Union. The means of achieving a higher rate of employment growth, sustained over a long enough period to bring the numbers out of work down to acceptable levels will, therefore, be a primary issue of policy concern for some time to come.

Moreover, both the scale and characteristics of the unemployment crisis in the European Union vary a good deal between countries and between regions, as do the potential for generating increased rates of job creation and the appropriate policies to pursue. In recent years, the unemployment problem has been most acute in Spain, Finland, Ireland, France and Italy – all with rates above the EU average. Belgium, the UK, Germany, Denmark,

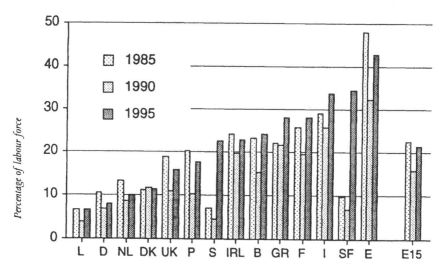

Figure 1.4: Unemployment Rates of Young People (Under 25 years) in European Union Countries, 1985, 1990 and 1995

Source: European Commission (1995a).

the Netherlands, Greece, Portugal and Sweden have tended to have rates below the EU figure but higher than the USA. Austria and Luxembourg have been the exceptions to the rest of Europe in having unemployment rates even lower than the US rate (Figure 1.2). This basic inter-country pattern holds for male, female and youth unemployment. Thus while unemployment rates for women tend to higher than those for men across most of the European Union (the exceptions being Austria, Denmark, Sweden and the UK), they are highest in the Catholic countries such as Spain, Ireland and Italy (Figure 1.3). Unemployment rates among those under 25 years of age are especially high (typically double the total rates) and also vary considerably across member states: in 1994 they ranged from a low of 6.5 per cent in Luxembourg to 45 per cent in Spain (Figure 1.4).[4] Across the Union as a whole,

4. The precise differences between the EU nations are, of course, constantly changing. For example, during 1995 and 1996 the British government made much of the fact that the UK's unemployment had fallen relative to the rest of Europe. While Britain's unemployment rate used to be higher than the EU average, it has now fallen below. This contrast should be viewed cautiously, however, for the evidence suggests that the fall in unemployment in Britain since late 1993 has not been mirrored in the growth of full-time employment, but by an expansion in part-time jobs and an increase in non-employment, that is, a decline in the labour force participation rate (see Morgan 1996). Also, throughout the 1980s Germany enjoyed one of the lowest unemployment rates in the EU, but since unification in 1990 its jobless rate has continued to rise, reaching a post-war peak of 4.14 million (10.8%) by March 1996.

roughly one in five young people are without jobs (compared with about one in eight in the United States).

While these national differences are important, it is at the regional, sub-regional and urban levels that variations in unemployment incidence are particularly significant and problematic (see European Commission 1996a; Symes 1995; Tomaney 1994). Regional and local unemployment disparities, far from being an incidental feature, are an integral component of the general 'jobs problem', and hence also have an important bearing on understanding the nature of that problem and devising policy responses to it. For 'national' labour markets are, in fact, spatially fragmented entities, intricate mosaics of regional and local labour markets. These spatial sub-markets not only mediate wider national and international processes and forces in ways that reflect the local particularities of economic structure, labour force supply and institutional forms, they also stamp their own autonomous imprints on such processes: the specific labour market conditions, opportunities and barriers that individuals face are, to some extent, regionally and locally constituted. In this sense, the unemployment process and the social inequalities which it produces have an intrinsic local level of operation, with the implication that the social exclusion effects that unemployment brings are likely to be compounded by the localised concentration of joblessness. Wide spatial differences in unemployment across the Union thus pose a real challenge to the EU's goal of social cohesion.

In addition, regional disparities in unemployment impinge upon the movement towards European economic and monetary integration. The larger are spatial unemployment disparities, the more they hinder the integration process, since regional and sub-regional imbalances in relative labour de-mand make it difficult to pursue growth in the Union without encountering inflation in the lower unemployment core areas of the Union well before the surplus labour in the high unemployment areas is fully utilised. But at the same time, given that productivity standards, competitiveness and monetary values will be set by the stronger core growth regions in the EU, economic integration and moves towards monetary union and a single currency will tend to exert additional adverse demand and supply pressures on the weaker, low productivity high unemployment regions. Economic and monetary union, therefore, could well exacerbate regional unemployment disparities, particularly in the absence of an EU-wide integrated system of automatic inter-regional fiscal transfers and stabilisers (see Eichengreen 1990, 1995; MacKay 1995).[5] The reduction of these disparities is thus seen as necessary for successful economic and monetary integration.

The problem is that regional differences in joblessness across the EU are considerable: 'The Union's unemployment problem is most acute at the regional and local level. The evidence confirms that it is in terms of unemployment that regional disparities are particularly acute and show little sign of narrowing' (European Commission 1996a, p.25).

For example, in 1995 the average unemployment rate in the 25 worst affected NUTS2 regions was 22.4 per cent, nearly five times the average rate (4.6%) in the 25 least-affected regions.[6] The range in unemployment rates at this regional level was from a low of 3.2 per cent in the Salzburg area of Austria to 33.3 per cent in Andalucia in southern Spain. Most of the areas with the highest unemployment rates (above 15.5%) are in the peripheral areas of the Union: in Finland, Ireland, the new German *Länder*, southern France, Spain and southern Italy (see Figure 1.5). These areas include economically lagging (the designated Objective 1) regions, areas of industrial decline (Objective 2 regions) and problem rural (Objective 5) localities. In contrast, most of the lowest unemployment regions (with rates less than 6.5%) tend to be more scattered across the more economically dynamic parts of the Union: in Luxembourg, southern and western Germany, Austria and northern Italy. Furthermore, there are often significant differences in unemployment rates within member states. In 1995, the difference between the least and worst affected regions was some 20 percentage points in Spain (from 13% in Navarra to 33.3% in Andalucia) and Italy (from just under 5% in Trentino-Alto Adige to 25 per cent in Campania), and almost 15 percentage points in Germany (from 4% in Oberbayern to more than 18% in Magdeburg). At a more local level, high unemployment rates also exist in some of Europe's capital cities, prime examples being Brussels, Berlin and London. More generally, urban unemployment has been a growing phenomenon throughout Europe, manifesting itself in particular parts of cities rather than across cities as a whole. The co-existence – and often close juxtaposition – of intra-urban areas of employment growth and high incomes with other intra-urban zones of high unemployment, low incomes and high

---

5. With monetary union, exchange rate autonomy becomes twice removed from individual regions (member states themselves are not free to devalue or revalue their currencies at will) so that as a necessary corollary of monetary union there will have to be a substantial EU centralisation of national budgets so that automatic federal European fiscal transfers can perform the required regional stabilisation role. This issue of fiscal federalism seems a long way off.

6. The NUTS (Nomenclature of Statistical Territorial Units) system refers to a four-fold hierarchical regional division of European countries for the purposes of collection and collation of various economic and social information in the REGIO data bank. The levels range from the national (NUTS0) down to the local province or district (NUTS3). The sub-national area units used to construct NUTS1, NUTS2 and NUTS3 regions differ from country to country.

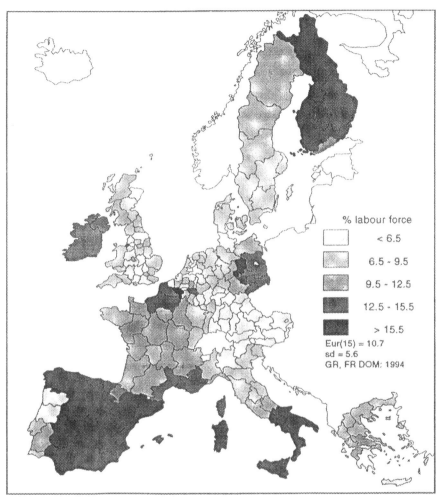

Figure 1.5: Unemployment Rates by Region, 1995 (NUTS2 regions)
Source: European Commission (REGIO)

dependence on welfare benefits, has become increasingly common. Unfortunately, few comparable statistics are available across Europe to capture the detailed extent of these intra-urban disparities, but national sources point to unemployment rates of 30 per cent and more – and occasionally as high as 50 per cent – in some inner city and suburban areas.

Not only are there marked regional and sub-regional disparities in the incidence of unemployment across Europe, there has also been a tendency for these regional differences to widen. As aggregate unemployment has risen, so the regional (and national) dispersion of unemployment rates – as measured,

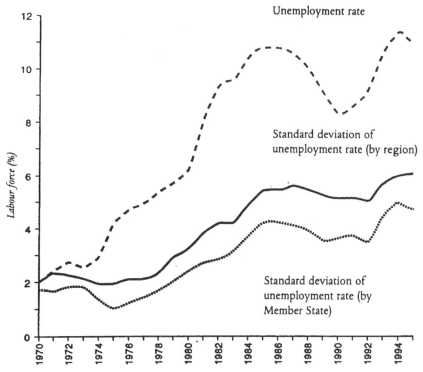

Figure 1.6: Unemployment Disparities Across the European Union, 1970–95
Source: European Commission (1996a)

for example, by the standard deviation – has increased (Figure 1.6). Thus the absolute dispersion of regional unemployment rates increased sharply from 1978 up to 1985, when aggregate EU unemployment peaked, and then fell slightly during the boom of 1986–90. However, with the subsequent rise in unemployment throughout Europe during the recession of the early 1990s, regional disparities widened once more. By 1995, the dispersion of regional unemployment rates across the EU was three times what it had been in the late 1970s. These movements in the dispersion of regional unemployment disparities reflect both the tendency for high unemployment regions to exhibit a greater cyclical sensitivity than low unemployment areas (see Decressin and Fatas 1994) and increasing differences in structural unemployment between areas.[7]

---

7. Using regional unemployment data for a number of EU countries for the period 1966–87, Decressin and Fatas find that the degree of cyclical sensitivity (as measured by the regression coefficient of the regional unemployment rate on the EU aggregate rate) is consistently greater than unity in high unemployment areas.

Table 1.1 Disparities in Unemployment by Region
(as Measured by the Standard Deviation), within Selected EU Member Countries, 1983–95

	1983	1984	1985	1986	1987	1988	1989	1990	1991	1992	1993	1994	1995
Belgium	0.5	1.0	1.4	1.3	1.3	1.6	1.4	1.3	1.0	0.9	1.0	1.4	1.4
Greece	0.7	0.9	1.8	2.6	1.9	2.1	1.9	1.9	2.1	2.1	2.4	2.4	2.4
France	1.6	1.9	2.0	1.8	1.8	1.9	1.8	1.7	1.8	2.0	1.9	2.1	2.0
Germany	1.7	2.0	2.2	2.2	2.2	2.2	2.0	1.8	1.6	1.9	1.8	1.8	1.9
Italy	2.8	3.0	3.3	4.0	5.2	6.4	7.1	6.4	6.7	4.3	5.4	6.4	5.9
United Kingdom	3.5	3.3	3.3	3.3	3.5	3.3	3.3	3.2	2.6	2.3	2.3	2.4	2.4
Spain	3.9	5.4	5.1	5.0	5.7	5.0	5.4	5.4	5.3	5.4	5.6	5.4	5.5
EU15 (by region)	4.2	5.0	5.4	5.4	5.6	5.5	5.3	4.9	5.0	4.8	5.6	6.0	6.0

Notes: 1. Germany refers to West Germany only.
2. NUTS2-level regions using REGIO data.

However, these EU-wide patterns conceal some interesting differences in dispersion trends within individual member states (Table 1.1). Some countries, such as Belgium, Greece, Italy and Spain, have experienced a steady rise in regional dispersion since the early 1980s. In others, such as Sweden, West Germany and France, the degree of regional dispersion has remained more or less constant. By contrast, in the UK the degree of regional dispersion has fallen over the period as a whole. These national differences reflect, among other things, the staggered and regionally differentiated nature of economic restructuring amongst the member states, national differences in macroeconomic policy and currency movements, and differences in their exposure and responses to international competition. Thus, for

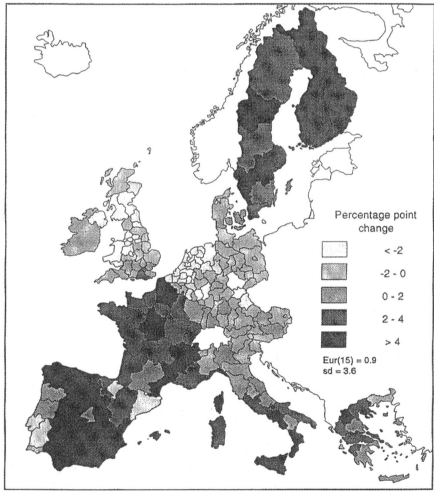

Figure 1.7: Change in Unemployment Rates by Region, 1983–93 (NUTS2 regions)
Source: European Commission (REGIO)

example, while in Italy the largest absolute increases in unemployment rates over 1983–93 occurred in the traditionally depressed southern regions, in the UK the largest increases were in the traditionally more buoyant South rather than the depressed North (Figure 1.7). Hence in Italy the dispersion of unemployment increased while in the UK it declined.

This decline in dispersion in the UK over this period has attracted considerable academic and political interest, and has elicited claims that a 'new geography of unemployment' is emerging there in which unemployment is now as much a feature of the southern regions of the country as it is of the traditionally depressed north (see, for example, Audas and MacKay 1996; Green, Owen and Winnett 1994). Thus the increase in unemployment in the customarily high unemployment northern regions of the country was far less in the 1990–93 downturn than in previous recessions (Table 1.2). As a result, regional unemployment differentials narrowed as national unemployment rose, rather than widening as has historically been the case. However, it is probably still too early to know whether these recent atypical

Table 1.2 Changes in Regional Unemployment Rates in the United Kingdom: Two Recessions Compared

| | 1980(I)–83(II) Recession | | 1990(II)–93(III) Recession | |
	Per cent Change	Absolute Change	Per cent Change	Absolute Change
South East	180.7	4.7	186.1	6.7
East Anglia	146.8	4.7	144.1	4.9
South West	121.0	4.6	148.7	5.8
East Midlands	151.3	5.6	100.0	4.8
West Midlands	184.4	8.3	101.8	5.6
Yorkshire – Humberside	145.6	6.7	62.5	4.0
North West	131.6	7.5	45.3	3.4
Northern	97.3	7.1	40.0	3.4
Wales	120.3	7.1	58.5	3.8
Scotland	90.6	5.8	10.8	1.5
Northern Ireland	80.9	6.8	4.6	0.8
UK	134.1	5.9	89.1	4.9

Notes:
1. Data from NOMIS.
2. Absolute change refers to change in percentage point unemployment rate.

Table 1.3 Persistence of Regional Unemployment in Selected EU Member Countries and the United States: Rank-Order Correlations, 1980–94

	1981	1982	1983	1984	1985	1986	1987	1988	1989	1990	1991	1992	1993	1994
United Kingdom	0.97	0.96	0.94	0.94	0.88	0.89	0.83	0.84	0.83	0.82	0.81	0.75	0.76	0.77
Germany	1.00	0.99	0.98	0.93	0.88	0.84	0.85	0.83	0.88	0.89	0.75	0.73	0.82	0.85
France	0.89	0.82	0.80	0.71	0.78	0.71	0.72	0.71	0.74	0.68	0.71	0.70	0.68	0.66
Denmark	0.90	0.88	0.90	0.91	0.87	0.86	0.80	0.85	0.89	0.84	0.83	0.80	0.81	0.83
Italy	0.97	0.94	0.97	0.98	0.96	0.98	0.94	0.94	0.86	0.91	0.89	0.90	0.92	0.88
Spain	0.98	0.93	0.84	0.88	0.95	0.98	0.93	0.76	0.73	0.71	0.70	0.70	0.72	0.74
United States	0.91	0.86	0.81	0.75	0.67	0.48	0.38	0.40	0.42	0.52	0.47	0.39	0.33	0.39

Notes: 1. Rank-order correlation coefficients of 1980 regional unemployment rates with those in subsequent years.

2. For EU countries, NUTS1-level regions, using national definitions of unemployment prior to 1983, adjusted to be consistent with REGIO data used for 1983 onwards.

3. For USA, state-level unemployment rates.

movements in regional unemployment disparities in the UK are merely temporary or whether they represent more permanent structural features of the country's economic landscape (for a discussion, see Martin 1993, 1997).

Persistence in the Regional Distribution of Unemployment

In any case, despite these different trends in regional dispersion amongst member states, the geography of unemployment within individual countries and across the Union as a whole has not in fact changed much. Indeed a distinctive feature of Europe's unemployment problem is the remarkable degree of rank-order stability that has characterised the regional unemployment structure over time.[8] Within the major member countries, the ranking of regions by unemployment rates in any given year is highly correlated with the ranking in subsequent years. For example, at the NUTS1 regional level, the United Kingdom, France, Germany, Italy, Denmark and Spain all show the same striking pattern of high correlations that decay only slowly over time (Table 1.3). Even regional rankings a decade and a half apart are highly

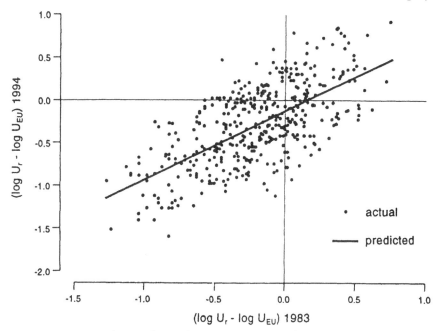

Figure 1.8: Persistence in the Map of Unemployment Disparities Across the European Union 1983–94 (NUTS3 regions)

Source: *Calculated from European Commission (REGIO) data.*

---

8. The dispersion of ranks is, of course, constant by definition. What is of interest is the identity of the regions in the various ranks over time.

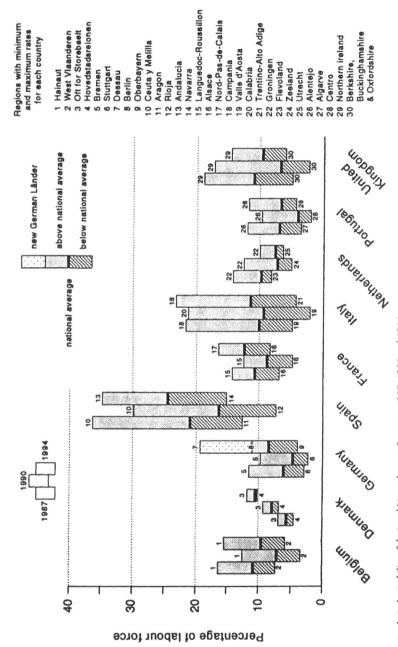

Figure 1.9: Rank-Order Stability of the Local Unemployment Structure, 1987, 1990 and 1994
Source: European Commission (1995a)

correlated. Thus in most cases, the rank-order correlations between regional unemployment rates in 1980 and those in 1994 are as high as 0.8 or more. This stability is even evident at the much more local level of NUTS3 areas. A regression of NUTS3 regional unemployment disparities in 1994 (as measured by differences around the EU average unemployment rate) against those in 1983 has a slope (b-coefficient) of 0.87, a t-statistic of 21.07 and an R^2 of 0.50 (see Figure 1.8). The slope of the regression is not statistically different from unity, which implies a high degree of persistence in the spatial pattern of unemployment differentials over this 11 year period. Furthermore, in almost every member state the identity of the NUTS3 areas with the highest and lowest unemployment rates was the same in 1994 as it was in 1987, and where it has changed the new area is usually located close to the old one, typically in the same NUTS1 region (Figure 1.9).

There is, then, a high degree of persistence in the regional and sub-regional unemployment structures of EU countries: the regional pattern of regional unemployment disparities does not change significantly from one year to the next, but rather remains relatively stable over several consecutive years (for a more detailed analysis of this persistence of regional unemployment disparities within Europe, see Baddeley, Martin and Tyler 1997). In this respect, regional unemployment structures in the European Union appear to behave quite differently from their counterparts in the US. There, regional and sub-regional unemployment trajectories are much more idiosyncratic, and one period's high unemployment regions can become the next period's low unemployment regions (see Bertola and Ichino 1996; Eichengreen 1990; OECD 1989). For example, Bertola and Ichino (1996) found that the inter-temporal rank-order correlation of state-level unemployment rates in the US in 1980 with those in subsequent years declines quickly, falling to less than 0.4 by 1985, and is much more variable than in European countries. Furthermore, in their study of the evolution of US regional labour markets, Blanchard and Katz (1992) found that the slope of a regression of state unemployment differentials in 1985 on those in 1975 was zero. Not only are regional unemployment differentials generally lower in the United States, there would appear to be much less persistence or stability in the regional unemployment structure in the US compared with that found across the EU (see Table 1.3). This raises some interesting issues with respect to possible differences in the operation of regional labour markets as between European countries and the United States.

Why should European regional unemployment disparities be characterised by a high degree of persistence? In standard economic theory, there should be no persistent inter-area differences in joblessness (apart perhaps from small differences in frictional or 'job-changing' unemployment). If unemployment becomes regionally unbalanced, for example as a result of a relative shift in demand away from some regions towards others, this should set in motion self-correcting movements in wages, workers and capital between regions. Wages would be expected to fall in the higher unemployment regions relative to those elsewhere, labour would migrate out to search for jobs in the lower unemployment regions, while capital would be attracted by the surplus labour and lower wages in the areas where unemployment had increased. As a result of these adjustments, differences in unemployment between regions would be quickly eliminated and equilibrium wages would tend to be similar in different areas (see Martin 1993).

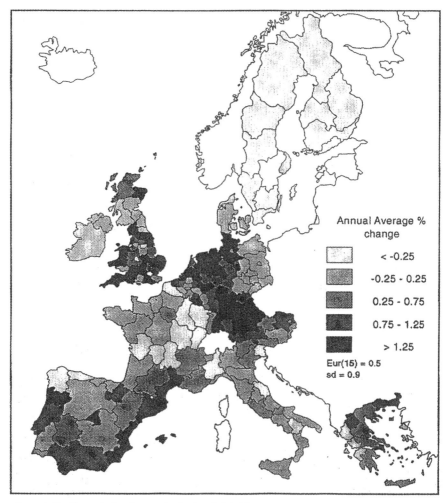

Figure 1.10: Change in Employment by Region, 1983–93
Source. European Commission (REGIO)

The fact that regional unemployment differences persist across Europe, and that the spatial pattern (rank-order structure) of those differences is remarkably stable, clearly indicates that actual labour markets do not function in this textbook way. In principle, the persistence of regional unemployment disparities that typifies European countries has two potential origins.[9] The first is that they represent a 'disequilibrium' phenomenon: regional unemployment disparities persist because labour market equilibrating mechanisms are very slow or weak. In these circumstances, regionally uneven demand,

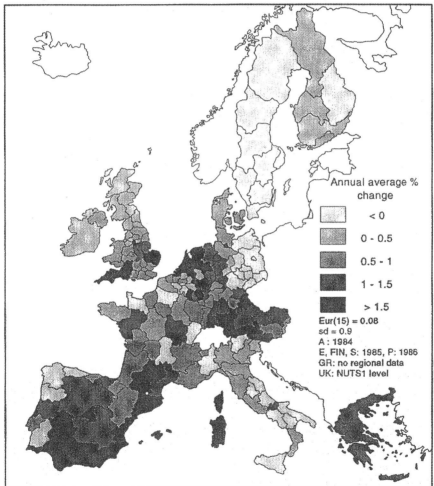

Figure 1.11: Change in Labour Force by Region, 1983–93
Source: European Commission (REGIO)

---

9. These two views seem to have been first elaborated by Marston (1985). More recently, the same framework has been used in the study of regional employment dynamics in the US by Blanchard and Katz (1992) referred to above.

supply and technology 'shocks' will have long-run effects on the geographical distribution of unemployment. If the inter-regional movements of labour and capital and relative wage adjustments are sluggish or incomplete, then regional unemployment differences will tend to be perpetuated. Since the late 1970s, the patterns of employment change and labour force growth have been very uneven across the Union (Figures 1.10 and 1.11), and it might be argued that it has been the slowness of different areas to adjust to these uneven labour market trends that has resulted in persistent inter-area differences in unemployment. For example, many of the regions of Northern Europe specialising in mining, steel, textiles and heavy manufacturing industry have experienced steep falls in employment. Although the process of de-industrialisation in these regions has promoted out-migration of labour to other areas, and while there has been some local economic redevelopment of new industries and services (often as a result of inflows of new capital), these adjustments have only been partial, and as a result the regions most affected by the contraction in traditional industry and manufacturing have tended to experience persistent unemployment. To compound matters, the skills possessed by the unemployed workers in these areas do not match those required by new expanding sectors, and retraining labour for alternative types of employment takes time. In other regions, particularly in Southern Europe, the decline of traditional agriculture has also put considerable strain on the local labour force and, again, although out-migration has occurred it has not taken place quickly enough or on a sufficient scale to prevent sustained high unemployment in these areas.

However, alternatively, persistent disparities in unemployment between areas can be viewed as a structural 'equilibrium' phenomenon. The argument is not that regional labour markets fail to equilibrate, or that labour, capital and wage adjustments are too slow or inadequate, but that different regions equilibrate at different levels of relative unemployment that reflect the different prevailing structural or 'real conditions' in different areas.[10] More specifically, in this explanation each region has its own 'equilibrium' unemployment rate, which can be thought of as composed of two parts: a nation-wide average equilibrium component which varies over time, and an equilibrium differential which is assumed to be constant for quite long periods. The nation-wide equilibrium component common to all regions might reflect geographically uniform supply-side factors such as the unem-

---

10. A somewhat similar equilibrium view is expounded by Adams (1985) and Topel (1986). According to Adams, in spatial equilibrium each region has to provide the same expected utility in terms of unemployment benefit, while in Topel, equilibrium occurs when expected real wages (that is, wages multiplied by the probability of being unemployed) are equalised between regions, a result that is consistent with the theory of 'compensating differentials'.

ployment benefit level, a national minimum wage, nationally set non-wage costs (such as employers' national insurance contributions for their employees), and so on. If these factors vary over time, then the common component of regional equilibrium unemployment rates will also change.[11] However, in addition, individual areas will have different equilibrium unemployment differentials, determined by their particular local economic, industrial-structural, institutional, social and environmental characteristics, for example, local industrial composition, the age and skill mix of the local labour force, customary local wage rates, the degree of union organisation in the area, local housing costs, the range and level of local amenities, and so on. Because such characteristics vary from area to area, and because these variations are not easily eliminated, there will be a corresponding pattern of 'structural' or equilibrium unemployment differentials across regions that is consistent with these locally specific circumstances.[12] This interpretation allows actual regional unemployment disparities, and hence the dispersion of regional unemployment rates, to diverge and converge over the short run, for example, with the economic cycle, but assumes these fluctuations are transitory and have no permanent effect on the regional unemployment structure. Of course, some structural factors do inevitably change over time, so that regional equilibrium unemployment differentials will also change. But in this view of persistence, such shifts are assumed to be slow, so that the regional unemployment structure remains relatively stable for quite long periods of time.

In the US, regional and local unemployment differentials appear to be an equilibrium phenomenon (see Blanchard and Katz 1992; Marston 1985), and there is some evidence to support a similar interpretation of the geographical distribution of unemployment in Europe (Baddeley *et al.* 1996; Decressin and Fatas 1994). However, what appear as equilibrium regional unemployment differentials may in fact be the result of a previous major cyclical or structural shock that impacts differently on different regions (as was the case, for example, with the oil price hikes of 1973–74, and 1979), creating a particular pattern of geographical unemployment disparities which then remains more or less unchanged for several years, not because of slow adjustment as such but because what starts as a 'disequilibrium' shock may

---

11. The claim of many monetarist and other supply-side economists, of course, is that the secular rise in unemployment throughout much of Europe since the mid 1970s has been due precisely to an increase in these factors.
12. Note that there is nothing inherent in this idea of equilibrium regional differentials to suggest that they are necessarily the result of 'voluntary' unemployment decisions of the sort emphasised by some monetarist economists. Although this account does imply that different regions have different 'natural' unemployment rates, it does not follow that these reflect different degrees of 'voluntary' unemployment between regions.

change the underlying structural characteristics of different regions and hence the map of equilibrium differentials. This would be a sort of inter-regional counterpart to the 'hysteresis' effect that economists often invoke in discussions of Europe's high unemployment problem.[13] The presence of hysteresis means that in practice it may not be possible to distinguish easily between equilibrium and disequilibrium explanations of the persistence of regional unemployment disparities.

This issue is of much more than just academic interest, for it has implications for the debate over policy. An equilibrium interpretation of regional unemployment disparities would imply that intervention is needed to change the economic, structural and institutional characteristics of high unemployment areas, so as to lower their equilibrium unemployment differentials. A disequilibrium view would emphasise the need for policies that improve the adjustment processes of regional and local labour markets and their responsiveness to changing economic and competitive conditions. As the above discussion suggests, it might not be easy to disentangle these two types of policy model. Much of the current debate about the causes of, and cures for, Europe's high unemployment reflects this difficulty. One of the main arguments advanced to account both for Europe's general unemployment problem and its large spatial unemployment disparities, is the 'rigidity' or 'sclerosis' of its labour markets (see, for example, Blanchard and Summers 1986; Krugman 1994a, b; OECD 1989). The policy challenge is seen to be one of improving the 'supply-side flexibility' of the labour market and the regions. However, while some appear to adopt a 'disequilibrium' position on this 'inflexibility' problem and see the solution to spatial unemployment differences in measures that speed up the adjustment of local labour markets, for example, through active training and retraining programmes and the promotion of new local indigenous business formation, others believe that regional unemployment disparities will only be reduced by dismantling those economic and institutional structures believed to be the basic causes of labour market rigidity and high equilibrium relative unemployment, such as local wage structures, strong local unions and nationally uniform social benefit levels. In reality, of course, attempts to distinguish between labour market processes and labour market structures as the basis of policy interventions may be both difficult and misleading.

---

13. The idea of hysteresis has been developed in an attempt to explain the progressive rise in the so-called 'natural' or structural equilibrium unemployment rate in Europe. It refers to the situation where the underlying equilibrium rate depends strongly on the past level of actual unemployment (see, for example, Blanchard and Summers 1986; Cross 1988; Layard and Bean 1990).

Regional Labour Markets and the Flexibility Debate

To compound matters, much of this debate about the problem of 'Eurosclerosis' has involved comparison with the US where, it is argued, labour markets are much more flexible in response to changes in demand, competition and technology (see, for example, Bertola and Ichino 1996; Krugman 1994a, b; Wood 1994). Typically, three basic factors are singled out by proponents of this view to account for the alleged rigidity of West European labour markets as compared with their counterparts in the US: (1) lower levels of worker mobility, especially geographical mobility; (2) a more institutionalised and regulated labour market, involving much higher levels of unionisation and collective wage bargaining; and (3) more generous state welfare and benefit systems.

In the US, it appears that labour migration is the main mechanism by which regional labour markets adjust to adverse shocks. If the demand for labour in a particular region falls relative to that elsewhere, so that unemployment begins to rise relative to the rate in other regions, workers tend to migrate out of the depressed region in significant numbers, and this helps to bring the demand for, and supply of, labour in the region in question back towards balance. Labour mobility is primarily a response to changes in unemployment rather than in wages, and this mobility seems to be sufficient to prevent local rises in unemployment from persisting (see Blanchard and Katz 1992). What evidence exists for Europe suggests that inter-regional labour mobility is much lower there. For example, Eichengreen (1993) found that net migration is much less sensitive to shocks in regional wages and unemployment in Britain and Italy than in the United States; while Houseman and Abraham (1990) found that regional employment shifts generate substantially more net migration in the United States than in Germany. The implication of such studies is that in Europe geographical labour mobility is not sufficient to remove regional unemployment disparities even within member states.[14] Moreover, given the linguistic and other cultural differences between countries in the EU, even with increasing economic and political integration in the Union, migration between regions in different member states is likely to remain substantially lower than geographical mobility across the US.

The problem, it is argued, is that not only does labour mobility fail to provide the necessary inter-regional adjustment within European countries, but so do wages. According to many proponents of the Eurosclerosis thesis, the inflexibility of wages, both in real and relative terms, is itself another major cause of high unemployment in the EU. Again, much has been made

---

14. Also, the generally higher unemployment conditions that exist in Europe may themselves dampen overall rates of worker mobility between regions.

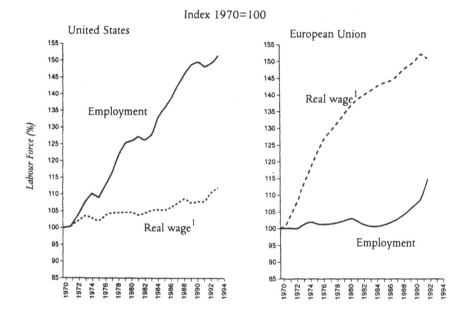

1. Total compensation per employee deflated by the GDP deflator.

Figure 1.12: Employment and Real Earnings in the EU and US Compared, 1970–93

Source: OECD Economic Outlook database

of the greater flexibility of wages in the United States. Between 1970 and 1993 real wages in the US increased by only about 10 per cent, whereas total employment grew by 50 per cent. This is in stark contrast to the European Union, where real wages increased by more than 50 per cent over the same period, whereas employment grew by only 15 per cent (Figure 1.12). As a result of these divergent trends, a substantially larger proportion of the working age population is employed in the United States than is the case in Western Europe. This American achievement has been highlighted by successive Economic Reports to the President (1991, p.3; 1992, p.81) and by numerous economists (for example, Applebaum 1990; Freeman 1995; Krugman 1990). The failure of Europe to replicate America's 'job miracle' is thus viewed by many to be evidence of the rigidity of Europe's wages. Strong real wage growth throughout the EU during the 1970s and 1980s is seen as having been at the expense of employment creation. Europe's problem, it is claimed, is that a higher degree of unionisation and more centralised wage bargaining systems combine to impart considerable fixity to real wages and the wages structure. To add to the predicament, the argument continues, social welfare benefit levels in many EU states are too high, and have the effect of raising workers' 'reservation wages' above what would otherwise be their market-clearing levels.[15] For these various reasons,

European workers are charged with having effectively 'priced themselves out of work'.

This line of argument has been used, largely unchanged, to explain the existence and persistence of regional unemployment disparities. Again, in the United States regional wages appear to be relatively flexible in response to shifts in labour demand, and unemployment benefits also vary across states. Since the early 1980s, regional wage differentials for different types of worker have increased substantially, supporting a geographical version of the 'wage flexibility' argument (Bertola and Ichino 1996). In contrast, regional wage structures in European countries have remained stable, or have even converged, despite wide regional differences in unemployment rates (Flanagan 1993). Union-based nation-wide or industry-wide wage bargaining, nationally uniform benefit levels and, in some cases, national minimum wage floors, have all been blamed for preventing local wages from responding flexibly to local variations in labour demand, supply and productivity. In this account, then, the existence of high unemployment in certain regions is the result of the relative wage being too high in such areas. Thus if wages fell in high unemployment regions, this would stimulate new jobs and bring down the local unemployment rate. The appropriate policy response, therefore, is to deregulate labour markets and promote greater flexibility of local wage-setting and employment practices.

However, such arguments have several weaknesses. Important new microeconomic research indicates that the degree of local wage flexibility (the elasticity of local wage levels to the local rate of unemployment) is remarkably similar across a wide cross-section of countries, including the US and the EU (Blanchflower and Oswald 1995).[16] This finding contradicts the view that the reason that some countries (particularly the United States) have had comparatively small increases in unemployment is that their wages are more flexible than those of other countries (particularly European states).[17] Furthermore, what is striking about the US case is that while wage 'flexibility'

---

15. Krugman (1994a) suggests that the social welfare aims of European states contrast sharply with those in the United States and that this difference in institutional arrangements goes a long way to explaining the high unemployment in Europe. Both the US and Europe, he argues, have been subject to similar technological and trade shocks, but the two economies have responded differently – with a widening income dispersion in the US and with high unemployment in Europe: it is, he comments, as if the same 'pebble' has been thrown into two different 'institutional waters', producing different 'ripple effects'.

16. More specifically, Blanchflower and Oswald find that the regression coefficient of the natural logarithm of wages on the natural logarithm of local unemployment to be -0.1 in the US, several European countries, Canada and Australia.

17. This new literature also contradicts the conventional 'compensating differentials' view that, since in spatial equilibrium all regions provide the same expected utility for workers, high unemployment regions ought also to be high wage regions.

may have contributed to the expansion of employment there, at the same time it has also promoted a marked widening of the country's earnings structure (OECD 1994a). This widening has not simply been due to a rapid growth in the incomes of high productivity, high skill employment groups (especially the top 10% of earners), but has also involved a substantial deterioration in the real earnings of the lowest wage groups (see Freeman and Katz 1994). Thus over the 1980s, the real earnings of the bottom decile of the US working population fell by 10 per cent and for younger unskilled men by almost 20 per cent. By the end of the 1980s, low paid male workers in the US were earning less in real terms than their predecessors in the early 1960s. A not insignificant proportion of the American 'employment miracle' of the past two decades has in fact consisted of relatively low skill, low productivity, low wage service sector jobs, many of which have been filled by women from low income households (Freeman 1995). The flip-side of 'wage flexibility' has thus been a substantial expansion in poorly paid and insecure employment, and an associated increase in the population of the working poor and the incidence of poverty (see Freeman 1995; Galbraith 1992; Krugman 1994b).

With one major exception, European wage distributions have not widened in this way, but instead have remained relatively stable. The striking exception is the UK, where the earnings distribution has widened even faster than in the United States (OECD 1994a, p.19). And like the US, the bottom 10 per cent of the workforce in particular have seen their relative position worsen considerably. Between 1978 and 1992, the real earnings of the bottom 10 per cent of the wages distribution remained static, while the median increased by 35 per cent and those of the top 10 per cent rose by 50 per cent (Gosling, Machin and Meghir 1994; Hills 1995; Machin 1996). Again, like the US, the real average hourly earnings of young workers (20–28-year-olds who had left school at 16) fell by 19 per cent over this period. Yet this wage 'flexibility' has not produced any corresponding British 'jobs miracle'. Instead the rate of employment expansion in the UK has fallen far short of that in the United States. Between 1979 and 1996 total employment (excluding those on government training programmes and in the armed forces) increased by only 0.5 million (or 2%). The number of full-time employees in employment actually *fell* by 2.6 million (3%), and all the growth that occurred was in part-time jobs (which increased by 1.8 million or 40%) and self-employment (which expanded by 1.3 million or 64%). These latter two categories are often celebrated in official and governmental circles as manifestations of the new 'labour market flexibility'. But they are also categories of employment that are often characterised by job insecurity, reduced employment rights and lower earnings. In many spheres of part-time work, the 'new flexibility' is simply a euphemism for increased exploitation of workers by employers.[18] It would seem that the UK labour market has suffered from the worst of both worlds: the high unemployment and slow employment growth that typify the EU, combined with the growing wage and earnings inequalities and employment insecurity that typify the US.

The 'Americanisation' of the European labour market would thus seem to be a questionable solution to the latter's unemployment problem. In Britain, for example, the decline in the relative wages of the low skilled and unskilled has done little to halt or reverse the decline in demand for such employees. Nor, if we accept the arguments of writers such as Wood (1994), is it likely to. In his view, the unemployment predicament in Europe is in significant part due to the increasing competition from, and expansion of trade with, the industrialising and developing countries. According to Wood, the dramatic growth of imports of low wage, labour-intensive goods from the developing world into Europe since the mid 1970s has undermined the demand for low skilled workers in European industries and, together with technological change, has shifted demand towards skilled labour. Although the increase in unemployment amongst unskilled workers that has ensued has been exacerbated by the rigidity of European wages, in Wood's view this does not mean that driving down unskilled wages by deregulating employment, legislating against unions and removing minimum wage provisions, will necessarily restore the demand for unskilled workers. Many of those jobs have been permanently lost, and more are likely to disappear as other developing countries compete for European markets and as technological advance continues in European industry itself. The relative underdevelopment of European services (as compared with the US) might be seen as one possible route through which wage flexibility could promote employment for unskilled workers. However, available evidence indicates that the price elasticity of demand for services is relatively low. Thus reducing wages in what are often already low paying service activities may not hold out much prospect for re-employing large numbers of unemployed unskilled workers. In any case, the distributional implications of such a strategy are likely to be highly inegalitarian: the worse paid sections of society and least favourable regions would have to bear the cost of reducing unemployment via cuts in wages, while the better-off sections and regions would benefit from access to the cheaper services. 'Wage flexibility' of itself, therefore, is unlikely to solve the European unemployment problem in general, or the plight of the

---

18. There is, in fact, a growing literature, both theoretical and empirical, that takes issue with the whole thrust of celebratory and advocatory accounts of the 'new flexibility'. For examples of such critical accounts see Rubery (1989), Pollert (1991) and Gilbert, Burrows and Pollert (1992).

worst affected regions more particularly, or only at the cost of increasing social and spatial income inequalities.[19]

The Problem of the Long-Term Unemployed

There is in any case another dimension to Europe's high unemployment that further complicates the flexibility argument: namely, the high level of long-term joblessness. Since the mid 1970s, the unemployment flow 'regime' in EU countries has typically been one of low unemployment inflow rates but high shares of long-term unemployment (that is, of more than a year). In 1994, for example, some 47 per cent of unemployed men and 50 per cent of unemployed women in the European Union had not worked for a year or more, while over half of these (26% of men and 29% of women) had not had jobs for more than two years. Furthermore, 10 per cent of the unemployed had been out of work for more than four years. These high proportions of long-term unemployment indicate the structural and deep-seated nature of joblessness in the EU. Like total unemployment, the incidence of long-term unemployment in the EU varies significantly across member states,

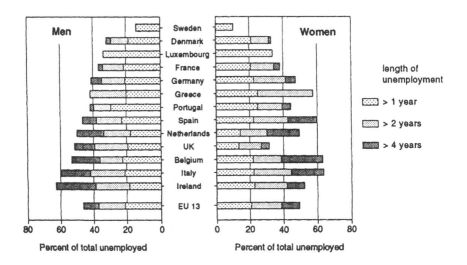

Note: A and SF no consistant data, S and L no data for <2 years or <4 years, GR no data for <4 years

Figure 1.13: Incidence of Long-Term Unemployment by Duration in EU Member States
Source: European Commission (1995a)

19. Freeman (1995) makes a somewhat similar point in his critical review of the impact of 'wage flexibility' in the United States.

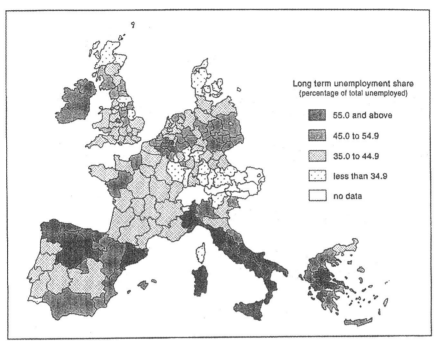

Long term unemployment share
(percentage of total unemployed)

55.0 and above

45.0 to 54.9

35.0 to 44.9

less than 34.9

no data

Figure 1.14: Incidence of Long-Term Unemployment (More than a Year) by Region, 1995
Source: European Commission (REGIO)

ranging from a low of about 12 per cent in the Swedish regions to more than 60 per cent in Italy and Ireland (Figures 1.13 and 1.14). In most countries in the Union, the unemployment flow 'regime' contrasts sharply with that in the US, where inflow rates are more than four times those in EU nations, but the share of long-term unemployed is very low, typically less than 10 per cent (it was 4.2% in 1979, 9.5% in 1985 and 5.6% in 1990: in Italy, for example, it increased from 51.2% to 71.1% over the same period).

Long average spells of unemployment tend to imply greater economic and social costs than shorter spells. The longer a person is unemployed the more that person's skills are likely to depreciate. Most long-term unemployed experience a loss of confidence and self-esteem, and this frequently leads to feelings of hopelessness in relation to finding work and a reduction in job search activity, often resulting in eventual withdrawal from the labour market altogether (Layard, Nickell and Jackman 1991). For their part, employers may use the length of time a person has been unemployed as a screening device and tend to discriminate against the long-term unemployed when making hiring decisions. The long-term unemployed can thus become effectively stigmatised by employers (Blanchard and Diamond 1989) and find themselves excluded from the labour market, 'outsiders' both in the sense that their prospects of returning into work fade with increasing duration of their joblessness and in the sense that they exert little external influence on wage-setting and employment processes within firms. The long-term unemployed thus find it difficult to 'price themselves into work', and do little to keep wages in check as the labour market tightens. In addition, in those cases where there are limits on the length of period over which an unemployed person is eligible for state social security and similar benefits, those out of work for long spells of time are also likely to suffer severe falls in their living standards and socio-economic welfare, and may drop out of the labour market altogether into inactivity.

It is understandable, therefore, why much recent analysis and policy discussion by economists has focused on the long-term unemployed. In fact it is widely believed that duration is the key variable explaining the rise and persistence of unemployment in Europe. Duration is seen as the central causal channel through which unemployment changes. Thus according to Flanagan (1987, p.195), 'European unemployment growth is almost entirely the result of the decline in the likelihood of leaving unemployment.' Likewise Layard (1989, p.6) argues that, 'unemployment in the EEC countries has grown mainly due to a rise in duration, not a rise in inflow. Thus to understand high unemployment we have to explain the long durations.' The grounds for this argument are as follows. Unemployment is a stock, and changes in this stock (U) can arise either from changes in the flows into unemployment (I) or in the flows out (X), or both.[20] Observers point to the fact that while the inflow rate $(i=I/E$, where E is the employed workforce) has remained relatively stable over the past two decades, outflow rates $(x=X/U)$ have fallen. As outflow rates have fallen, so the average duration of unemployment and the proportion of long-term unemployment have increased. The growth in long-term joblessness is thus blamed for the rise in the overall unemployment rate. The positive correlation across countries between the rate of unemployment and the proportion of unemployment that is long term (more than a year) is taken as evidence supporting this argument (see Figure 1.15).

This suggests that geographical differences in unemployment might also be 'explained', to some extent at least, in terms of the differential spatial incidence of long-term unemployment. The spatial counterpart of the duration argument outlined above would imply that differences in the spatial incidence of unemployment are primarily due to regional differences in

---

20. By definition, $U=I-X$. In a steady state, unemployment is constant, that is, $\Delta U=0$, and thus $I=X$. Under this condition, the unemployment rate is related to the inflow and outflow rates by the expression $u=(1+x/i)^{-1}$, where u is the unemployment rate (U/L), x the outflow rate (X/U), and i the inflow rate (I/E).

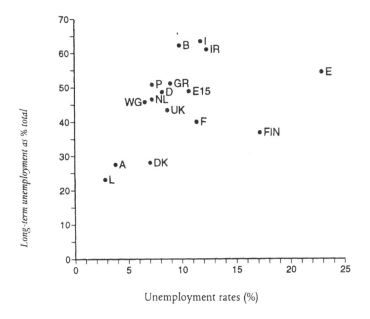

Figure 1.15: Unemployment Rates and Long-Term Unemployment in Member States, 1995
Source: European Commission (1996a)

unemployment outflow rates, and hence the incidence of long-term unemployment. Unfortunately, the flow data necessary to examine this proposition are not generally available across the various regions of the EU. However, some flow data do exist for the UK regions, and these throw some interesting light on this issue (see Jones 1992; Martin and Sunley 1997). For it appears that contrary to what the Layard-type argument might suggest, during the 1980s high unemployment regions in the UK owed their above average jobless rates to high unemployment inflow rates rather than to low outflow rates. Conversely, low unemployment regions were characterised by below average inflows. These findings imply that spatial differences in the incidence of long-term joblessness are probably a *consequence* rather than a cause of geographical disparities in unemployment.[21]

---

21. This finding is consistent with Burgess's analysis of aggregate unemployment flows in the UK labour market (1989). He argues that the fall in the unemployment outflow rate in the UK is more a symptom of rising unemployment than a direct determinant. His case is based on decomposing the outflow rate, $x = X/U$ into $(X/L)/u$, where X is the number of people leaving unemployment, L is the labour force, U is the number of unemployed and u is the

One of the possible reasons for this has to do with the fact that the 'labour turnover regime' – the interaction of flows of worker hires, quits and lay-offs – seems to vary between different regional and sub-regional labour markets, and in ways that depend on local unemployment conditions (see Jones 1992; Jones and Martin 1986; Martin 1984). In areas of high unemployment, 'natural' labour turnover – voluntary quitting of jobs by workers – tends to be significantly lower than in areas of low unemployment, mainly because under conditions of high unemployment employees are much more inclined to hold on to their jobs rather than quit to search for alternative employment. This lack of voluntary mobility in high unemployment regions limits movement of both the employed and the unemployed. When the propensity of the employed stock to 'turn over' voluntarily is low, employers will resort much more to enforced lay-offs and redundancies in order to adjust their workforces in response to instabilities in demand. Thus in high unemployment areas, a much greater proportion of total separations from employment, and thus of the inflows into unemployment, will be involuntary. In such circumstances, the 'qualities' of those workers who are laid off and made redundant are likely to be significantly different from those who make up a 'normal' voluntary flow. They are more likely to be the less skilled, less productive employees, precisely those who will experience greater difficulty in finding new employment, especially in slack labour markets. Thus those made unemployed in this way are more prone to end up as a 'hard core' of long-term unemployed which then becomes absorbed into the high 'equilibrium' unemployment differential of such areas.[22]

Not only is this an example of the way in which geography shapes the operation of the labour market and the unemployment process, it also raises some key questions for policy. Over the past decade or so, EU countries have developed a bewildering array of measures designed to help the long-term unemployed (see OECD 1994c; for an evaluation of some of these, see Alogoskoufis *et al.* 1995). Many of these measures are based on some form of hiring subsidy designed to encourage employers to take on and train long-term unemployed workers. Few would disagree that long-term unemployment is one of the most pressing socio-economic problems in Europe, or that greater efforts should be made to reduce this particularly corrosive dimension of joblessness. On equity grounds this is certainly desirable.

---

unemployment rate (U/L). Using this decomposition he finds that the fall in the outflow rate over the 1970s and 1980s comes from the rise in the unemployment rate, and that by contrast X/L hardly varies at all. Burgess's result thus contests arguments of the Layard type.

22. This is a spatial counterpart to the sort of thesis advanced, for example, by Cross (1988), who argues that the long-term unemployed have acted as a mechanism for the operation of hysteresis effects in the rise and persistence of the EU unemployment rate.

Furthermore, such policies may help to reduce regional unemployment disparities. However, if long-term unemployment is as much a consequence as a cause of high unemployment, to intervene with policies only when the stage of long-term unemployment has been reached would be to disregard the role that unemployment inflows play in shaping regional unemployment differentials. The loading of labour market policies towards the long-term unemployed is unquestionably socially desirable, but such policies alone may be seriously deficient, and need to be combined with other measures directed at limiting or intercepting the inflows into unemployment in the first place.

Unemployment as Social and Spatial Exclusion: The Issue of Market- Versus Welfare-Regulation

The labour market is a key factor through which the contours and cohesiveness of society are shaped. It is where the various structural, technological and institutional forces that drive the process of economic development intersect and where the effects of those forces are directly felt, on jobs, working conditions and incomes. It is where the economic well-being of individuals and their families is determined and their social values and relationship to society as a whole are in large part moulded. Full employment performs an integrative and social harmonising role: it promotes social inclusion, cohesion, citizenship and a sense of participation in the wider community. Such social inclusion was basic to the underlying rationale of the post-war welfare state policy model followed by most European economies until the late 1970s. That model was based on two key assumptions concerning both the level and the composition of employment. The pursuit of full employment was justified not only in terms of economic efficiency, of utilising all available labour resources, but also as a means of securing social harmony and integration. Furthermore, full employment maintained the flow of taxes needed to finance the national welfare system whilst simultaneously limiting the claims made on that system. A national social insurance scheme would only work if unemployment could be contained within reasonable limits and long-term unemployment was more or less abolished. In addition, however, the social security system of most countries was also based on the assumption that the typical worker was a male who normally earned sufficient to support himself, his wife and a family of at least one child. The onset of endemic high unemployment, the increasing insecurity of employment and the ongoing shifts away from male to female employment, and from full-time to part-time jobs, all have profound implications for the social security systems of European states.

High unemployment is both wasteful of human resources and economically inefficient. At the level of the economy and society as a whole, every person unemployed means a loss of output and taxes whilst simultaneously adding to the costs of social welfare. Moreover, unemployment has a disintegrative effect, leading to the economic marginalisation and social exclusion of the individuals and families involved. Unemployment, especially if prolonged, promotes social corrosion: it erodes people's skills and 'employability' and can lead to a vicious downward spiral in their living standards, economic freedom and social citizenship. It is no accident that as unemployment has risen and the labour market in the Western advanced economies over the past two decades has become more uncertain, volatile and fragmented, so the incidence of poverty, homelessness, ill-health and crime has also risen, and concerns have grown over the emergence of a deprived and socially excluded 'underclass' (see, for example, Freeman 1994; Galbraith 1992; Glyn and Miliband 1994; Gregg and Machin 1994; Hutton 1995; Phillips 1990).

These exclusionary effects of unemployment are the more pronounced because of the uneven incidence of joblessness across the labour force. Unemployment does not fall equally on the different members of the working age population, but instead tends to be concentrated amongst particular social groups, especially young labour force entrants, the less educated, the manual and unskilled, ethnic minorities and older workers. These groups tend to experience much greater job insecurity than other members of the labour force, resulting in repeated spells of unemployment and long periods of joblessness. But not only does unemployment tend to be focused within particular social-economic groups, in Europe it is also markedly uneven in its geographical impact. Moreover, these spatial disparities in European unemployment tend to be large, self-reproducing and persistent. They operate, therefore, to reinforce the concentration of unemployment and its social exclusion effects within particular communities. In other words, the unemployed become spatially as well as socially excluded, geographically marginalised from the employment and income growth opportunities available elsewhere. Significant and persistent geographical differences in joblessness thus constitute an important, but insufficiently understood, component of the 'unemployment puzzle' (Oswald 1994).

The access of all individuals to employment opportunities is one of the two key defining elements of the European Union's model of social cohesion (the other being an equitable distribution of income with minimal levels of poverty: see European Commission 1996). The reduction of social and spatial disparities in unemployment is thus central to the achievement of this model. The problem facing much of Europe, however, is that within most member states labour market trends have frustrated progress towards social cohesion (Verhaar *et al.* 1996). Not only have social and spatial disparities in unemployment remained considerable or even widened, at the same time government policies have shifted increasingly away from the welfarist mode of regulation that – in its several national variants – had previously provided some measure of local social support against the impact of unemployment. Instead the current trend is towards more market-orientated forms of regulation. As a result, labour markets across Europe are now caught in a powerful predicament.

On one side, advancing technologies and rapidly intensifying global competition require the constant and intense restructuring of regional and local economies, with destabilising consequences for the employment prospects of large sections of their workforces and potentially rising demands on state welfare, social benefits and training programmes. On the other side, European states are busy deregulating labour markets and decentralising labour market policies so as to increase the flexibility of regions and localities to global competition and new technologies, while at the same time seeking ways of cutting expenditure on welfare and social security as part of their attempts to control public spending, reduce personal taxation, contain inflationary pressures and meet the criteria required for European monetary union. Contrary to the post-war Keynesian-welfarist model of economic regulation, the present underlying political-economic ideology of most European governments is that states cannot influence the level of employment directly but can only help markets to operate more efficiently. To this end, policies have become much more 'supply-side' orientated, for example providing better education and training schemes; nurturing an entrepreneurial climate; enhancing the diffusion of technological knowledge; increasing wage and labour cost flexibility; dismantling job security provisions; increasing working time flexibility; encouraging a switch from passive to 'active' labour market measures; curbing the power of unions; and reforming benefit systems (see Alogoskoufis *et al.* 1995; OECD 1994b). The UK in particular is leading the way in this shift towards a 'flexible labour market' approach to the unemployment problem, and is even seen as the model that other European states, such as Germany and Sweden, want to emulate.[23]

23. In 1994, interestingly the 50th anniversary of the UK's 1944 White Paper on Full Employment, several official statements and discussions seemed at last to push the jobs issue to the top of the public agenda, including the White Paper by Jacques Delors, President Clinton's G7 'Jobs Summit' in Detroit, the European Commission's labour market meeting in Essen and the influential OECD Jobs Study. However, although there may now be a common concern about bringing unemployment levels down, Clinton's Jobs Summit in March 1994 also exposed the lack of agreement as to how this should be done. Whereas Clinton stressed

Some observers interpret this shift to a new mode of labour market regulation as the emergence of a decentralised, market-orientated Schumpeterian 'workfare' or 'trainingfare' state, in which social policy is becoming subordinate to the needs of labour market flexibility (Geddes 1994; Jessop 1994). Two features are frequently alleged to be central to this new model. The first is the idea of introducing 'workfare' into the welfare system, that is, the requirement that the unemployed should be made to undertake compulsory work (or, in the 'trainingfare' version, compulsory training) for their benefits. The US has already moved in this direction, and following visits to observe the US workfare system, the UK government has also recently implemented local trials of a similar scheme. However, the idea of a 'workfare' mode of regulation is problematic, for substantial gaps exist between conservative (that is, neo-liberal) and social-democratic visions of such a system.[24] In the conservative vision, workfare is meant to have a strong 'deterrent' and cost-saving element, in that if the unemployed are made to work for their welfare benefits this should deter 'voluntary' unemployment and 'work-shyness', and thus save public spending on benefits. Essentially, for the conservative policy-maker, 'workfare' is a welfare-retrenchment strategy. This contrasts with the more social-democratic conception of 'rehabilitative' workfare, in which strategies to link welfare benefits to work should lead potential workers back into the labour force. To be successful, this implies associated heavy investments in the training of the unemployed, and efforts to make jobs available and attractive, for example by underpinning the labour market by a national minimum wage and improved employee protection rights. Under this model, substantial additional public expenditures are needed in the short term in order to make workfare schemes cost-effective in the long run. Given this political flexibility in the interpretation and objectives of 'workfare', a policy consensus is likely to remain elusive. In any case, actual experience with workfare policies in the United States has thus far proved disappointing, both in terms of creating jobs and equipping the unemployed with the skills needed to compete in the labour market.

---

the need for expansionary policies to boost demand for labour in the world economy, this strategy was rejected by the UK, which instead rehearsed its usual litany of flexibility, deregulation and enterprise as the key factors for reducing unemployment. The jobs shortfall in Europe was also a key issue at the EU inter-governmental conference in Lille in early 1996, at which the UK again stressed its belief in the 'flexible labour market' approach to the problem.

24. Jessop (1994) in fact distinguishes between three workfare models, neo-liberal, neo-statist and neo-corporatist, but insists we will witness its continuing consolidation in successful capitalist economies because, 'the hollowed out Schumpeterian workfare state could prove structurally congruent and functionally adequate to post-Fordist accumulation regimes' (p.27).

The second feature identified as a key element of the emerging Schumpeterian workfare state is what might be termed the 'hollowing out' of the state through the transfer of its regulatory powers and responsibilities to regional and local governmental, quasi-governmental and even private sector bodies whose interventions and activities are closer to local labour markets and related sites of competitiveness. Given the high degree of persistence of regional unemployment disparities across the European countries, a case can certainly be made for labour market policies and programmes to be much more locally focused and tailored so that they can be more responsive to the varying employment needs and opportunities of individual areas. However, whilst in theory the 'decentralisation' and 'de-nationalisation' of labour market interventions and programmes may increase their flexibility and local impact, in practice their success will depend on sufficient levels of funding, measures to ensure a consistent level and quality of policy delivery between different local areas, and by no means least a supportive macroeconomic programme of economic growth. For the decentralisation of labour market programmes leaves individual regions and localities potentially vulnerable to changes in central state funding arrangements. As the 'New Federalism' welfare initiative in the US demonstrated, neo-liberal central states may see decentralisation as a means of cutting expenditure on labour market and welfare programmes, leaving local states and agencies to fund the shortfall. The more central states withdraw from the direct implementation and funding of labour market programmes and initiatives, and the more these are 'marketised' and 'contracted out' to local agencies and bodies, the more the success of such programmes is likely to vary between different localities. Under such a decentralised and marketised mode of labour market regulation, the areas worst affected by entrenched unemployment would be the least able to fund labour market and associated welfare programmes from local resources. Although many academic and political commentators would like to see greater decentralisation of state policies and spending, and increased local autonomy over economic governance and regulation, such a model may do little to reduce, and might even intensify, spatial inequalities in employment opportunities and incomes.[25] Moreover, unless the macroeconomic

---

25. Complete decentralisation and de-nationalisation of labour market regulation seem a long way off. Nevertheless, given the spirit of the times it seems almost inevitable that eventually it will occur to Western politicians that deregulation and privatisation of the unemployment insurance system (in much the same way that is already beginning to happen in the realm of pensions) offers them a way out of one of their most pressing political-financial problems, particularly as the US has just moved a step nearer to this position. Whether this radical form of 'welfare marketisation' would help alleviate the social and spatial disparities in unemployment and labour market exclusion across Europe is altogether another question.

climate is favourable for capital investment and job creation, local schemes and initiatives may have little prospect of sustained success.

In sum, the benefits of an American-style 'flexible', decentralised, work-fare-based labour market policy model for the solution of Europe's unemployment problem are doubtful. The drive for greater labour market flexibility might be a necessary condition for a return to higher rates of employment across Europe, but of itself it is not sufficient. Flexibilisation is creating less stable patterns of employment and a growth of part-time work rather than increasing the number of stable full-time jobs, and is a key factor contributing to the widening of social and regional income inequalities in some European states (for the case of regional income inequalities in the UK, see Martin 1995). At the same time the distinctions between 'in work' and 'out of work', and between unemployment and inactivity, are becoming blurred. Greater social and spatial fragmentation of employment, income and welfare are hardly consistent with the goal of social cohesion. The European Commission is right, therefore, to view the fight against unemployment as, 'an overriding priority for the European Union and the Member States' (European Commission 1996a, p.121), and is right in its moves to focus its various Structural Funds and cohesion policies on this objective. However, as the Commission recognises, member state policies remain the primary instrument for influencing unemployment and labour market cohesion across the Union. Thus how these national policies evolve in the near future, and whether and to what extent they reinforce or resist those of the Commission, are key elements of the challenge of European integration. In this respect, as in others, the solution to Europe's unemployment problem is as much political as it is economic.

Acknowledgement

This paper was presented at seminars at Cambridge University and Liverpool University. I am grateful for the useful comments made by colleagues on those occasions, and have tried to incorporate as many of their suggestions as possible.

CHAPTER 2

Unemployment as Exclusion
Unemployment as Choice
R. Ross MacKay

Introduction

High unemployment in the 1930s provided the background to the Keynesian revolution. Keynesian economics emphasises that resources often remain unemployed, underemployed and unrecognised, that economies can become stuck at levels of demand at which there is persistent involuntary unemployment. Under these circumstances, labour with a strong desire for opportunity (and willingness to accept employment on terms less generous than currently offered to those in jobs) cannot insist on work. Rising unemployment in the 1970s and 1980s provided the background to a new view of unemployment. There are various strands to this counter-revolution (monetarist, rational expectations, neo-classical, new classical macroeconomics), but all stress the importance of individual flexibility and choice. The 'natural rate' of unemployment, which is regarded as the market-clearing rate, is consistent with voluntary unemployment and adjustment unemployment: the 'natural rate' of unemployment can be reduced if individuals are more flexible and less selective in their employment search (by occupation, industry and region) and the wage they will accept. The individual has control over his/her labour market state – employed, self-employed or unemployed.

The counter-revolution (which emphasises unemployment by choice) and the Keynesian revolution (which emphasises unemployment by exclusion) provide quite different explanations of joblessness. On micro/macro, individual/collective, supply side/demand emphasis, flexibility and mobility as a solution to unemployment/flexibility and mobility as developing from opportunity – on all of these, as well as the timing and targets of policy, the counter-revolution and the Keynesian revolution are opposed. The key question is which perspective provides an appropriate framework for under-

standing unemployment and for framing policy. The following section of
this chapter considers the nature of labour market adjustment, turnover, quits,
redundancies, and flows in and out of unemployment, in the context of the
counter-revolution theory and the new view of unemployment. The third
section then examines regional development (structural change) in the
context of the Keynesian revolution and the traditional view of unemployment. This is then followed by a discussion of the differential success in
reconciling inflation and unemployment across countries. The final section
proffers some conclusions.

Labour Market Adjustment

All of the different strands of counter-revolutionary economics argue that
the economy would return towards full employment given flexibility of
wages and prices, and all identify government involvement in the economy
as a source of reduced wage and price flexibility. Also common to the
different strands of this school of thought is an emphasis on a 'natural rate'
of unemployment which provides a limit to demand management. The
'natural rate' of unemployment is not fixed – it depends upon several factors.
First, the efficiency with which information circulates in the labour market
and the ease and efficiency with which mobility takes place; second, the
demographic structure of the labour force; third, the degree of government
intervention in the market-place, for example minimum wage legislation,
wage councils, unemployment benefits and other income supports; and
finally, the importance of institutional factors, particularly the strength and
militancy of trade unions and the extent of centralised wage bargaining.

The 'natural rate' will be high when the market-clearing process takes
time and proceeds inefficiently, when public policies remove the incentive to
adjust and adapt, and when the labour force is ageing. It will also be high if
public policy holds wages above the competitive level which would be set
in the market-place, for example, as the result of minimum wage provisions
or the protection afforded by wage councils. Furthermore, the natural rate
of unemployment will be high when trade unions use their monopoly power
to press for and obtain higher wages than would be set in 'free' labour
markets. In sum, the more that labour markets deviate from the competitive
ideal, the higher will be the natural or equilibrium unemployment rate.

Unemployment as choice places the emphasis on the individual. The
unemployed can find a way into work by demonstrating a willingness to
accept lower wages, less attractive working conditions, longer journeys to
work or by transferring to other occupations, industries and locations.
Insufficient flexibility results in unemployment 'by choice'. The counter-

revolution represents the relationship between employer and employee as remarkably shallow. The loss of job security for an individual, the loss of a way of life for a community are depoliticised and described in a way that minimises their consequences. Unemployment is seen as a voluntary choice or as the result of government policies that provide incentives to workers to remain unemployed. The new view of unemployment also emphasises productive search, transitional (brief) unemployment and selective choice. These are always part of unemployment. The question is how important these features actually are in explaining high and rising unemployment in the 1970s, 1980s and 1990s (see MacKay 1993; MacKay and Jones 1989).

The evidence shows that the number of people moving between jobs declines, and voluntary quits (a proxy for productive job search) fall as unemployment climbs. There is a tendency for workers to hold on to their existing jobs (even if they are not entirely satisfactory) in difficult labour markets. When labour markets are tight, transfer between jobs is high and movement is predominantly voluntary; when labour markets are slack, transfer is reduced and voluntary quits account for a declining proportion of job separations. Choice, experiment and productive job search decline in significance as unemployment climbs: they cannot explain high and rising unemployment.

High unemployment emerges from a background where redundancies (which mean that jobs no longer exist) substitute for voluntary quits. The higher the level of unemployment (by region or over time), the more important redundancies become relative to voluntary quits (Jones and Martin 1986; Martin 1984). The evidence clearly shows (see Mackay 1993; MacKay and Jones 1989) that those who move as a result of redundancy are less successful in the labour market than those who move by choice. This is not surprising. Those who quit by choice not only have different characteristics, they also tend to move at a time of their own selection and often in response to positive labour market signals. Redundancy, in contrast, implies labour surplus to requirements: the labour market signals are negative and often redundancies involve large numbers of workers, including many who saw their future in particular internal labour markets and specific industries. The balance of labour market adjustment shifts away from choice in slack labour markets.

The counter-revolution, the new view of unemployment, emphasises buoyant flows into and out of unemployment. In the early 1970s, annual flows out of unemployment in the UK were close to 7 times the unemployment stock, whereas in the mid 1980s they were only about 1.4 times the stock. Unemployment involves an unusual or perverse queue. The longer one stands in line (the longer the spell of unemployment), the lower the probability of movement back into employment. In the tight labour conditions of the 1960s, the strength of flow relative to reserve ensured that the risk of long-term unemployment (more than a year) was slight. Rising unemployment is mainly down to longer spells of unemployment, and flows out account for a diminishing share of the unemployment pool. Moreover, outflows change their nature as unemployment climbs. The more slack the labour market, the more likely it is that flows out of unemployment feed labour force inactivity (or hidden unemployment).

The optimistic view of unemployment (which connects to the counter-revolution perspective) is that it represents a constantly shifting mix of short-term unemployed who are making the sensible adjustments (investments) that will provide long-term labour market stability. The metaphor for the new view is a flow that delivers labour to new opportunity. The pool may appear deep, but the waters are continually refreshed by flows in and out. UK male unemployment rates in the 1980s were two and a half times those in the 1970s, more than four times those in the 1960s and more than six times those in the 1950s. As unemployment climbs, long-term unemployment grows as a proportion. By 1984, long-term male unemployment (continuous unemployment of more than a year) was higher than total male unemployment in 1979. By 1986, extended male unemployment (continuous unemployment of more than two years) was only 17 per cent below total male unemployment in 1975. Long-term unemployment (male and female) was only 52,000 in 1965; male long-term unemployment was 132,000 in 1975 and over 1 million in 1985. The unemployment pool has developed dangerous waters and also isolated lakes which are barely touched by flows into work.

From the mid 1970s, unemployment in the UK has consistently been higher than vacancies (even after allowing for non-recording of the latter) and during the 1980s the gap grew substantially. An excess of unemployment over vacancies implies that the unemployed are not scarce resources on the road from one opportunity to another. The new view of unemployment, the counter-revolution, is one possible way of describing unemployment. The reality is that it provides predictions which are unreliable and an account of unemployment which is difficult to reconcile with the evidence. The peculiarity of the counter-revolution is that it has grown in influence, even as it has become increasingly unrepresentative. Ironically, the interpretation of unemployment as voluntary choice, selective search and temporary transfer is more relevant to the 1950s and 1960s than the 1970s, 1980s and 1990s.

Most of what happens in the labour market lies between the extremes of choice and compulsion. In slack labour markets, balance moves away from choice and, as the balance shifts, the potentially flexible find it increasingly difficult to discover opportunity. Ideas are powerful and their power is demonstrated when they mislead. The counter-revolution explanation of high unemployment focuses primarily on the impact of government policies which have reduced mobility and adjustment; public policies and union power which hold wages above market-clearing levels; and unemployment benefits and social security which add to the attractions of unemployment and raise the reservation wage – the minimum wage which labour will accept. The problem with this account is that the counter-revolution has been politically persuasive. It was the inspiration for policies which address the (hypothesised) 'natural' rate unemployment. In the UK, government policies have sought to deregulate and 'flexibilise' the labour market by abolishing wage councils and minimum wages, reducing unemployment benefits (relative to average wages), restricting access to welfare, removing trade union power and privilege, decentralising wage bargaining, removing safety standards and employee protection for those in work, and encouraging private home ownership rather than public housing. These policies have been consistently followed and are consistently market-led. They are designed to provide clear market signals and incentives. As unemployment rose during the 1980s so the pursuit of these policies became more intensive, with little apparent positive effects on employment.

The counter-revolution has been influential not only in shaping the nature of official employment and labour market policies, but also their timing. In the UK, there are few retraining and redeployment policies at the point of redundancy. Instead policy concentrates on the long-term unemployed. Little attention has been directed to the pace of employment loss, and employers (public and private) face few checks in declaring large-scale redundancies. There is no pressure on employers to signal vacancies (inside or outside the organisation) to employees when jobs are removed. Neither is consultation with unions or employees over cutbacks and closures given a high priority (see Rubery 1992a). In short, we do not have an active labour market policy which reacts quickly and effectively to employment loss by providing positive signals and direction. The delayed, dilatory response that typifies current policy practice follows directly from the counter-revolution and its emphasis on inflation reduction as the key economic objective. The short-term unemployed and flows into unemployment are assumed to maintain the effective labour reserve. Policies which reduce their numbers would add to inflationary pressure. Labour market policy should thus address flows out of unemployment, and particularly the long-term unemployed because they are so far removed from opportunity that a reduction in long-term unemployment will do little to add to the bargaining power (inflationary threat) of labour. The claim that we should react to those without work only when it is quite clear that loss of opportunity is lasting deserves a direct challenge. Probability of escape from unemployment certainly declines the longer people are without work. With long unemployment, skills deteriorate; the habit of regular work may be lost; the self-respect and self-confidence of the individual and the view of the potential employer change. But it is surely preferable to prevent the flows into unemployment in the first place. A policy approach which develops from the counter-revolution will be hard on the unemployed, but soft on the causes of unemployment. If one wishes to understand – rather than disguise or deny – unemployment, the counter-revolution is not the ideal philosophy.

Recognising Unemployment: Regions and Structural Change

Involuntary unemployment is the product of a cumulative process which is triggered by an initial decline in key sectors of the local economy. Modern unemployment takes its characteristic form from the employment relationship within large industrial units. Such employment requires a clear separation between the formal and the informal economy: a clear divide between organised and casual work. When this form of secure employment disappears, a gap or space emerges within the community and around the individual. That gap or space is the essence of unemployment (see Piore 1987). It cannot simply be assumed that work is always available to those who are truly flexible; to bridge the gap may require a collective response as well as individual initiative. Experience in work does not necessarily translate into alternative productive activity and without capital, without organisation, the individual and the community lack direction. The unemployment which follows major plant closures and cutbacks is not indicative of a sudden taste for leisure on the part of the workers involved. Neither can it be explained in terms of productive job search.

The internal labour market literature (see Doeringer and Piore 1985) is one way to escape from the restrictions of market-clearing theory and policies, with their assumption of unfettered substitution and transfer. There is not one but many fragmented labour markets, and substitution across them can be difficult. The most effective barriers to movement are often those around the individual plant or organisation. Employers and employees value continuity. The majority of established employees are not actively in the broader labour market, but tend to consider their prospects to be determined by the opportunities that emerge within the organisation. Employment policies and attitudes which weaken internal labour markets and make the workforce insecure are not the most obvious way to add to human capital.

Modern economies are not accurately described as a series of small-scale gambles, nor naturally compatible with contestable markets which guarantee ease of entry and exit. They are marked by long-term commitments, by heavy sunk costs and by pronounced specialisation of physical and human capital. The essence of division of labour is interdependence, not independence. The individual has to be part of a working team to be productive. The exchange value of a worker is at the mercy of a division of labour which adjusts to competitive forces beyond the control of the individual and the local community: employees do not own or control the means of production.

'Creative destruction' is Schumpeter's felicitous phrase describing the process of structural change (Schumpeter 1943). With capital and labour fixed and organised in particular employments, structural change implies real loss in exchange value for physical and human capital. Failure to consider the realities and costs of structural adjustment encourages economists to overstate consistently the speed with which resources transfer between employments and locations. Specialisation and division of labour tend to make employment more unstable, more precarious of tenure and less certain in market value. The effects are not obvious in an economy where new employment broadly compensates for, and matches, jobs lost. But they create real problems when employment decline leaves large numbers of workers without effective labour market opportunity. Innovation and structural change – the compensatory 'gale of creative destruction' – does not merely check existing developments, it puts an end to them. The employment relationships that dissolve involve external economies. Different kinds of unemployment interact and build from each other, and the loss of a locality's economic base has implications for employment in the local service sector. What might have been frictional unemployment (requiring little change and limited search by potential employees) becomes structural unemployment (possibly requiring extensive labour retraining and changes in occupation, industry and/or location), and what may have been structural unemployment translates into extended unemployment or even withdrawal from the labour force altogether.

Unemployment, in the Keynesian view, is associated with loss of markets and a lack of effective demand. Effective demand depends on a host of economic decisions, both private and public, and especially on investment. Since this in turn depends on demand for particular products and services in a future which cannot be known, there are limits to markets and to market signals. The Keynesian and post-Keynesian claim is that wages (and other) prices are less flexible and less effective in clearing markets than the counter-revolution suggests. Wages (and more generally prices) are not as sensitive as market-clearing implies and when wages are flexible, falls in money wages do not necessarily lead to falls in real wages and these do not necessarily stimulate new employment. Reductions in real wages also reduce effective demand which in turn depresses the demand for labour.

The Keynesian argument is complex (see Chick 1983), but examining labour market adjustments in relative wages and employment opportunities at the regional level can add to understanding. Figure 2.1 shows the contrast between the Outer Regions of the United Kingdom (Northern Ireland, North, Scotland, Wales, Yorkshire and Humberside, North West) and the Inner Region Core (South East, East Anglia, East Midlands, South West). As unemployment rose to notably higher levels in the 1980s, the gap between the more and less prosperous regions also increased. Household income excluding social security is a rough measure of family income from work. In the Outer Regions, household income without social security fell from 86 per cent of the Inner Region Core average in 1978–79 to 70 per cent in 1990–91 (Figure 2.1). The household income gap (or income from work gap) can be divided into a wage (price of labour) gap and an employment (opportunity) gap – the gap between relative wages and relative household incomes reflects both higher unemployment and lower activity rates in the Outer Regions. In 1978–79, the household income gap was about 14 per cent, with 5 per cent attributable to lower earnings for those in work in the Outer Regions and roughly 9 per cent the result of inferior employment opportunities (higher unemployment, lower activity rates) in the Outer Regions. By 1990–91, the household income gap had doubled to 30 per cent, with 15 per cent explained by lower earnings for those in work and 15 per cent the result of fewer employment opportunities. The key point is

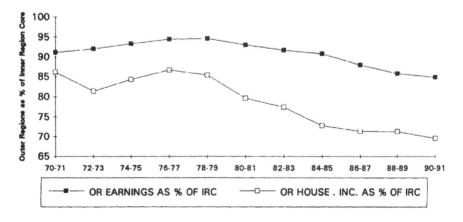

Figure 2.1. *Outer Regions Compared with Inner Region Core Earnings Gap and Household Income Gap Net of Social Security*

Source: *New Earnings Survey and Family Expenditure Survey.*

that when wages move against the Outer Regions so does opportunity. We cannot simply assume that wage adjustment will provide the responses that market-clearing approaches anticipate.

The counter-revolution argument accepted by Conservative governments is that this regional divergence was the product of wage signals that are insufficiently flexible. The natural adjustment of labour markets implies lower wages and unit costs in high unemployment regions. The wage signals would then be more effective in promoting labour migration from, and capital movement to, the parts of the country where wages are low. As we have seen, relative wages did move strongly against the Outer Regions in the 1980s, but so did relative employment as well. The counter-revolution 'solution' has real difficulties. The true implication of the apparently neutral and objective search for regional balance is wage reduction even for secure jobs in high unemployment regions.[1] A related argument is that the number of secure jobs be reduced against a background of cuts to and restrictions on the welfare state. These are controversial solutions, particularly if our objectives include a more even spread of labour market opportunity and a reduction in regional imbalance.

The counter-revolution highlights the failure of economics as a science to understand the nature of unemployment. It is a reflection of the attempt of economists to seek a market solution to a problem which is caused by market failure. The two great faults of capitalism, suggested Keynes, are its failure to provide for full employment and its arbitrary and inequitable distribution of income and wealth. All too often counter-revolution 'solutions' tend to add simultaneously to both unemployment and inequality. They do so against a background which encourages, even draws comfort from, an atmosphere of pervasive employment insecurity.

The Keynesian revolution suggests that the image of a relentlessly 'taut' economy can be a check to curiosity and a bar to true enquiry. The equilibrium assumption (which lies at the heart of the counter-revolution) is that all resources released in the process of structural change find alternative employment. The assumption is heroic when unemployment is under 3 per cent, even more so when it is in double figures. A proper search for understanding must relax the assumptions of fully informed wage and price

---

1. Wage bargaining is difficult, contentious, time-consuming and emotional. It is a means of reaching an often untidy compromise rather than a precise means of rewarding contribution. Wage bargaining can create divisions and reduce goodwill, even as it consumes resources. The potential for all of these is enhanced with wage bargaining encouraged plant by plant and organisation by organisation. Introducing wage differentials across regions where there were common scales is unlikely to be conducive to good labour relations.

signals and automatic and flexible responses on the part of both employees and employers. Only then can one develop a realistic conception of the economic system where bargains and contracts are made at prices which do not clear markets, where resources remain unemployed, and where there are problems in encouraging adjustment to constantly changing opportunities. In such an imperfect, but realistic economy there may be a role for public policy.

Figure 2.2 indicates the impact of one policy response: an automatic stabiliser which comes into play when there is loss of economic base and loss of income. The upper line shows household income in the Outer Regions relative to household income in the Inner Region Core when social security payments are included, and the lower line relative income without social security. Expenditure on social security raised relative household income in the Outer Regions by only 1 per cent in 1974–75 (low national unemployment, low regional divergence in unemployment rates), but by 6 per cent in 1982–83 (high national unemployment, strong regional divergence). As wage (price) and opportunity (quantity) move strongly against the Outer Regions (Figure 2.1), social security becomes more important in maintaining relative income (Figure 2.2). The counter-revolution identifies non-market forces as imperfections and identifies only negative effects (encouraging families to rely on welfare rather than their own efforts and weakening

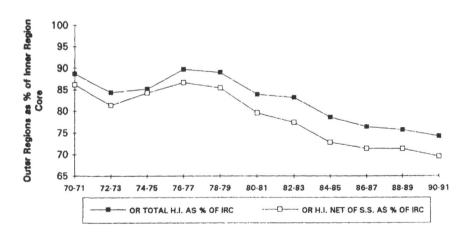

Figure 2.2. Outer Regions Compared with Inner Region Core: Total Household Income Gap and Household Income Gap Net of Social Security, 1970–71 to 1990–91
Source: New Earnings Survey and Family Expenditure Survey

alternative support systems). However, in practice non-market forces, including the welfare state, have a more positive side. They can complement market adjustments by reducing fear of change and resistance to it. They can act as a counter to the loss of effective demand and they can provide a direct, and immediate, response to regional inequality.

Social security is only one example of social and spatial stabilisers. Social security and other transfer payments act to check the adverse secondary impacts which flow from loss of markets. Non-market forces, including automatic stabilisers, are deeply embedded in mixed economies. They provide greater socio-economic stability and security than would otherwise exist. They are a response to a weakness of capitalism. At times of rapid structural dislocation in the economy, automatic stabilisers provide stability until new economic and employment opportunities emerge. Without such transfers and guaranteed social wages, cumulative forces of decline may be set in motion which are likely to be difficult to check once they gain momentum. The Keynesian revolution emphasis is quite different from the counter-revolution. Early response is more effective than delayed reaction, and prevention and managed adjustment are most effective of all.

Inflation, Unemployment, Corporatism

> By far the most successful and durable method [of checking inflation] has been that of corporatism... It depends not only on sufficient consensus about aims and methods, but also on cohesive organisation: the employers' associations and the trade unions must be able to rely on, or secure, their members' compliance with the agreements they reach. (Phelps Brown 1990, pp.18–19)

Keynes identified two considerable problems for the Keynesian revolution. The first is inflation prior to full employment. High employment shifts the balance of labour market advantage in favour of workers' bargaining power and under these circumstances it becomes more difficult to reconcile two desirable policy objectives: low inflation and low unemployment. Figure 2.3 indicates the problems in reconciling high employment and low inflation. The figure records average unemployment and average inflation for 16 market economies.[2] Prior to the late 1960s unemployment rates were low and inflation was moderate (there are some signs of a Phillips curve

2. The 16 countries are those selected by Maddison (1991). In order of inflation bias average, 1954–93 – highest first, lowest last – they are Italy, the UK, Canada, Denmark, France, Finland, Australia, the US, Belgium, Netherlands, Sweden, Norway, Austria, Japan, Germany, Switzerland.

relationship with price changes moving in the opposite direction to unemployment). A favourable interpretation of the Keynesian revolution would connect the years of record growth and low unemployment to state policies which accorded central importance to full employment. From 1968, and with increasing force after the oil price rises of 1973–74 and 1979–80, the economic climate changed considerably. Inflation rose prior to 1973 and without any fall in unemployment, but it was the oil price rises of 1973–74 (when oil prices quadrupled) and 1979–80 (when they doubled) that signalled major problems for inflation and unemployment. The extent of the problem is summarised in a measure of inflation bias, which is simply the sum of consumer price increases and unemployment rates (see Figure 2.3). An increase in inflation bias implies growing problems in reconciling low unemployment and moderate price increases. The inflation bias index for the 16 countries rose from an average of 5.8 in 1954–67 (low inflation and low unemployment), to 7.6 in 1968–72 (rising inflation), to 14.4 in 1973–78 (first oil price shock) and to 14.5 in 1979–85 (second oil price shock), before falling to 10.9 in 1986–93 (high unemployment) as oil and energy prices moderated.

There are four key points. First, inflation began to rise prior to the oil price shock of 1973–74. Second, energy price changes are critical to understanding the more difficult economic climate and the breakdown of the Phillips curve in the early 1970s. Third, problems with stagflation (low growth and rising unemployment combined with uncomfortable levels of price increase) undermined Keynesian-style policies that were designed to

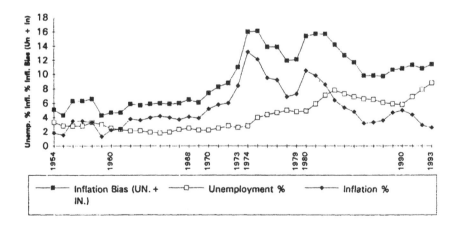

Figure 2.3. Shifts in Inflation and Rising Unemployment Average for 16 Market Economies, 1954–93
Source: Maddison (1991) and Main Economic Indicators (OECD)

achieve full employment. Fourth, low inflation has coincided with higher unemployment in recent years. Inflation was low in all 16 market economies by 1993, when unemployment also reached its highest post-war level in 11 of the 16 countries. As each country abandoned its employment objectives and substituted inflation targets, the level of unemployment rose.

There may be no clear solution to inflation at or prior to full employment, but Keynes and post-Keynesians connect inflation to the nature of wage bargaining institutions and practices. Wage bargaining is an important part of the inflation process. The degree of direct responsibility of each wage bargaining unit for inflation may be small, or large, depending on its scale.

When there are many unions and no general agreement on wages (as in the UK), the temptation for each wage bargaining group to pursue the shadow (money wage increases) at the expense of the substance (real wage gains) is strong. When there are many unions, compromise and consensus on acceptable wage increase is difficult to reach and to hold. The reduction of inflation then emerges as a public good. In such situations self-interest dictates that others bear the costs and responsibilities. As with other public goods, it may be difficult to find a solution which is consistent with each unit taking decisions that are independent of the decisions made by others.

Olson (1965) provides a framework for the above theme with his 'encompassing' concept. There are special interest groups which embrace a significant part of the societies to which they belong. They are forced by their scale to limit the burdens they place on society. The notion of 'encompassing' suggests that union structure may be important to restraint. Encompassing implies a small number of large unions and/or a general consensus on wage policy. It limits distributional conflict and contributes to reconciling high employment and moderate wage and price increases. Union structure in Austria and Germany (16 unions in both) encourages unions to recognise individual responsibility for inflation, while unions in the UK have less incentive to exercise restraint. In Austria and Germany there are powerful central union organisations, but in the UK the Trades Union Congress has limited authority and provides little co-ordination on pay. It is important to note that a responsible policy appears to follow not from union weakness, but from an orderly, settled, concentrated union structure where unions with real power and authority are accepted as social partners.

The idea of 'encompassingness' can be embraced in a broader framework. Tarantelli's Index of Corporatism ranks countries by three criteria: centralisation of wage bargaining, the degree of ideological and political consensus, and the existence of arbitration rules. A country with a high ranking for corporatism is one where concentrated wage bargaining encourages each social group to recognise responsibility for inflation, but a high ranking also implies a process of consultation, compromise and consensus. Figure 2.4 considers the relationship between corporatism and inflation bias in the years 1954–67, when inflation bias was low, and in the years 1973–85 when inflation bias was high.[3] The Index of Corporatism clearly captures a substantial degree of country-by-country variation in inflation bias in the years 1973–85 (the degree of correlation is 0.90 and each unit of corporatism reduces inflation bias by 1.19, while for 1954–67 the correlation is 0.52 and each unit of corporatism reduces inflation bias by 0.19). The contrast suggests that corporatism is particularly important in times of inflationary turbulence.

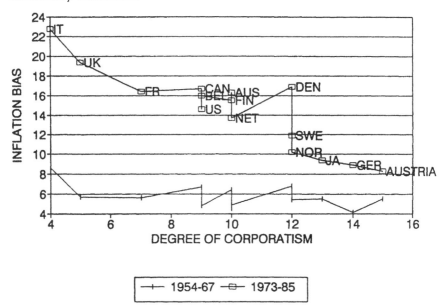

Figure 2.4. Inflation Bias and Corporatism, 1954–67 and 1973–85
Source: Maddison (1991) and Main Economic Indicators (OECD) and Tarantelli (1986) and
Pekkarinen et al. (1992)

3. The relationships are shown for 15 of Maddison's 16 countries. There is no measure of corporatism for Switzerland. The Swiss model has been described as paternalistic-liberal, though the term 'liberal corporatism' has also been used to denote a decentralised, consensus-generating system. The industrial relations system is characterised by the avoidance of conflict – see Pekkarinen, Pohjola and Rowthorn (1992) and, in particular, the chapter on Switzerland by Blaas. Cornwall (1990, p.111) claims that a, 'spirit of trust and compromise permeates Swiss society'. Compromise involves negotiation followed by binding arbitration rather than industrial action; agreement to cut wages and profits and dividends in recession; and work sharing rather than redundancies. Compromise and trust mean that labour has a real stake in the wage restraint and industrial harmony which promotes full employment and rising living standards.

Corporatism is useful in illustrating an important Keynesian theme. Co-ordination and consensus can be an important restraint on wage and price inflation. That efficiency wages may creep up in spite of best efforts was the Keynesian warning, but best efforts are more impressive in some countries than in others. Corporatism is a product, 'of a certain social and historical ground, from which it is not readily transported' (Phelps Brown 1990, p.19). Corporatism depends on the attitudes and compromises which define the nature of the societies in which we work. Corporatism may be difficult to import, but the relative success of compromise and consensus suggests that movement in the opposite direction (the UK choice) may not have favourable results. Current government policy in the UK is to promote more bargaining units, local negotiation and plant-by-plant bargaining. The assumption is that wage restraint will then develop from market weakness against a background of unemployment. There is a problem with this scenario, however. As Sawyer (1992, p.20) points out, 'the more negotiating units there are, the less each one pays attention to the overall impact of their own settlement, and the less effect will any call for wage restraint have'. Decentralised wage determination makes it more difficult to approach full employment. The Phelps Brown emphasis is similar. Shifts in pay negotiation to the local level move the UK economy further away from corporatist approaches that have been effective in the past.

Unemployment as Exclusion

Priestley, in his *English Journey* (1934 [1994]), discovered unemployment (notably higher in Northern England) as a series of personal tragedies and also a national calamity. Darwin (1890) described labour as the prime basic condition for all human existence. And Freud (1930) insisted that work is our strongest tie to reality: there is no satisfactory substitute. Marx (1975) claimed that productive activity makes sense of life by giving meaning to human energy, and Conrad (1899 [1983]) suggested that while we may not consistently enjoy work, employment is one way we discover ourselves and our potential. For Adam Smith (1776 [1904]), our labour is our most important property: it provides the natural, the healthy access to the necessaries and conveniences of life.

Employment is income, but more than income. Employment contributes to deep needs in people who struggle to make sense of their lives (see Jahoda 1982). We need to structure our days; we need wider social experience than is provided by the family; we need to participate in collective effort; we need to know what and where we are in society; we need regular activity. The exclusion imposed by unemployment can only be understood by considering employment as a structure which adds meaning to life. Employment provides organisation, identity, contact, collective purpose and a target for energy. Unemployment benefit may be partial compensation for income loss, but not for the meaning and purpose which work provides.

The counter-revolution and the 'natural rate' view employment and unemployment from a perspective of choice. The individual is deemed to have control. Employment and leisure are substitutes: any reduction in employment involves compensation in leisure. The wage return is the sum required to compensate for the disutility or inconvenience of employment at the margin. Individual preferences are seen as operating within a labour market where supply and demand for labour interact to provide equilibrium wage and employment levels. Those without employment offer labour services that they value (price) at a higher level than the market. Unemployment as either voluntary choice or transitional adjustment emerges from a labour market which clears. If individuals are willing to take employment at less than the ruling wage, the wage falls to clear the market. Involuntary unemployment, in all but the short run, is inconsistent with continuous bargaining and with profit maximisation: it implies that industrialists ignore significant and obvious opportunities to trade. In doing so they ignore the possibility of labour cost reduction and profit increase. Behaviour that is inconsistent with the underlying assumptions is deemed irrational and therefore not important: the assumptions are allowed to dictate the view of reality that is acceptable. An overly narrow equilibrium approach is erected as a barrier to economic thought (see Kornai 1971; Shackle 1972).

The assumptions of the counter-revolution are seldom admired for their realism. The Keynesian Revolution develops from observation. For Keynes, the most important source of the conservation of errors is the absence of strong claims based on actual experience. Writing in 1933, Keynes (1933 [1972], p.350) expressed a keen sense of frustration with economists who tried, 'to solve the problem of unemployment with a theory which is based on the assumption that there is no unemployment'. The *General Theory* is the Keynesian escape map. It is not required by the counter-revolution. Substitute 'avoid' for 'solve' in the above quotation and the accusation applies to the counter-revolution. An approach which concentrates on inflation and ignores the need for a theory of the supply and demand of output as a whole is not value-free. A cautious and conservative approach to macroeconomic policy has a major effect on real variables (output, employment) as well as nominal ones (wages, prices). In achieving its effect, it adjusts the balance of power between employer and employee firmly in favour of the former (see Kalecki 1943 [1972]). It also denies work to many who seek opportunity.

It is always possible to argue that the effect would be different if it were not for unions, the welfare state and other imperfections introduced by public policy. The only sensible response is that the world described by the theory does not exist and cannot be created. Unions are a response to the weakness of isolated labour in industrial economies. Some imperfections introduced by government (including regional transfers and possibly welfare benefits) are in fact important in maintaining effective demand and in adding to, or supporting, employment. The nature of the employment contract, the importance of trust and loyalty in the employer/employee relationship, means that price is only one of the important signals and that wages are sticky. In the counter-revolution, the simplified hypothesis of rapid adjustment is described as health, the complexities of the real world are regarded as disease. The counter-revolution is part of an ambitious attempt to explain the economy within one general, idealised framework. That set of ideas is at its weakest and most vulnerable when applied to the labour market.

The counter-revolution argues that if a surplus appears on the market it will drive down the real wage. The labour market does not behave in this fashion. Unemployment in the UK rose above 3 million in 1983 and remained above 3 million into 1987. Real wage increases were average in 1984 and 1985 and above average in 1986. High unemployment and real wage resistance were consistent with government policies designed to limit unions and reduce the generosity of the welfare state. The evidence is difficult to reconcile with the counter-revolution's emphasis on unemployment as choice and the real wage adjusting to bring supply and demand for labour into balance. The counter-revolution pays little attention to the circumstances which make the labour market a non-clearing market. Had attention been paid to the inherent difference between labour and other markets, the costs of containing inflation by means of monetary restraint might have been better understood.

An explanation of unemployment (the 'natural rate') which sees unemployment as often too low (with employees deceived into accepting employment that they do not really desire at the wages paid) is perhaps not the ideal way to explain high and rising unemployment, or a level of unemployment well above that of vacancies. An approach which derives from tight, prior market-clearing and which believes in a strong underlying tendency to full employment is not the only road to understanding.

Conclusion

The Keynesian revolution (unemployment by exclusion) and the counter-revolution (unemployment by choice) are difficult to reconcile. An important

Keynesian theme is that it is the battle of ideas which counts. The theory, the philosophy, the approach to understanding which wins acceptance sets the policy agenda. But theories are even more important: they check, they guide the way we interpret events, they control what we allow ourselves to see. This chapter is an attempt to understand how and why a set of ideas which provides a good understanding of unemployment and labour market adjustment has lost position to a less effective explanation.

It is no surprise that rising inflation and growing inflation bias should lead to problems for demand management and demand maintenance. There is real, not imaginary, policy conflict when macroeconomic policy restricts output and employment in one direction, but raises wages and prices in the other. What is puzzling is that growing problems in reconciling unemployment and inflation provide such fertile soil for models and explanations of unemployment that emphasise market-clearing: where rising unemployment is explained in terms of individual preference and lack of flexibility, and where the individual is assumed to have control over the state of the labour market. Economic systems are capable of more than one market failure. It is not just inflation that developed a rising trend in the 1970s: unemployment continued on an upward path through the 1980s and has remained high into the 1990s. Growing inflation bias implies increasing conflict between desirable objectives. It does not mean we can redefine full employment in terms of price behaviour (see Cornwall 1990, p.12).

The Keynesian revolution and corporatism suggest that capitalism can compromise without losing its defining characteristics. Both were inspired by a humanity and compassion which is less important to the counter-revolution. In important respects, both proved consistent with improved performance. The Keynesian revolution did prove important in containing the business cycle, and corporatism was important in checking inflation without resort to high unemployment. However, what is reasonably effective at one stage of economic development and in a particular economy is not necessarily appropriate to other countries and/or times. The nature of the relevant compromise alters with circumstance, *but there is little to suggest that performance only improves when policy is inspired by a search for market solutions.*

The market has limits. Recognising those limits is important to understanding the labour market and developing appropriate policies. We have, in important respects, a more difficult economic climate. The experience of recent years (with Japan a possible exception) suggests that high and stable employment is difficult to reconcile with wage and price restraint. It is possible to check inflation, but only by running economies at margins of unused capacity which are uncomfortable. There are difficulties in deriving and applying a successful social bargain appropriate to the 1990s (Cornwall

1990). However, without an alternative to the control of inflation by prolonged and high unemployment, the problems of mixed economies grow more complex.

We know that the pace of change is important to labour market adjustment. Labour markets can accommodate structural change, but as with most sensitive systems there are limits. The way in which help is extended to those unable to fend for themselves is of profound importance to any society. One critique of the welfare state is that it encourages people to look to the system rather than their own (and family) efforts. But traditional ties and supports are disturbed by more than welfare. We are constantly told that the only certainty in market economies is change. There is continuous revolution in production and in social conditions, a background of perpetual flux. A complex and shifting division of labour does not necessarily produce security. The ability of the individual and the community to look after its own connects paradoxically to the possibility of drawing upon a larger pool of resources in circumstances widely accepted as providing proper grounds for state assistance. Social transfers, including regional transfers, are not just about compassion. Automatic fiscal stabilisers are deeply embedded in advanced mixed economies (see MacKay 1994). Prevention and early response are more effective than delayed reaction. Given a loss of markets and a reduced valuation of human and physical capital, built-in stabilisers provide time and opportunity to find a new sense of direction.

In this chapter an attempt has been made to understand and comment on opposed economic-political philosophies. Four broad policy themes follow from the argument. First, employment is important not just to income, but to involvement in society. The weight we place on employment varies with the life cycle and according to family responsibilities. Substituting voluntary leisure for forced leisure (unemployment) has considerable attractions. Keynes (1933 [1972]) refers to this response as 'spreading the bread' (opportunity) more evenly in economic systems where wealth continues to accumulate, but the labour content in output declines.

Second, Keynesian stabilisers and corporatism are nation state solutions. They were designed to retain the search for efficiency without offending our ideas of a satisfactory way of life. As nation state solutions they possibly lose energy as the nation state loses power. A key characteristic of capitalism is that capital hires labour. The critical decisions are made by those who own and control capital. The 'right of investment' and the 'right of relocation' are the right to sabotage employment (see Veblen 1978). Given mobile capital, the key decisions are often taken outside the economy. The threat of relocation and capital flight suggests that socio-economic compromise may have to embrace groups of countries (EU, NAFTA, ASEAN) rather than nation states.

Third, capitalism is not so fragile as to lose all meaning if parts of the economy obey non-market rules. Apart from other considerations, the sectors that remain outside the market are potentially important in avoiding the speculative excesses and spectacular dislocations that spread through the private sector.

Fourth, microeconomics is about constrained choice, its key theme being scarcity. Macroeconomics is not simply the principles and techniques of microeconomics extended to a broader stage. It has a different agenda; its concerns embrace the circumstances that remove effective choice for labour and make it more difficult to provide direction for education, training and mobility.

CHAPTER 3

Regional Unemployment Changes in Britain

Anne Green, Paul Gregg and Jonathan Wadsworth

Introduction

Britain's regions have experienced differential economic performance for decades. Typically, the Southern regions have prospered relative to those further north. Hence the existence of a 'North–South divide' popularised in the media. When measured by the relative unemployment rate, this North–South divide was at its greatest during economic booms and smallest during recessions. In contrast, the absolute unemployment differential tended to rise in recessions and narrow during recovery. The persistence of these differentials across regions over time, however, assumed the status of stylised fact.

The late 1980s was a period of strong economic growth which, if anything, reinforced previous regional patterns of economic performance. At the height of the boom, in 1989, in towns such as Crawley in the South East of England the unemployment rate fell as low as 1.4 per cent, whilst the unemployment rate in Newcastle in the North of England remained over 14 per cent. The onset of recession in 1990 appeared to change this regional pattern radically. For the first time in 50 years, the unemployment rate in the South East of England rose above that of Scotland. Both relative and absolute regional unemployment differentials narrowed.

This chapter attempts to assess the extent to which the early 1990s were an exceptional period with respect to regional economic performance or whether this was indeed part of a general convergence in local unemployment patterns. The issue of whether the unemployment rate can be considered as an adequate measure of a region's economic performance is assessed in the first section. Indeed the question is posed whether the standard region or the unemployment rate are any longer useful concepts with which to measure the extent of social exclusion. The second section describes the main empirical features underlying the regional patterns in unemployment, labour supply, earnings and migration which motivate this analysis. The third section examines unemployment variation at more disaggregated levels, namely counties, travel to work areas (hereafter TTWAs) and census wards, and explores whether alternative formulations of geographical variation in unemployment are more informative about changing relative fortunes. The final section draws some conclusions about the relevance of regional policy in this new environment.

Regional Unemployment, 1965–95

Table 3.1 uses claimant count data to outline the pattern of relative unemployment rates at five year intervals for the ten standard regions of Great Britain. Relative unemployment rates exhibit a clear secular convergence over the period. The dispersion of regional unemployment rates in 1995, as captured by the coefficient of variation, is around 75 per cent lower than in 1965. However, this general convergence disguises changing regional fortunes, as is apparent from Table 3.1. The West Midlands, for example, undergoes a transformation from low to high unemployment status. Unemployment rose by 60 per cent relative to the national average between 1965 and 1995. In contrast, Scottish unemployment fell by 110 per cent relative to the average over the same period, half of which occurred after 1990. Likewise, relative unemployment in the South East rose by 36 points after 1990. So does this sudden reversal of fortunes herald the end of the North–South divide or is there something peculiar about regional labour market performance in the early 1990s?

Table 3.1 Relative Unemployment Rates Across Standard Regions, 1965–95

	1965	*1970*	*1975*	*1980*	*1985*	*1990*	*1995*
North	1.77	1.76	1.33	1.52	1.44	1.61	1.28
Yorkshire – Humberside	0.77	1.08	0.94	1.03	1.12	1.23	1.07
East Midlands	0.69	0.88	0.86	0.93	0.91	0.89	0.93
East Anglia	0.92	0.88	0.86	0.80	0.76	0.60	0.78
South East	0.62	0.64	0.72	0.64	0.75	0.65	0.99
South West	1.15	1.08	1.11	0.90	0.87	0.74	0.87
West Midlands	0.46	0.80	1.08	1.17	1.19	1.07	1.03
North West	1.08	1.08	1.28	1.29	1.27	1.40	1.06
Wales	2.00	1.44	1.33	1.40	1.27	1.19	0.99
Scotland	2.08	1.76	1.19	1.36	1.20	1.54	0.97
Great Britain (%)	**1.3**	**2.5**	**3.6**	**5.8**	**10.8**	**5.7**	**8.0**
Coefficient of variation	0.51	0.34	0.20	0.26	0.22	0.33	0.15
Standard deviation	0.73	0.93	0.74	1.60	2.45	1.98	1.02

Source: Department of Employment Gazette

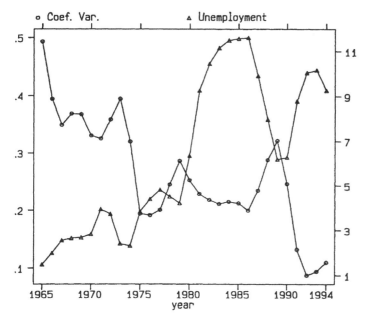

Figure 3.1a. National Unemployment and Coefficient of Variation Across Standard Regions, 1965–94
Source: Authors' calculations

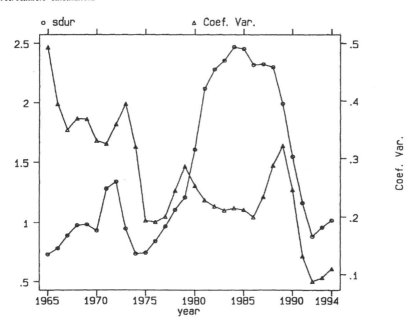

Figure 3.1b. Coefficient of Variation and Standard Deviation of Unemployment Across Regions, 1965–94
Source: Authors' calculations

As the path of the coefficient of variation in Figure 3.1 indicates, relative unemployment rates usually converge as national unemployment rises. However, the standard deviation of regional unemployment, a measure of dispersion in the absolute rates, usually rises with aggregate unemployment. Hence relative regional unemployment rates converge during recessions and diverge during economic booms, while, conversely, the absolute variation in unemployment rates follows the opposite pattern (see also Martin 1997). However, the data suggest that the most recent recession had a radically different impact across regions than those of the past. The standard deviation and coefficient of variation both began to move in the same direction after 1989. Regional dispersion in the 1990s, whether measured in relative or absolute terms, is now at its lowest for 30 years.

The extent of, and changes in, persistence in unemployment differentials over time is captured in Table 3.2, which gives correlation and regression coefficients for relative unemployment rates across time. The larger the correlation coefficient, the greater the correspondence in relative unemployment rates in the two periods. Panel (a) indicates a strong degree of persistence in relative unemployment rates, particularly over the period 1970–90.[1] The five year correlation is normally in excess of 0.9 and after ten years around 0.8. After 1990, the regional pattern weakens somewhat, (see final column). Neumann and Topel (1991) produce, for US census regions, correlations in excess of 0.8 after 25 or 30 years to 1985. To the US observer, regional persistence in Britain looks low.[2] Within Britain, however, the degree of persistence is lower than at any time in the past 30 years.

The regression coefficients give the direction of movement in the relative pattern of unemployment. The coefficients in panel (b) in Table 3.2 are derived from a regression of relative unemployment at time t on relative unemployment at time t-x and a constant. A coefficient greater than one suggests diverging regional performance; a coefficient less than one suggests convergence. Hence Table 3.2 suggests that the North–South divide has been redrawn a number of times before the last recession, though never to the same extent. Whilst the regression of 1995 relative regional unemployment on 1965 rates produces a coefficient of 0.05 and an implication of complete convergence, the intermediate years suggest alternating periods of convergence and divergence, with coefficients below and above unity.

---

1. See Evans and McCormick (1994) for some complementary evidence.
2. Blanchard and Katz (1992), however, find a considerable degree of convergence at state level. Also, as Martin (1997) shows, in the case of differentials rather than relativities, regional unemployment disparities in the UK exhibit greater persistence than do the US states.

**Table 3.2 Correlations of Relative Unemployment Rates
Across Standard Regions, 1965–95**

	1970	1975	1980	1985	1990	1995
(a) Correlation coefficients						
1965	0.93	0.74	0.73	0.57	0.64	0.23
1970		0.77	0.83	0.73	0.81	0.46
1975			0.92	0.87	0.81	0.50
1980				0.97	0.95	0.65
1985					0.96	0.79
1990						0.75
(b) Regression coefficients						
1965	0.61	0.27	0.70	0.23	0.36	0.05
1970		0.43	0.62	0.44	0.68	0.16
1975			1.23	0.95	1.22	0.31
1980				0.80	1.07	0.30
1985					1.32	0.44
1990						0.31

Source: Department of Employment Gazette

The penultimate column of Table 3.2 indicates that relative unemployment rates widened between 1980 and 1990. Yet the aggregate level of unemployment was approximately the same. The late 1980s boom was therefore a period in which the North–South divide was exaggerated. The extent of the convergence after 1990 in a period of rising unemployment is unprecedented and it is this issue which we pursue further in the following sections. The 1985 relative unemployment pattern rate is correlated more with 1995 than 1990. This suggests that at least part of the convergence is a reversal of the effects of 1980s boom.

Accounting for Convergence

Convergence in regional unemployment rates can come about through adjustments to employment or to labour supply. Convergence through changing relative employment patterns across regions can be thought of as a positive adjustment. It captures changes in relative economic performance, whilst labour supply responses are likely to reflect divergent economic performance across regions. Relative wage movements and migration are two key forces in any equilibrating process. Wages can induce decisions to relocate or change local producer competitiveness. Migration from areas of high unemployment reduces the labour supply in the origin region whilst raising it in the destination region. Labour supply may also adjust through participation decisions which are influenced by changing wages or job opportunities within a region. This section therefore highlights the extent of migration and relative wage shifts across regions and explores the importance of employment and labour supply shifts in explaining the regional convergence.

Migration

Table 3.3 shows that the pattern of net migration is broadly consistent with regional differences in the level of unemployment and labour market performance. Individuals gravitate towards economically prosperous regions. The size of these flows is, however, rather small when expressed as a percentage of the population of working age. The economically prosperous regions of East Anglia and the South West grew by 10 and 8 per cent, respectively between 1975 and 1993 as a direct result of migration.[3] All other regions of Britain lost between 1 and 2 per cent of their populations in the 18 year period. The West Midlands witnessed the largest emigration.

Table 3.3 Regional Employment and Migration, 1975–93

	Employment Growth (%)		*Net Migration Rate (%)*	
	1975–84	*1985–93*	*1975–84*	*1985–93*
North	-14.48	1.30	-0.62	0.40
Yorkshire – Humberside	-9.07	4.30	0.04	-1.03
East Midlands	-0.62	5.22	3.92	1.86
East Anglia	8.54	10.21	7.37	2.29
South East	0.91	-1.52	-1.06	-0.25
South West	4.23	11.44	4.78	2.25
West Midlands	-9.43	-0.10	-3.72	-1.83
North West	-11.81	0.67	-0.43	-1.18
Wales	-7.46	5.92	-1.01	2.45
Scotland	-6.62	5.56	-0.25	-0.53

Note: Includes employees and self-employed.
Source: LFS

3. These numbers are based on LFS retrospective data where individuals are asked to recall their region of residence one year prior to sampling.

After 1988, however, many Northern regions reversed part of the population loss observed in the previous decade. Thus since 1989, the period of greatest convergence, net migration has not behaved in a manner consistent with a movement towards equilibrium.

Figure 3.2 casts further doubt on whether migration is responsible for convergence in unemployment rates. Figure 3.2a plots the national gross migration rate and the share of the employed and unemployed in these flows (the residual is migration by the economically inactive). Figure 3.2b gives the gross migration rate by employment status. Migration in Britain is highly pro-cyclical, rising in good times and falling in bad.[4] This holds for both the employed and unemployed. Thus migration fails to exercise an equilibrating effect in the periods when it is needed most (see also Gordon 1980). Whilst the unemployed are more mobile as a group, (Figure 3.2b), they never constitute more than 12 per cent of the migrant stock. Further, the gap between employed and unemployed migration propensities fell steadily over the period, reaching near parity, at around 1 per cent a year, by 1994. Between 60 and 70 per cent of all moves were undertaken by the employed. This ratio is remarkably stable from GDP peak to peak or trough to trough. It is perhaps not surprising, then, that migration follows employment changes more than unemployment differences across regions. Many of these employed moves are, presumably, (pro-cyclical) within-company transfers. Gross migration fell by 70 per cent between 1989 and 1993. It is therefore improbable that migration from high unemployment to low unemployment regions was a significant factor in regional convergence of unemployment rates.

Employment

Table 3.3 also summarises the pattern of employment changes between 1975 and 1993. Throughout the period only East Anglia and the South West grew continuously. The West Midlands was in continual decline, whilst the other regions underwent fluctuations in economic fortunes. Of those regions experiencing a decline in employment during the first half of the period, only Scotland and Wales came close to reversing the employment falls of the early 1980s. It appears, then, that relative regional differences are persistent over time, but that after 1990 a modest reversal of past patterns began. This

---

4. This confirms the implications of Pissarides and Wadsworth (1989) who compare migration at two points in the economic cycle.

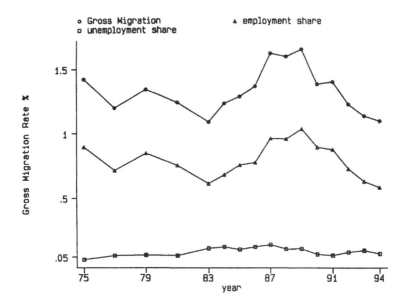

Figure 3.2a. Gross Migration as a Percentage of Working Age Population and Employment Status Shares, 1975–94

Source: LFS

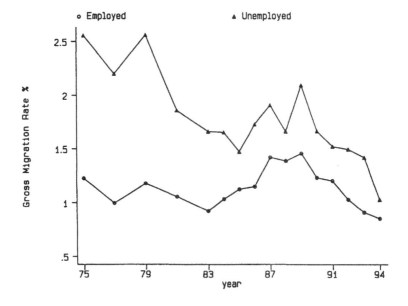

Figure 3.2b. Gross Migration by Employment Status, 1975–94

Source: LFS

Table 3.4 Percentage Changes in Relative Male Weekly Earnings by Standard Region and Selected Characteristics, 1975–91

	All Men			Age 16–30			Low Qualifications		
	1975–85	1985–91	1975–91	1975–85	1985–91	1975–91	1975–85	1985–91	1975–91
North	-1.00	-6.18	-7.14	-2.02	-6.19	-8.08	-2.00	3.06	1.00
Yorkshire – Humberside	-6.25	0.00	-6.25	-4.08	-7.45	-11.22	-2.02	0.00	-2.02
East Midlands	-3.16	0.00	-3.16	-6.00	-3.19	-9.00	-1.03	0.00	-1.03
East Anglia	4.40	-4.21	0.00	1.06	0.00	1.06	4.40	0.00	4.40
South East	4.55	1.74	6.36	1.06	3.53	10.38	2.80	0.91	3.74
South West	-2.11	1.07	-1.05	0.00	10.00	10.00	-4.30	4.49	0.00
West Midlands	-3.19	0.00	-3.19	-3.12	3.22	0.00	-4.00	2.08	-2.00
North West	-4.08	-4.25	-8.16	-8.91	-2.17	-10.89	0.00	-5.15	-5.15
Wales	-6.32	2.25	-4.21	-1.09	-3.29	-4.35	-6.25	2.22	-4.17
Scotland	2.13	-2.08	0.00	-1.01	-8.16	-9.09	6.38	-3.00	3.19

Note: Figures represent three year moving averages centred around indicated year. Low qualifications represents bottom 50 per cent of education distribution.
Source: GHS

reversal typically takes the relative employment position of a region back to that observed in the mid 1980s.[5]

Earnings

Neither have wages responded in recent years in a manner which would indicate a shift in the pattern of demand. Table 3.4 shows that male relative earnings fell in every region except the South East between 1975 and 1991. There is little evidence of a significant turnaround after 1985. As Topel (1986) shows for the United States, the size and timing of relative wage changes in Britain are not distributed equally across age and education groups. The relative wage gains of low skilled workers in the South East, for example, are half the gains of the regional average.

Elsewhere, however, low skilled earnings are no more volatile than the regional average, although the wages of younger workers are more sensitive to the local labour market environment. Earnings of this latter group rise furthest in growing regions and fall more than average in declining regions.[6] That all the adjustment occurs prior to 1985 suggests that recent changes in wages have not altered the patterns of employment. If wages are responsible for changing relative employment patterns then it must imply a heavily lagged process. Strong lags would tend to suggest a slow evolution process at odds with the rapid accentuation and narrowing of the North–South divide between 1986 and 1993.

Labour force participation

Regional unemployment can also be affected by changes in labour force participation rates. Unemployment may rise if more people are attracted into the labour force. Unemployment may fall if individuals leave the labour force and become economically inactive. Unemployment may not fall as much in good times if the majority of employment growth comes from those previously outside the labour force. Convergence in unemployment rates can therefore occur as a result of convergence in employment levels or a divergence in economic activity rates. These relationships are summarised in

---

5. A test for the existence of a unit root in relative employment based on the regression: $\Delta e_{rt} = a_{0t} + a_{1r} \Delta e_{rt-1} + a_{2r} e_{rt-2} + a_{3r} \Delta e_{rt-1} + a_{ar}T + u_{rt}$ where e_{rt} is the log of employment in region r minus the log of the national employment growth in time t, cannot reject the hypothesis of a unit root for any region. See Blanchard and Katz (1992) for similar results for US state employment growth.
6. See Jackman and Savouri (1991) for evidence that regional wages, with the exception of male manual workers, are largely unresponsive to local unemployment rates.

Table 3.5. The change in unemployment rates, U/L, between 1975 and 1993[7] can be decomposed into its constituent components: the employment–population ratio, E/P, and the participation rate, L/P. Using the fact that: $(1-U/L) = (E/P)/(L/P)$, Table 3.5 takes logs of this equation so that the change in unemployment is given by:

$$\Delta \text{Log} (1-U/L) = \Delta \text{Log}(E/P) - \Delta \text{log}(L/P)$$

The results suggest that regional convergence in unemployment rates is not necessarily the result of a convergence in economic performance. The first column gives the change in the unemployment rate between 1975 and 1993. Thus, for example, the unemployment rate in Scotland and the South West of England rose by 2.1 and 2.8 log points, respectively (column 1 is $1-(U/L)$). Yet this apparent convergence in unemployment rates, both relative and absolute, has been achieved by diametrically opposite movements. The unemployment rate in the South West has grown largely because of an increase in activity rates of 3.9 log points (column 3), whilst Scotland has suffered a fall in employment demand of 5.3 points (column 2), partially offset by a *decline* in labour supply of 1.6 points.[8]

Hence the relatively prosperous regions have experienced the smallest declines in employment and the largest increases in labour supply, whilst the traditionally depressed regions have experienced the largest falls in employment and falls in labour supply. Columns 4 to 9 repeat the analysis for the sub-periods 1975–89 and 1989–93. The years 1975 to 1989 had roughly equal employment rates. Around half of any change in employment (also relative employment) is observed in changes in unemployment and half in participation. During the latter period, the typical high unemployment regions of the North of England, Scotland and Wales had smaller employment falls but also the highest participation falls, producing a more rapid convergence in unemployment rates than would otherwise have occurred. Even at the standard regional level, reliance on the unemployment rate as a measure of an area's relative advantage can produce misleading results.

Households

One way in which these differential regional labour market trends may be manifested is in the distribution of employment across households. Table 3.5

---

7. These years are both GDP troughs, so we are comparing points at the same stage of the economic cycle.
8. See Schmitt and Wadsworth (1994a) for evidence of the decline in male labour force participation rates in Britain.

Table 3.5 Unemployment, Employment and Inactivity Rates Across Standard Regions, 1975–93

	1993–75			1989–75			1993–89		
	$\Delta Ln(1-U/L)$	$\Delta Ln(E/P)$	$\Delta Ln(L/P)$	$\Delta Ln(1-U/L)$	$\Delta Ln(E/P)$	$\Delta Ln(L/P)$	$\Delta Ln(1-U/L)$	$\Delta Ln(E/P)$	$\Delta Ln(L/P)$
North	-0.030	-0.070	-0.042	-0.042	-0.059	-0.017	+0.013	-0.012	-0.025
Yorkshire – Humberside	-0.036	-0.048	-0.012	-0.027	-0.035	-0.008	-0.009	-0.013	-0.004
East Midlands	-0.011	-0.023	-0.012	-0.016	0.006	0.022	-0.019	-0.028	-0.010
East Anglia	-0.037	-0.001	0.036	+0.001	0.036	0.035	-0.039	-0.037	0.002
South East	-0.054	-0.056	-0.002	-0.009	0.003	0.012	-0.045	-0.059	-0.015
South West	-0.028	0.011	0.039	+0.008	0.050	0.042	-0.037	-0.040	-0.003
West Midlands	-0.066	-0.083	-0.017	-0.029	-0.035	-0.006	-0.038	-0.048	-0.010
North West	-0.043	-0.107	-0.064	-0.035	-0.070	-0.035	-0.009	-0.037	-0.028
Wales	-0.010	-0.059	-0.049	-0.021	-0.034	-0.013	+0.011	-0.025	-0.036
Scotland	-0.021	-0.053	-0.032	-0.024	-0.042	-0.018	+0.004	-0.010	-0.014

Source: LFS

Table 3.6: Employment Polarisation Across Standard Regions, 1975–94

					Region					
	North	Yorkshire	East Mids.	East Anglia	South East	South West	West Mids.	North West	Wales	Scotland
1975										
No Work	5.6	4.3	3.7	3.7	3.6	5.5	3.6	4.6	6.6	4.7
All Work	48.3	53.7	54.1	53.8	57.8	50.6	54.5	56.4	44.7	50.8
1985										
No Work	16.5	13.6	11.7	9.7	8.6	8.4	14.3	14.2	16.0	13.4
All Work	41.3	49.8	52.1	53.1	55.1	56.0	48.1	50.2	42.3	45.8
1994										
No Work	18.5	15.0	11.9	9.7	12.8	10.5	13.8	16.0	16.5	14.5
All Work	51.8	58.2	59.6	64.1	61.1	64.4	58.1	56.1	51.9	57.9

Source: LFS

shows that labour force participation has risen most in areas with the highest employment growth. Gregg and Wadsworth (1996) show that employment has risen fastest in households where an occupant was already in work. Conversely those jobless individuals living in households with non-employed partners face the greatest difficulty in obtaining work. Table 3.6 summarises these trends, whilst documenting the proportion of individuals of working age living in households with no working adult, and the proportion in fully employed households over the sample period. All regions exhibit the same pattern of employment polarisation: a secular decline in partially employed households replaced by a simultaneous rise in fully and non-employed households. The crucial difference between regions is in the extent of polarisation and, correspondingly, in the levels of non-employed and fully employed households. In East Anglia, by 1994, 64 per cent of working age individuals were living in fully employed households and just 10 per cent of the population were resident in non-employed households, though this represents a tripling on the 1975 figure. In contrast, the North of England had 15 per cent of its population resident in workless households. Significantly, in those regions which have performed relatively well over the last decade, Wales and Scotland, the incidence of workless households has continued to rise. Most new jobs have therefore gone to households with an occupant already in work. More than ever the evaluation of a region's labour market performance needs to be based on a broader set of measures.

Local Unemployment Change

The evidence of the previous section suggests that there may be differential experience of unemployment within regions. We therefore introduce a further disaggregation to identify whether standard regional variation in unemployment is important in explaining the different experiences of groups in society. We disaggregate first by education and then by local labour markets within regions. The total variation in unemployment can be written as:

$$\sum_{ij} (u_{ij} - u)^2 = \sum_{ij} (u_{ij} - u_i)^2 + \sum_i n_i (u_i - u)^2$$

where u_{ij} is the unemployment rate in locale/skill group j in region i, u is the national unemployment rate, u_i is unemployment in region i and n is the number of regions. The first term measures the extent of variation in unemployment within regions and the second the amount of variation in unemployment between regions.

Figure 3.3 decomposes the total variation in unemployment rates across the regions and four skill groups, defined to represent the 50 per cent of the population with the lowest educational qualifications, the next 25 per cent, the next 15 per cent and the top 10 per cent. These categories are chosen so as to net out composition changes in education qualifications across time. Standard regions represent only a small proportion of the total variation in unemployment by skill. The regional component accounts for no more than 25 per cent of the total variation and normally less than 10 per cent. Hence knowledge of an individual's region adds little to predicting the likelihood of unemployment after education is controlled for.

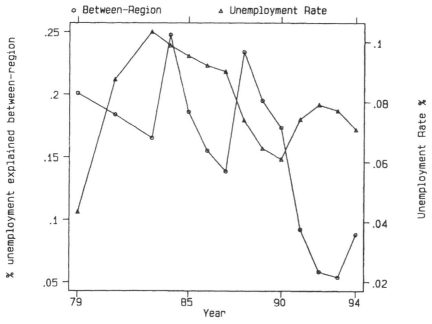

Figure 3.3. Between-Region Variation in Unemployment Rates by Education
Source: LFS

Analysis of geographical variation within regions as well as between regions allows us to assess whether there has been a general convergence in local unemployment rates. As a first step, Table 3.7 repeats the exercises of Table 3.2 using county and TTWA unemployment data instead of that for standard regions. These below-regional level correlations are much more persistent than the equivalent figures for standard regions. Figure 3.4 decomposes the variation of unemployment rates across 62 counties into that explained by the standard regions and that which occurs within regions. In Figure 3.4a the decomposition is deflated by the average level of unemployment.[9] The between- and within-group variation move together until the late 1980s. Thereafter, the between-region component declines rapidly, but the within-region component remains in line with previous periods. In other words, convergence at the standard region level is not mirrored within regions. Figure 3.4b shows that within-region absolute unemployment rates widened after 1989 whilst the between-region rates continued to converge.

Table 3.7 Correlations of Relative Unemployment Rates
Across County and LLM

	1980	1985	1989	1993
(a) County				
1975	0.86	0.79	0.75	0.69
1980		0.92	0.89	0.66
1985			0.92	0.78
1989				0.74
(b) TTWA				
1983		0.98	0.83	0.78
1985			0.88	0.80
1989				0.74

Note: Figures based on correlations of 62 counties and 320 TTWAs.
Source: Department of Employment Gazette

Quah (1994) argues that a clearer insight into convergence can be obtained by examining the entire distribution of cross-area economic performance and its evolution over time. Thus Figure 3.5 ranks counties in order of rising relative unemployment rates. Figure 3.5e plots the 1975 rankings against 1975 relative unemployment. Figures 3.5a–d compare, in ascending order, the 1979, 1981, 1989 and 1992 rates with the 1975 rankings. In a situation of no change each panel would show a monotonic upward sloping line with the same slope as in 1975. If Britain experienced convergence in its relative unemployment rates, for example a 3 percentage point rise in the unemployment rate in every county (perhaps after a country-wide employment shock), then the slope of the line would become shallower but the county rankings would remain unchanged. Any sharp upward or downward spike indicates a re-ranking of county unemployment rates. The height of the spikes indicates the scale of movement. The slope of the graph in 1992 (Figure 3.5a) has indeed become shallower compared with 1975, consistent with

9.   In practice this is achieved by examining the variance of the natural log of unemployment.

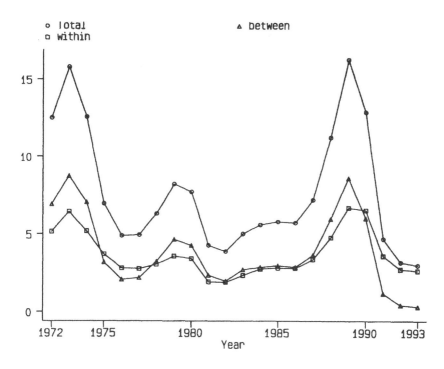

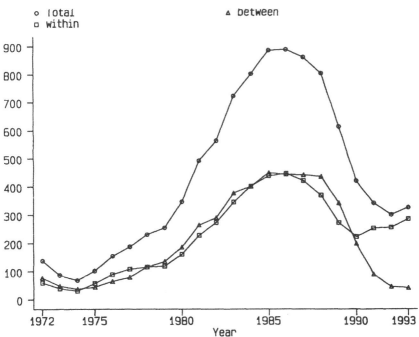

Figure 3.4. Within- and Between-Group Variation in Log County Unemployment Rate

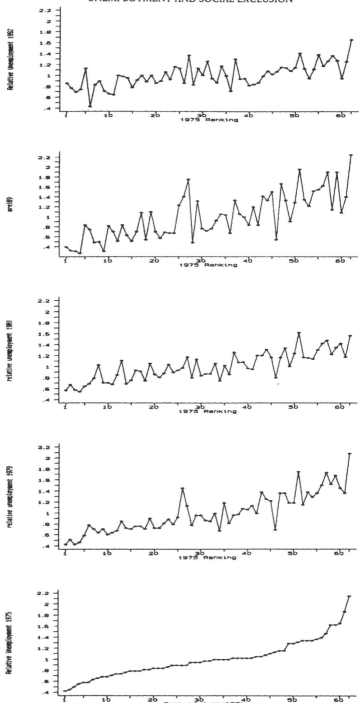

Figure 3.5. County Unemployment Rates Relative to 1975 Ranking
Source: Department of Employment Gazette

general convergence. However, the jagged line indicates a lack of uniform convergence. In other words, some counties have done better than others. For example, Clwyd moves from 60th to 26th in the rankings, whilst Greater London falls from 5th to 45th. Other counties exhibit a strong degree of persistence. Merseyside was 62nd in 1975 and in 1992. Berkshire moves from 3rd to 4th in the ranking over the period. Figures 3.5b–d confirm the tendency for convergence of relative unemployment in recessions and divergence in economic booms. The chart shows that 1989 was the period of greatest volatility. There is no evidence of monotonic convergence over the period 1975 to 1989. If anything the slope is steeper. Rather, there is considerable within-distribution movement over time.[10] Counties which improved their ranking most (the major peaks in Figure 3.5) were all in the West country and rural Wales: Dorset, Clwyd, Wiltshire, Powys, Cornwall and Devon. The biggest losers were South Yorkshire, Greater London, Derby, West Yorkshire, Nottingham and Grampian. Thus this period was one largely of an accentuated North–South divide, with the North Midlands and Yorkshire losing out to the more rural parts of western Britain.

The 1989–92 period was a return to previous patterns of rankings after the exceptional changes between 1981 and 1989. The spikes are far less marked in 1992. The big losers were Essex, East Sussex, Dorset, Bedfordshire, Kent and Cornwall. The big gainers were Borders, Grampian, Tayside, Cumbria, North Yorkshire and Central Scotland. Greater London and the West Midlands were the only counties to lose significantly in both periods, whereas Clwyd, Cumbria, Dumfries, Powys and Shropshire witnessed noticeable improvement in both periods.

Taking this analysis one stage further, Table 3.8 presents transition probabilities of the county relative unemployment distribution across several time periods between 1975 and 1992. Panel (a) gives the 17 year transition matrix between the GDP trough years of 1975 and 1992. The columns indicate the counties' positions in the 1975 unemployment rankings divided into quartiles (top 25% to bottom 25%). The row headings indicate the position in subsequent years. The entries in each cell indicate the probability of observing a county's unemployment rate in the rankings in both years. For example, the first entry, cell $(1,1)$, indicates a probability of 0.6 that a county will remain in the top 25 per cent of unemployment rates for both periods. Hence the degree of persistence is indicated by the size of the coefficients on the main diagonals.

---

10. See Barro and Sala-I-Martin (1991) for an analysis of 'ß' and 'σ' convergence of regional GDP in Britain.

Table 3.8 Relative (County) Unemployment Transition Matrices, 1975–92

	Quartile				
	1	2	3	4	N
(a) 1975–92					
1	0.60	0.27	0.13	0.00	15
2	0.20	0.27	0.40	0.13	15
3	0.19	0.38	0.25	0.19	16
4	0.00	0.13	0.25	0.62	16
(b) 1989–92					
1	0.50	0.31	0.13	0.06	
2	0.40	0.27	0.27	0.07	
3	0.07	0.33	0.40	0.20	
4	0.00	0.13	0.25	0.62	
(c) 1979–81					
1	0.87	0.07	0.07	0.00	
2	0.19	0.62	0.19	0.00	
3	0.00	0.19	0.50	0.31	
4	0.00	0.07	0.20	0.73	
(d) 1975–89					
1	0.60	0.40	0.00	0.00	
2	0.40	0.20	0.27	0.13	
3	0.06	0.31	0.37	0.25	
4	0.00	0.06	0.31	0.62	

Note: 1 = lowest relative unemployment quartile; 4 = highest.
Source: Department of Employment Gazette

A majority of counties in the top and bottom quartiles remain in the same part of the distribution over the sample period. The degree of persistence is much lower in the intermediate quartiles. Two counties move from the top 50 per cent of the distribution to the bottom quartile, and three counties move from the bottom 50 per cent to the top quartile. Panel (d) indicates that movements of similar magnitude had occurred by 1989. However, panel (b) reveals a substantial degree of mobility after 1989. Essex, for example, moved from being among the lowest quartile in 1989 to the highest in 1993.

Despite this apparent rise in mobility, 80 per cent of counties that made no transition between 1975 and 1989 remained in the same quartile between 1989 and 1992. This suggests that the labour market is characterised by a hard core of persistent under- and over-performing localities, with remaining rankings determined by a series of region-specific shocks across time. More than ever, it appears that standard regions are not the most relevant level of aggregation for understanding (or counteracting) geographical variation in unemployment.

Finer geographical disaggregations are available from the Census of Population every ten years. Aggregate unemployment levels in 1981 and 1991 were approximately the same, so that absolute and relative analysis makes no difference. The smallest cell size offers 10,000 separate Census ward unemployment observations. It can also be aggregated to the district local authority, TTWA level and standard region level to enable comparison. Table 3.9 repeats the analysis of variance within and between regions at each scale available in the Census. The substantial degree of convergence in the total variation at the TTWA level is confirmed, largely caused by convergence *between* regions, while within regions variation has become relatively more important.

Table 3.9 Between- and Within-Region Variation Unemployment at Different Levels of Aggregation, 1981–91

Aggregation Level	*280 TTWAs*		*459 Local Authority Districts*		*10,000 Census Wards*	
	1981	*1991*	*1981*	*1991*	*1981*	*1991*
Total Variation	2520.5	1944.9	4719.7	4992.5	220.6	283.6
Between-Region variation	775.2 (30.7%)	373.8 (19.2%)	1191.5 (25.2%)	436.7 (8.8%)	24.6 (11.2%)	12.7 (4.5%)
Within-Region variation	1744.9 (69.2%)	1571.1 (80.8%)	3528.2 (74.8%)	4555.8 (91.3%)	195.9 (88.8%)	270.8 (95.5%)

Source: Census of Population 1981 and 1991.

However, at local authority level this overall convergence disappears altogether. Any between-region convergence is offset by within-region divergence. At ward level, the total variation in unemployment rates rises substantially. Again this suggests that it is not true that local unemployment patterns have converged. This only holds at higher levels of aggregation and is therefore unlikely to be the result of forces driving towards a general equilibrium of unemployment. However, identifying a growing divergence at such a micro level is not very helpful unless we can identify the characteristics of the areas losing out or gaining.

Table 3.10 Area Characteristics and Unemployment Rates
for Census Wards, 1981–91

	1981	1991	Change, 1991–81
Local Characteristics:			
Proportion Rented	0.0792	0.1752	0.0198
	(0.0019)	(0.0022)	(0.0014)
Proportion Degree	-0.1337	-0.1252	-0.0258
	(0.0057)	(0.0047)	(0.0043)
Proportion Intermediate	0.0416	0.0179	-0.0001
Skill Occupations	(0.0042)	(0.0048)	(0.0012)
Proportion Low Skill	0.0964	0.0616	0.0111
Occupations	(0.0039)	(0.0043)	(0.0030)
Major Cities	0.7103	2.3460	1.9632
	(0.0925)	(0.0921)	(0.0697)
Other Cities	0.3817	0.8720	0.5116
	(0.0818)	(0.0817)	(0.0617)
Rural Areas	-0.6502	-0.9099	-0.0733
	(0.1158)	(0.1151)	(0.0874)
Standard Regions:			
South East	-1.7844	-0.3975	1.2634
	(0.1499)	(0.1488)	(0.1131)
East Anglia	-1.3954	-1.3919	-0.0989
	(0.1929)	(0.1916)	(0.1456)
South West	-0.6567	-0.2657	0.1315
	(0.1673)	(0.1665)	(0.1253)
West Midlands	0.4341	-0.2711	-0.9195
	(0.1768)	(0.1759)	(0.1335)
East Midlands	-1.1694	-0.5601	0.2355
	(0.1738)	(0.1728)	(0.1312)
North West	1.4314	1.5677	0.0479
	(0.1772)	(0.1757)	(0.1337)
Northern	1.0338	0.5578	-0.4853
	(0.1864)	(0.1849)	(0.1407)
Wales	2.5020	2.1325	-0.4889
	(0.1818)	(0.1806)	(0.1372)
Scotland	0.2685	-0.8812	-0.7612
	(0.1729)	(0.1704)	(0.1305)
Constant	0.4624	0.8818	-1.2902
	(0.2735)	(0.2710)	(0.2064)
Adjusted R-Squared	0.477	0.598	0.2117
No. Observations	10,000	10,000	10,000

Characteristics of areas with diverging unemployment rates: the urban/rural split

The Census offers a range of useful indicators covering region, socio-economic make-up, worker qualifications (which will proxy skill/education levels), housing types (which will proxy earning power) and the urban/rural nature of the area. Table 3.10 presents regression estimates of the determinants of local area unemployment. In both years, the explanatory power of these regressions is high and the key correlations are the same.

The percentage of rental housing, the proportion of lower socio-economic groups in the population and the percentage of the workforce with higher qualifications are the driving factors. Region is of secondary importance, especially in 1991. The final column gives the change in unemployment rate between the two periods and it is here we can see which factors are associated with growing variation in unemployment at the micro level.

The South East experienced a substantial adverse shock between these two dates – not so the other southern regions. The West Midlands, Scotland, Wales and the North of England have improved relative to the base area, Yorkshire. Most striking is the deteriorating position of the large British cities, and to a lesser degree other smaller cities, relative to the small town or rural areas. Further, those with a larger rented sector in 1981, a greater proportion of workers in the lowest socio-economic group (semi- and unskilled manual workers and labourers) and those with few highly educated people, have all suffered disproportionately. All of these factors are typical of groups with lower earning power and consistent with the growing literature about the deteriorating economic position of the less educated (see, for example, Schmitt and Wadsworth 1994 and Gregg and Machin 1994, amongst others). The dominance of the urban–rural split rather than traditional cross-regional patterns since 1981 suggests that the North–South divide is no longer relevant as a description of the patterns of unemployment across the country.

Recovery

As the economy emerges from recession can we expect any change in the economic position of the less skilled? Table 3.11 provides a simple insight into the likely pattern of regional performance of the less skilled based on the previous recovery in the 1980s. The table arranges 17 areas of Britain by the area unemployment rate prevailing in 1989. The columns document the economic position of less skilled males[11] resident in those areas at the

---

11. We define the less skilled as those in the bottom half of the education distribution in each period.

Table 3.11 Effect of Area Unemployment on Employment, Unemployment and Inactivity Rates of Low Skilled Workers, 1984–89

Area Unemployment Rate 1989	Group Unemployment Rate			Group Employment Rate			Group Inactivity Rate		
	1989	1984	Difference (1989–84)	1989	1984	Difference (1989–84)	1989	1984	Difference (1989–84)
<4%	7.0	11.3	-4.3	88.2	85.3	2.9	4.9	3.7	1.2
4–7%	11.1	13.1	-2.0	82.9	82.8	0.1	6.8	4.7	2.1
7–9%	16.9	18.4	-1.5	74.5	76.8	-2.3	10.2	5.9	4.3
9–11%	20.1	18.8	-1.3	69.6	74.8	-5.2	12.8	7.6	5.2
11%+	22.4	23.9	-1.5	65.3	70.1	-4.8	15.8	7.9	7.9

Source: LFS

start of the recovery in 1984 and at the end in 1989. Low unemployment areas in 1989 were not necessarily low unemployment areas in 1984, so Table 3.11 allows for an area fixed effect. There is a strong monotonic relationship between area unemployment and the economic position of the less skilled. The more prosperous an area the higher the employment rate and the lower the unemployment rate of the less skilled (see Wadsworth 1995 for more details). Through the recovery, employment of less skilled men grew fastest and unemployment fell further in those areas with the best aggregate performance. This finding gives support to the idea that expansionary demand policies at the sub-regional level could help to mitigate the economic position of the economically disadvantaged.

Conclusions

Changes in aggregate unemployment are unequally distributed across and within regions over time. This reflects the geographic dispersion of industry and the non-neutral effect of aggregate economic shocks across sectors in different time periods. There has been a profound convergence in standard region unemployment rates since 1989, untypical of any previous period. Relative and absolute differences across regions have declined. Yet in terms of the overall variation in unemployment across groups in Britain, regional variation in unemployment has never been important. Rather, skill differences and dispersion within regions are more significant determinants of the total variation. Convergence observed at the standard region level has not been mirrored at other levels of geographic disaggregation. Moreover, there is evidence that convergence in unemployment rates has in part been due to differential regional behaviour in employment and participation rates. In other words, the unemployment rate no longer provides a unique satisfactory measure of the extent of social exclusion within a locality. The patterns of unemployment across standard regions are more than ever a poor guide of jobless concentration. Inequality has increased markedly, but within rather than between regions. A better description is increasingly shown by the urban/rural split in unemployment patterns and across skill groups. If we are to tackle social exclusion, then greater efforts should be targeted in these directions.

Acknowledgement

Anne Green is at the Institute of Employment Research at the University of Warwick. Jonathan Wadsworth is at the Centre for Economic Performance and Royal Holloway College, London. Much of this work was carried out whilst Paul Gregg and Jonathan Wadsworth were at NIESR and the Centre for Economic Performance. We would like to thank the Employment Department for supporting the research on which this paper draws. As usual the disclaimer applies that the views expressed herein are not necessarily those of the Department or the Centre. We would like to thank Dave Wilkinson and Richard Dickens for help with the data. LFS and GHS data were supplied with the permission of OPCS and made available through the ESRC Data Archive at the University of Essex.

CHAPTER 4

The Changing Geography of Non-Employment in Britain

Anne Green

Introduction

This chapter provides an evaluative overview of selected key features of continuity and change in the geography of non-employment in Britain in the 1980s, using a range of indicators from various data sources at different spatial scales. The concepts of unemployment, inactivity and nonemployment are reviewed in the first section of the chapter, and the different statistical sources and geographical units referred to subsequently are outlined. In the second section the main emphasis is on outlining selected features of changing geographical patterns of non-employment, rather than attempting to 'explain' them in a comprehensive fashion. Amongst the changes reviewed are the convergence of regional unemployment rates in the late 1980s and early 1990s, and geographical variations in timing of entry into recession in 1979 and 1989/90. Substantial intra-regional variations in unemployment are highlighted, and the tendency for an increasing proportion of variation in local unemployment rates to be accounted for by intra-regional, rather than inter-regional, differences is reviewed. The disproportionate relative increase in unemployment in the country's large urban areas is identified as a major feature of change in the 1980s, with non-employment becoming increasingly extensive in many urban labour markets. A discussion of the concept of segregation follows in the third section of the chapter. A range of measures of different aspects of segregation are operationalised using data from the Census of Population, and the main features of geographical patterns of segregation of non-employed sub-groups are outlined. In particular, the increasing segregation of the non-employed in the largest cities is highlighted. The final section is concerned with synthesising the empirical evidence presented and highlighting the implications for policy.

Unemployment, inactivity and non-employment

Despite the fact that the unemployment rate is a widely used economic and social indicator, the task of defining and measuring unemployment in a clear and unambiguous fashion is a difficult one. There is considerable debate about who should be and who is counted as *unemployed*, and who is not. Moreover, in comparing the incidence of unemployment between local areas, against what baseline population should an *unemployment* rate be calculated? The answers to such questions are not clear-cut.

There are three main 'official' sources of unemployment data which may be used for local-level analyses in Great Britain: the Employment Department claimant count, the Census of Population and (to a lesser extent) the Labour Force Survey (the latter two also contain data on inactivity and non-employment). These data sources differ in their coverage, scope and basis of definition, disaggregation – both spatially and by individual characteristics – and frequency (for further details see Green 1995a; Royal Statistical Society 1995; Sly 1994; Woolford and Denman 1993). In some areas these sources may be supplemented by data from local surveys, often allowing a variety of different 'definitions' of unemployment to be operationalised. Hence it is likely that the detail of the geographical patterns of unemployment observed will vary in accordance with the statistical source used and the section of the population covered.

To illustrate how estimates of unemployment can vary quite markedly according to the definition of unemployment used, Table 4.1 provides a breakdown of the 'self-defined' unemployed by claimant status and job search activity in three local areas – Central London, north east Wales and southern Derbyshire – using data from local labour force and skills surveys.[1] The proportion of the self-defined unemployed who were claiming benefits and seeking work at the time of the surveys ranged from less than one in two in central London, to two in three in southern Derbyshire and three in four in north east Wales. In central London less than two-thirds of the self-defined unemployed were claimants, and nearly 16 per cent were neither claimants nor 'actively seeking work' (and hence would be excluded from

---

1. For further information on these local labour force surveys undertaken by the Institute for Employment Research, University of Warwick – collecting a variety of information on economic (in)activity, qualifications and work history – see Hasluck (1994a, b) and Hasluck, Siora and Green (1995).

the 'official' International Labour Organisation (ILO) definitions of unemployment). While there are variations between the three local areas in the composition of the self-defined unemployed by job search and claimant status, a key point emerging from the analysis is that a significant proportion of the 'self-defined' unemployed fall outside the category of claimants 'actively seeking work' (that is, those who would be included in the monthly 'headline' unemployment count and the 'official' ILO definition of unemployment).

Table 4.1: The Self-Defined Unemployed: Job Search and Claimant Status

Category	Claimant		Unregistered		Total	
	no.	% of grand total	no.	% of grand total	no.	% of grand total
Central London						
Seeking work	31,260	45.7	14,205	20.7	45,465	66.5
Not seeking work	12,213	17.9	10,727	15.7	22,940	33.5
Total	**43,473**	**63.6**	**24,932**	**36.4**	**68,405**	**100.0**
North East Wales						
Seeking work	13,683	73.1	1,222	6.5	14,905	79.6
Not seeking work	2,471	13.2	1,350	7.2	3,821	20.4
Total	**16,154**	**86.3**	**2,572**	**13.7**	**18,726**	**100.0**
Southern Derbyshire						
Seeking work	13,946	64.2	3,327	15.3	17,273	79.5
Not seeking work	2,744	12.6	1,711	7.9	4,455	20.5
Total	**16,690**	**76.8**	**5,038**	**23.2**	**21,728**	**100.0**

Sources: Central London Skills and Labour Force Survey, north east Wales Skills Survey, Southern Derbyshire Skills Survey (see footnote 1).

Not only is the concept of unemployment somewhat amorphous, it has also been noted that the boundary between unemployment and inactivity is becoming increasingly fuzzy (Bryson and McKay 1994). Analyses of Labour Force Survey data reveal that compared with the position in the early 1980s, by the early 1990s an increasing proportion of people leaving unemployment moved into inactivity and fewer were leaving for a job: in 1981 three-quarters of those leaving unemployment went into a job, but by 1993 this had fallen to only 60 per cent (Gregg and Wadsworth 1995). It would seem that there are all kinds of grey areas on the fringes of 'complete unemployment' (Nicaise et al. 1994).

In the face of such ambiguities and the various needs of social scientists and economists for unemployment data (Gregg 1994), some commentators have argued for the development and use of a range of different *parallel* measures of unemployment (ranging from restrictive measures of long duration 'hard core' unemployment, to broader measures including discouraged workers and those on government training schemes in addition to those who are unemployed according to the 'official' count), to serve different objectives (Miller 1988; Sorrentino 1993). Various such measures can be operationalised using data from the Labour Force Survey. A suite of alternative measures of unemployment from the relatively 'narrow' (U1) to the relatively 'broad' (U6) are outlined in Table 4.2, and counts of the number of unemployed in 1991 and 1993 in two regions – the South East and the Northern region – are presented in Figures 4.1 and 4.2, respectively. It is apparent that the two regions have rather different profiles of unemployment. For example, in the Northern region the proportion of unemployed prime age males (U1) is greater, and government training schemes (included in measure U6) are relatively more entrenched, than in the South East. The presentation of data for both 1991 and 1993 also illustrates the differential impact of the increase of unemployment on different categories of the unemployed – the rise in long-term unemployment in the South East over the two year period is particularly notable.

Table 4.2: Measures of Unemployment

Measure	Description
U1	males aged 25–54 years unemployed for one year or over
U2	all males unemployed for one year or over
U3	all males unemployed
U4	ILO unemployment count
U5	U4 plus discouraged workers
U6	U5 plus those on government training schemes

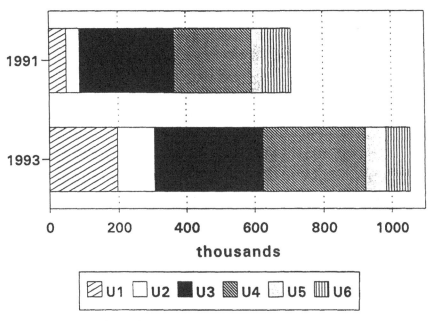

Figure 4.1. Measures of Unemployment: South East Region
Source: Labour Force Survey.

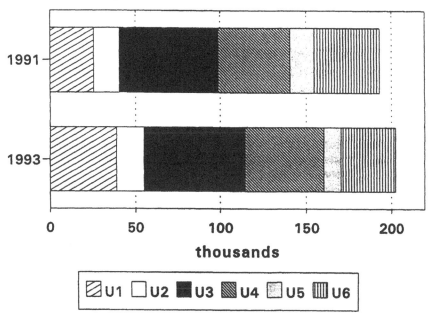

Figure 4.2. Measures of Unemployment: Northern Region
Source: Labour Force Survey.

Geographical perspectives

Four sets of geographical units are referred to in the subsequent analyses. In descending order of geographical size these are:

- standard regions: the economic planning regions for which a wide range of economic data are available
- 280 local labour market areas (LLMAs): relatively self-contained commuting areas (originating from the CURDS Functional Regionalisation of Britain (Champion *et al.* 1987))
- 459 local authority districts (LADs): administrative areas
- approximately 10,000 1981 Census wards.

These spatial frameworks have been defined in different ways for different purposes. Clearly, the *way* in which the boundaries of an area are drawn, and *where* they are drawn, have an impact on the picture of unemployment or non-employment that is obtained. The use of more than one areal framework in the analyses below permits a variety of perspectives and enables insights into confirmatory or contradictory patterns of spatial variation at different geographical scales. However, it should be borne in mind that the interpretation of indicators may vary at different spatial scales.

Key Features of Continuity and Change in the Geography of Unemployment and Non-Employment

'Explaining' changes in the spatial distribution of unemployment and non-employment

Changes in unemployment may arise for a number of different reasons, since unemployment is a function of the interaction of changes in labour supply and labour demand (see Beatty and Fothergill 1994; Green and Owen 1991). In simplistic terms, unemployment increases may occur in the face of employment growth if growth in the population seeking work (as a result of natural change, in-migration or participation increase) outstrips the increase in jobs available, as well as in circumstances of employment decline (when labour supply reductions through out-migration and withdrawal from the labour force are outstripped by job losses). Hence in attempting to 'explain' unemployment changes in different areas, it is important to bear in mind how supply and demand factors interact in different ways in different areas to produce such changes.

Application of a labour market accounts methodology to local labour market areas shows that some large cities (such as Liverpool) would have had a higher unemployment rate if it were not for net out-migration, while in some towns (such as Milton Keynes) net in-migration and natural increases have been key factors in increasing the unemployment rate despite the expansion of employment opportunities. Similarly, research on recent changes in employment and unemployment in coal-mining communities reveals that in the face of the demise of jobs in mining and related industries, many working age adults 'withdrew' from the labour force (that is, became inactive) rather than becoming unemployed (Beatty and Fothergill 1994; see also Chapter 5, this volume). Different interactions between labour supply and demand in different local areas may complicate analyses of the changing geography of unemployment, and perhaps suggest that a broader focus on non-employment is more appropriate.

The demise of the regional dimension of variation

There has been much debate about the changing regional relativities in unemployment during the 1980s, and in particular about convergence in regional unemployment rates during the early 1990s recession. Table 4.3 presents regional unemployment indices for selected years over the period 1978–94. North–South regional unemployment relativities were particularly marked in 1979/80 (before the doubling of unemployment in the early 1980s recession), and again in 1989/90 (before the massive increase in

Table 4.3: Regional Relative Unemployment Rates

Region	1979	1986	1989	1993
South East	64.1	75.5	65.0	100.0
Rest of South East	61.5	67.3	48.3	89.2
London	69.2	83.6	85.0	114.7
East Anglia	79.5	78.2	58.3	80.4
South West	100.0	84.5	73.3	93.1
East Midlands	82.1	90.0	106.7	93.1
West Midlands	100.0	116.4	90.0	107.8
Yorkshire – Humberside	102.6	113.6	121.7	101.0
North West	128.2	125.5	140.0	105.9
Northern	161.5	139.1	165.0	117.6
Wales	135.9	125.5	123.3	101.0
Scotland	46.2	122.7	156.7	96.1
Great Britain	**100.0**	**100.0**	**100.0**	**100.0**

Source: Department of Employment seasonally adjusted unemployment rates (via NOMIS)

unemployment in the early 1990s recession).[2] There is evidence for convergence of regional unemployment rate relativities in the mid 1980s (when unemployment peaked before recovery in the late 1980s) and again in 1993 (before unemployment began to fall).

Although the focus on selected years in Table 4.3 disguises some of the detail of the pattern and timing of movements in regional unemployment disparities, some key features are evident. Figure 4.3 shows general trends in unemployment for London and Scotland over the period 1978 to 1994, as measured by changing shares of total UK unemployment. Perhaps the two most notable features are, first, the deterioration in the relative fortunes of London: as it moved from a situation of a below average to above average incidence of unemployment its share of national unemployment rose from under 10 per cent in 1980 to about 17 per cent in 1993 and 1994; and, second, the upturn in the relative fortunes of Scotland – which moved from a situation of a much higher than average to a lower than average unemployment rate over the period.

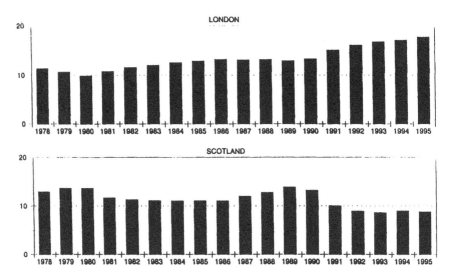

Figure 4.3. Annual Unemployment Rates as a Percentage of UK Total: London and Scotland
Source: Department of Employment seasonally adjusted unemployment rates (via NOMIS)

---

2. It should be noted that different results are obtained if regional unemployment disparities are defined as absolute differentials (the regional unemployment rate minus the national rate) rather than the relativities (ratio of regional unemployment rates to the national rate) used here (see Martin 1997 for an analysis based on differentials).

Analyses of data from the monthly unemployment series at the LLMA scale provide a more detailed insight into the changing geography of recession in the early 1980s and early 1990s. Using a 19-fold classification of LLMAs on the basis of urban and regional system characteristics, Green, Owen and Winnett (1994) identified some intra-regional variations in the changing geography of unemployment overlying a simple North–South regional distinction. Northern Britain led into the first recession, with the metropolitan areas, large cities and manufacturing towns being the first to experience increases in unemployment. By contrast, in southern Britain, parts of the London metropolitan region were the last areas to experience an unemployment upturn. However, these same areas were the first to experience the effects of the second recession, while the largest urban areas of northern Britain were the last: a clear reversal of fortunes compared with the first recession. These patterns are indicative of the different structural impact and geographical consequences of the two recessions, and also highlight the significance of intra-regional differentials in experience alongside regional variations.

Intra-regional variation: rising non-employment in large urban areas, 1981–91

Application of analysis of variance techniques to Census of Population data on unemployment, inactivity and non-employment rates at LLMA, LAD and ward scales reveals that most of the geographical variation in the experience of non-employment in both 1981 and 1991 is accounted for by intra-regional, rather than inter-regional, variation (see Table 4.4). In the case of local unemployment rates, over the 1980s there was a convergence in total variation at the LLMA scale, and intra-regional variation became relatively more important. However, such overall convergence in local unemployment experience between 1981 and 1991 is not evident at LAD or ward scale; but intra-regional variation again became relatively more important in explaining local differentials in unemployment. There is no evidence for convergence in total variation in inactivity rates (for 20–59-year-olds) or non-employment rates at any of the three scales of analysis between 1981 and 1991, and the shares of total variation accounted for by inter- and inter-regional components remained similar in 1981 and 1991. Hence the picture emerging tends to be one of growing local complexity in experience of unemployment, inactivity and non-employment.

Table 4.4: Inter- and Intra-Regional Variations in Local Unemployment,
Inactivity and Non-Employment Rates, 1981–1991

Indicator Component	LLMAs 1981	LLMAs 1991	LADs 1981	LADs 1991	Wards 1981	Wards 1991
Unemployment rate						
Total variation	2520.1	1944.9	4719.7	4992.5	220568.6	283551.5
Inter-regional variation (%)	30.8	19.2	25.2	8.8	11.2	4.5
Intra-regional variation (%)	69.3	80.8	74.8	91.3	88.8	95.5
Inactivity rate (20–59 years)						
Total variation	1647.4	2902.2	2935.0	4712.0	240337.3	286038.2
Inter-regional variation (%)	39.8	40.8	32.5	33.3	11.0	10.2
Intra-regional variation (%)	60.2	59.3	67.5	66.7	89.0	89.9
Non-employment rate						
Total variation	5475.2	7534.6	10029.8	13360.0	667699.8	916830.4
Inter-regional variation (%)	28.3	31.7	27.3	25.7	11.3	10.0
Intra-regional variation (%)	71.7	68.3	72.7	74.3	88.7	90.0

Source: Census of Population

Some insights into the factors underlying continuity and change in the characteristics of areas experiencing high and low unemployment rates may be obtained through regression analysis. Table 4.5 presents such analyses at the ward scale using local unemployment rates in 1981 and 1991, and percentage point change in unemployment rates between 1981 and 1991 as the dependent variables. Selected socio-economic indicators are used as explanatory variables alongside standard region and urban size dummies.

In both 1981 and 1991 the proportion of households in rented accommodation and the proportion of the economically active population in semi-skilled and labouring occupations display the largest positive coefficients, while the proportion of adults with higher level qualifications exhibits a negative coefficient, thus confirming the importance of socio-economic factors in understanding local variations in unemployment. Urban size factors are relatively more important in 1991 than in 1981, with the largest conurbations displaying particularly high rates of unemployment in 1991. Relative to Yorkshire and Humberside (the base case), the Southern regions and the East Midlands had lower unemployment in both 1981 and 1991, but the relative deterioration in the fortunes of the South East is apparent from the analysis of 1981–91 unemployment change. By contrast, the unemployment situation improved in the West Midlands, Scotland, the Northern region and Wales relative to Yorkshire and Humberside over the inter-censal period. However, the most striking feature emerging in the 1981–91 regression analysis is the deterioration of the unemployment

Table 4.5: Determinants of Unemployment Rates: The Ward Scale

Indicator	1981			1991			1981–91 change		
	b	SE(b)	t	b	SE(b)	t	b	SE(b)	t
Socio-economic characteristics									
% renter households	0.079	(0.002)	41.795*	0.175	(0.002)	79.710*	0.020	(0.001)	13.874*
% adults with higher qualifications	-0.134	(0.006)	-23.408*	-0.125	(0.092)	-26.348*	-0.026	(0.004)	-5.990*
% skilled manual/artisans occupations	0.042	(0.004)	9.820*	0.018	(0.005)	3.817*	-0.0001	(1.125)	-0.304
% semi-skilled and labourers	0.096	(0.004)	24.129*	0.062	(0.004)	14.235*	0.011	(0.003)	3.670*
Urban size									
Large dominants	0.710	(0.092)	7.681*	2.346	(0.092)	25.471*	1.963	(0.070)	28.132*
Cities	0.382	(0.082)	4.667*	0.872	(0.081)	10.743*	0.512	(0.062)	8.288*
Rural areas	-0.650	(0.116)	-5.617*	-0.910	(0.115)	-7.907*	-0.108	(0.088)	-1.225
Standard regions									
South East (London + ROSE†)	-1.784	(0.150)	-11.899*	-0.398	(0.149)	-2.671*	1.205	(0.114)	10.555*
East Anglia	-1.395	(0.193)	-7.230*	-1.392	(0.192)	-7.266*	-0.099	(0.146)	-0.679
South West	-0.657	(0.167)	-3.925*	-0.266	(0.167)	-1.595	0.132	(0.126)	1.042
West Midlands	0.434	(0.177)	2.454	-0.271	(0.176)	-1.541	-0.920	(0.133)	-6.889*
East Midlands	-1.169	(0.174)	-6.727*	-0.560	(0.173)	-3.242*	0.236	(0.131)	1.795
North West	1.431	(0.177)	8.077*	1.567	(0.176)	8.914*	0.048	(0.134)	0.359
Northern	1.034	(0.186)	5.545*	0.558	(0.185)	3.016*	-0.485	(0.142)	-3.449*
Wales	2.502	(0.182)	13.759*	2.133	(0.181)	11.806*	-0.489	(0.137)	-3.563*
Scotland	0.268	(0.173)	1.553	-0.881	(0.170)	-5.171*	-0.761	(0.130)	-5.835*
Constant	0.462	(0.274)		0.882	(0.271)		-1.290	(0.206)	
Adjusted R Square	0.477			0.598			0.212		

Note: The 'Towns' urban size category and Yorkshire and Humberside standard region are excluded from independent variables included in the regression analyses.   † Rest of South East

* Coefficient is significant at the 0.01 per cent confidence level.

Source: Census of Population

situation in the largest urban areas, and to a somewhat lesser extent in smaller cities, relative to towns and rural areas. These results are indicative of the increasing salience of the urban size dimension in 'explaining' geographical variations in unemployment rates in the 1990s as compared with the 1970s and 1980s. Areas which in 1981 had relatively high proportions of renting households and workers in lower skilled occupations, and with relatively low proportions of people with higher level occupations, also suffered disproportionately in the face of unemployment change over the decade.

The Changing Segregation of the Non-Employed

Does segregation matter?

Concerns have been expressed from varying quarters about the possible consequences of the 'segregation' of the non-employed from the rest of the population, particularly in those areas of multiple disadvantage where the most vulnerable groups are spatially concentrated in certain localities (Mingione 1993; Wilson 1987). It has been argued that if severely disadvantaged groups are spatially concentrated (in areas of 'extreme poverty' (Greene 1991; Hughes 1989)) rather than dispersed, they will become isolated from the economic and social mainstream; and there is evidence to suggest that the social networks of the long-term unemployed consist disproportionately of other unemployed people, so 'isolating' them and potentially reducing the number of employment opportunities available to them (Dawes 1993; Griffin, Wood and Knight 1992; Morris 1993). Partly in the light of North American experience, throughout Europe there are fears of increasing socio-spatial polarisation and exclusion, resulting from processes of economic restructuring and changing welfare states (see Martin, Chapter 1, this volume). Liberalisation of labour markets, reductions in taxes and erosion of universal benefits, all serve to stimulate social polarisation; while the demise of employment in public services, and a reduction of social housing, tends to contribute to greater socio-spatial segregation in cities.

Measures of segregation: a review

Although the concept of segregation has been of interest to social scientists and policy-makers for some time, what is meant by 'segregation' is far from clear. From a sociological perspective, segregation may mean the absence of interaction among social groups. From a geographical perspective, it may mean an unevenness in the distribution, or separation, of social groups across physical space (White 1983). Since segregation does not stem from a single process, but from a complex interplay of many different social and economic processes that generate various constellations of outcomes interpreted as 'segregation', it seems appropriate to consider several different measures.

Massey and Denton (1988) identify five conceptually distinct – but overlapping – axes of measurement, each corresponding to a different aspect of segregation and each with different social and behavioural implications:

1. *Evenness*: a sub-group may be distributed so that it is over-represented in some parts of a local area and under-represented in others.

2. *Exposure/isolation*: a sub-group may be distributed so that its exposure to other sub-groups is limited by virtue of rarely sharing a neighbourhood with them; isolation refers to the extent to which sub-group members are exposed only to one another.

3. *Concentration*: a sub-group may be spatially concentrated within a very small area, occupying less physical space than the rest of the population; (the term 'concentration' is also often used as a substitute for evenness (as described above)).

4. *Centralisation*: a sub-group may be spatially centralised, congregating around the urban core and occupying a more central location than other sub-groups.

5. *Clustering*: areas of sub-group settlement may be tightly clustered (that is, adjoining one another in space) to form one contiguous enclave, or be scattered widely around the urban area.

While acknowledging that segregation is a multi-dimensional concept, some other commentators dispute the distinctiveness of these axes of variation (see Green 1995a for further information). For example, Morrill (1991) makes a broader two-fold distinction between *structural* indices of segregation (subsuming evenness, exposure and isolation) and *spatial* indices of segregation (incorporating some interaction component incorporating the spatial relationships between areal units).

Using data from the Census of Population it is possible to operationalise a range of measures of different aspects of segregation[3], and so gain a more rounded insight into the various dimensions of segregation. The following analyses refer to five indices of segregation; calculated at the ward scale for LLMAs:

---

3. For some further segregation analyses see Green (1995b).

1. *Index of dissimilarity (D)*: This is the standard, most widely used structural measure of segregation. It compares the spatial distribution of two population sub-groups – for example, the unemployed with those who are not unemployed – by measuring the percentage of the population sub-group of interest (that is, the unemployed) which would have to move their residence for the spatial distribution of the two sub-groups to be the same. Hence it is a measure of 'evenness'. Segregation is maximised (and 'evenness' minimised) when no sub-group and other members share a common area of residence. Values on the index of dissimilarity fall within the range 0.0 to 100.0; the higher the value the more segregated the population sub-group of interest.

2. *Index of isolation*: This measures the probability for a member of a sub-group (for example, the inactive of working age) that someone else randomly chosen from the same area will be a member of the same sub-group (that is, it measures the extent to which members of the sub-group in question are exposed only to one another). Values on the index of isolation vary between 0.0 and 100.0; the higher the value the more isolated the population sub-group of interest.

3. *'Weight-modified' index of dissimilarity (D(w))*: This (and the following) spatial measure of segregation attempts to take the geographical arrangements of micro areas within a city into account by assuming that interaction between areas is proportional to the *length* of their shared boundary (that is, more interaction is assumed across a long common boundary than across a short one) (see Wong 1993).

4. *'Shape-modified' index of dissimilarity (D(s))*: This represents a further enhancement of the 'weight-modified' measure, in which it is assumed that the more compact the areal units (that is, the lower the perimeter–area ratio), the lower the chance for residents to interact with residents of other areal units.

5. *A measure of spatial autocorrelation*: This measures the tendency for neighbouring areas to share similar values (that is, in this case to have similar proportions of non-employed residents).The higher the value on the spatial autocorrelation measure the greater the tendency for similar areas to be 'clustered' together, and the lower the value the greater the tendency for similar areas to be more widely scattered.

Empirical evidence on the segregation of the non-employed

SEGREGATION OF THE UNEMPLOYED

Different patterns of segregation of the unemployed emerge using the different indices, although the patterns of variation on the index of dissimilarity and adjusted dissimilarity indices (D(w) and D(s)) are very close. Of the 280 LLMAs in Great Britain, only 17 fall into the 'top' quartile of the distribution on all five segregation measures operationalised using unemployment rate data from the 1991 Census of Population. Twenty LLMAs were so categorised in 1981. Of these, nine LLMAs are common to the 'top' quartile in both 1991 and 1981. All nine (Preston, Middlesbrough, Blackburn, Birmingham, Manchester, Derby, Hull, Leeds and Leicester) are large cities – the majority with a higher than average incidence of unemployment. The list also includes some of the LLMAs with the largest shares of ethnic minority populations in Britain – which in turn have been shown to exhibit pronounced spatial segregation (Owen 1994) and in many cases are characterised by labour market disadvantage and concentrated poverty (Green 1994; Owen 1993).

In all LLMAs common to the 'top' quartile in 1981 and 1991, a key feature emerging from a comparison of the 1981 and 1991 values on all five segregation measures is that the degree of segregation increased over the decade. Hence in LLMAs exhibiting a relatively high level of segregation of the unemployed at the start of the analysis period, the 'unevenness'/'clustering' of the unemployed became even more pronounced, so that the 'isolation' of the unemployed from the rest of the population had become even more marked by 1991.

Studies from the US and Europe suggest that processes fostering social exclusion and spatial segregation – including industrial restructuring, professionalisation of the employment structure, decentralisation of jobs, and immigration and *in situ* growth of ethnic minority populations – are more advanced in the largest cities (Fainstein, Gordon and Harloe 1992; Sassen 1991). Indeed the increasing salience of the urban size dimension in 'explaining' geographical variations in unemployment rates, with some of the most pronounced increases in unemployment during the 1980s evident in parts of the largest cities, has already been outlined.

Table 4.6 shows the 1981 and 1991 values of selected unemployment rate distribution and segregation measures for the six largest LLMAs in Britain. With the exception of Birmingham, city-wide unemployment rates were higher in 1991 than in 1981.[4] In four of the six cities, the 'extensive-ness' of high unemployment rates at the micro-area level became more pronounced, with the number of constituent wards falling within the 'top' decile group of the national distribution of wards ranked on the unemploy-

Table 4.6: Unemployment Rate: Distribution and Segregation Measures
for the Six Largest LLMAs in Britain

Measure	London	Birmingham	Glasgow	Liverpool	Manchester	Newcastle
Unemployment rate (%)						
1981	7.4	12.1	13.7	16.7	11.3	11.8
1991	10.8	11.7	14.3	18.3	12.7	12.0
% wards in 'top' decile group						
1981	5	23	33	58	26	30
1991	24	19	35	64	36	27
Dissimilarity index						
1981	21.06	22.58	25.41	23.75	21.97	17.90
1991	22.43	26.83	30.73	25.99	26.62	21.58
Wong's D(w)						
1981	19.45	19.41	21.30	17.78	18.38	14.19
1991	20.31	23.69	26.03	19.41	21.88	17.23
Wong's D(s)						
1981	20.97	21.47	25.27	21.07	20.55	17.24
1991	22.32	25.76	30.58	22.89	24.67	20.74
Index of isolation						
1981	9.00	15.08	17.62	20.56	13.99	13.83
1991	13.45	16.21	20.52	23.18	17.04	15.29
Spatial auto-correlation						
1981	0.19	0.24	0.21	0.13	0.21	0.13
1991	0.22	0.26	0.10	0.16	0.23	0.13

Source: Census of Population

4. Adjustments for social and spatial differentials in 'under-enumeration' in the 1991 Census of Population would have the effect of increasing unadjusted 1991 unemployment rates. Hence, 1981–91 differentials in Table 4.6 are likely to be understated.

ment rate increasing over the decade. This increase in the extensiveness of high unemployment rates is particularly pronounced in inner London (Green 1994, 1995b). With a single exception (on one segregation measure for one city), there was an increase in segregation – across all of the different dimensions of segregation measured – between 1981 and 1991. Hence the analyses suggest that in both absolute and relative terms the unemployed in the largest cities became increasingly segregated from the rest of the population over the 1980s.

SEGREGATION OF THE ECONOMICALLY INACTIVE

Considering the six largest LLMAs in Britain once again, Table 4.7 shows the 1981 and 1991 values of the inactivity rate distribution and segregation measures. In London, Birmingham and Newcastle there was little change in city-wide inactivity rates for 20–59-year-olds over the decade, whereas Liverpool, Glasgow and Manchester recorded increases. This aggregate picture disguises marked increases in inactivity rates amongst working age males in all of the largest cities (ranging from an increase of 3 percentage points in London to 8 percentage points in Liverpool) and generally somewhat smaller reductions in inactivity rates for working age females.[5] More pronounced than the aggregate changes in city-wide inactivity rates is the marked increase in the extensiveness of high inactivity rates: in Liverpool one in two of the constituent wards fell within the 'top' decile group of the national distribution of wards ranked on the inactivity rate measure in 1991, compared with less than one in ten in 1981. (This pattern of increased extensiveness of high inactivity rates is apparent for both males and females.) There was a near universal increase in segregation of the economically inactive from the rest of the population in all of the largest cities on each of the dimensions of segregation, with the index of dissimilarity measures recording particularly marked increases in the unevenness of the distribution of the inactive at the micro-area level over the period.

---

5. The reductions in female inactivity rates over the period from 1981 to 1991 tend to be smaller in larger cities than at lower levels of the urban hierarchy.

Table 4.7: Inactivity Rate – 20–59-Year-Olds: Distribution
and Segregation Measures for the Six Largest LLMAs in Britain

Measure	London	Birmingham	Glasgow	Liverpool	Manchester	Newcastle
Inactivity rate (%)						
1981	19.8	20.4	21.8	21.9	20.7	21.9
1991	19.3	20.4	24.4	25.7	22.6	21.7
% wards in 'top' decile group						
1981	1	3	8	7	4	4
1991	7	12	36	49	31	22
Dissimilarity index						
1981	6.33	6.77	8.35	6.34	7.44	6.10
1991	9.58	12.39	17.33	12.81	14.97	10.90
Wong's D(w)						
1981	4.03	3.78	4.49	3.74	4.74	2.68
1991	6.99	9.32	12.75	8.43	10.07	6.47
Wong's D(s)						
1981	6.23	5.91	8.25	5.23	6.39	5.56
1991	9.12	11.42	17.21	10.78	13.11	10.12
Index of isolation						
1981	20.11	20.81	22.53	22.21	21.27	22.36
1991	21.65	21.90	26.78	26.93	24.35	22.69
Spatial auto-correlation						
1981	0.23	0.04	0.04	0.03	0.09	0.02
1991	0.40	0.20	0.03	0.14	0.17	0.07

Source: Census of Population

ASSESSMENT

On both unemployment and inactivity rate indicators, the picture that
emerges is one of increased segregation of the non-employed in the largest
cities across all dimensions of segregation investigated. This is in accordance
with hypotheses regarding the 'quartering' of cities and the expression of
divisions in society in spatial terms. Hence the results of these empirical
analyses are unlikely to dispel concerns that the 'losers' from the processes
of economic restructuring (notably those who would wish to work but are
non-employed for long periods) may become 'isolated' from the socio-economic mainstream and 'dislocated' from majority norms and values as they

become increasingly geographically concentrated and spatial disparities widen.

Synthesis and Policy Implications

Many of the key themes emerging in this review – most notably the deterioration in the fortunes of parts of the largest conurbations and the consolidation of high levels of unemployment and non-employment in many areas already suffering disproportionately in the early 1980s – are captured in Table 4.8, which lists those LADs with the highest proportion of households with no economically active residents in employment in 1991. In four inner London boroughs (Hackney, Tower Hamlets, Newham and Southwark) and four LADs from the large metropolitan areas of northern Britain (Knowsley, Liverpool, Manchester and Glasgow) more than one in ten households containing one or more economically active residents in 1991 had no earners in 1991. If the 'no earner' indicator is broadened to include all households, the proportion of households containing no earners increases to nearly one in two in many large cities, old industrial areas and (former) coalfield communities.

Table 4.8: LADs with High Proportions of 'No Earner' Households, 1991

| *No economically active residents earning* | | *No earners* | |
LAD	*% households*	*LAD*	*% households*
Hackney	12.8	Glasgow	49.0
Tower Hamlets	12.4	Rhondda	48.6
Knowsley	12.2	Manchester	48.2
Liverpool	11.5	Liverpool	48.2
Manchester	10.4	Merthyr Tydfil	46.8
Glasgow	10.3	Easington	46.6
Newham	10.3	Knowsley	46.5
Southwark	10.3	Cynon Valley	46.5

Source: Adapted from Green (1994)

In the light of evidence for the increasing spatial segregation of the unemployed and economically inactive, the concept of space becomes central to non-employment, as those without jobs are increasingly insulated from those with jobs in other parts of cities. Gaffikin and Morrisey (1994) use the phrase 'social containment' to describe this condition. It is within some of the largest cities that the increase in the extensiveness of high levels of non-employment, and the concentration, isolation and clustering of those

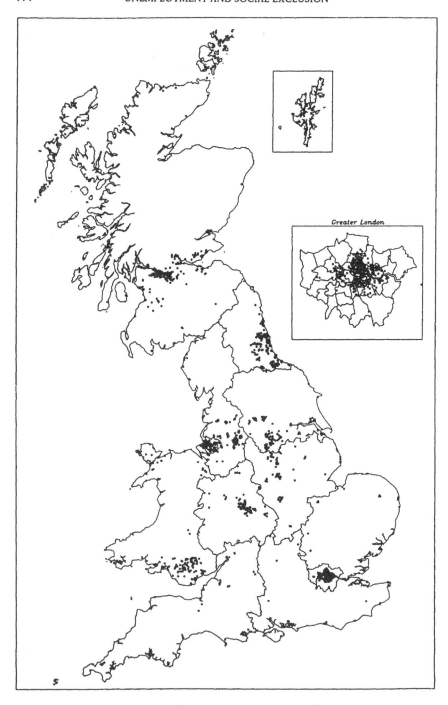

Figure 4.4. Wards in Great Britain Suffering Extreme Labour Market Disadvantage
Source: *Green and Owen*

sub-groups concerned, are furthest developed. As the duration of non-employment increases and other cumulative disadvantages persist, so the non-employed slip further and further back in the 'queue' for available employment opportunities. The main dimensions of the likely spatial expression of this sub-group are shown in Figure 4.4, which maps those wards in Great Britain scoring values at least 150 per cent greater than the national average on unemployment, non-employment and long-term unemployment indicators.

While many policy statements (at local, national and European level) have stressed the scope for achieving greater competitiveness through investment in human capital so as to increase the skills base and enhance the level of qualifications and competencies of the population, it is also recognised that a broadly based policy approach is needed – as emphasised by the principle of 'multi-dimensionality' in the European Poverty 3 Programme (Duffy 1994) – at area, individual and institutional scales. At the local scale, it is increasingly recognised that the different constellations of local circumstances call for different policy measures. For example, examining the spatial pattern of deprivation within a subset of 94 of the most deprived English local authority districts, Robson, Bradford and Tye (1995) identified seven descriptive categories of spatial patterning, and suggested that different area-based policy approaches may be more appropriate in some local authority districts than in others, depending on the character of the spatial pattern of deprivation. From a more specific labour market perspective, in recognition of the different dimensions and associated spatial manifestations of labour market disadvantage, research has been undertaken for the Department of Education and Employment on the construction of an enhanced local classification of labour market disadvantage in Great Britain, to be used as an improved spatial framework for detailed labour market and associated policy analyses at the local scale (Green and Owen 1995). In this way, it is hoped that policies can be integrated and adapted in ways that best address specific local conditions.

Acknowledgements

This paper draws on research undertaken for the Joseph Rowntree Foundation, the Leverhulme Trust and Department of Employment. It includes data derived from the 1981 and 1991 Census of Population which are Crown Copyright, and Employment Department unemployment statistics accessed via NOMIS.

CHAPTER 5

Registered and Hidden Unemployment in the UK Coalfields

Christina Beatty and Stephen Fothergill

Introduction

A remarkable thing has happened in Britain's coalfields. Despite the well-publicised dismantling of the coal industry, which by the mid 1990s had reduced its employment by nine-tenths in a decade, registered unemployment in the coalfield areas has not risen. Indeed the official unemployment figures suggest that coalfield unemployment in the mid 1990s is lower than a decade ago, and that the gap between the coalfields and the rest of the country has narrowed.

Closer examination suggests that this paradox may not be so unusual. Elsewhere in the United Kingdom, and in Western Europe and North America, the collapse of employment in formerly dominant industries rarely has quite the impact on recorded unemployment as is generally feared. An area may shed 20 or 30 per cent of its employment, but it is rare for unemployment to rise by more than a few percentage points. In particular, long-established disparities between local and national rates of unemployment rarely seem to be disturbed after the initial impact of the redundancies has worn off.

The stability in patterns of unemployment points towards powerful labour market adjustments. These may involve the vigorous creation of new jobs in other industries, taking up the slack in the local economy. Or there may be a downward adjustment in labour supply, for instance through out-migration in response to the lower levels of local labour demand. There is also another possibility, not necessarily incompatible with the other two. This is that some of the resulting unemployment may not be recorded. A large number of people may simply disappear into the ranks of those who are neither employed nor unemployed, at least in terms of official statistics. This third possibility – hidden unemployment – is particularly pertinent in the UK, where the official unemployment statistics are frequently regarded with suspicion. The most widely used figures are no more than a monthly count of those claiming unemployment-related benefits. As such, even the Royal Statistical Society (1995) has recognised that they can be no more than a partial measure of unemployment.

The traditional approach to the study of job loss is to trace the impact on the redundant workers themselves. How many find new work? How many opt for early retirement? How many stay unemployed? In the context of the UK coal industry, two of the best recent examples in this tradition are by Witt (1990) and Guy (1994). Such studies are illuminating but their limitation is that they are partial. They do not tell us what is happening in the local labour market as a whole and therefore how unemployment responds or fails to respond to changes in employment. For example, if an ex-miner finds new work this does not necessarily indicate successful labour market adjustment. The miner may simply fill an existing vacancy that would otherwise have been filled by another worker in the locality, thereby transferring unemployment from one individual to another.

Our approach in this chapter is to take an overview of the labour market in the UK's coalfields. We do this first by constructing local 'labour market accounts'. Logically, a loss of jobs must feed through into one or several adjustments in a local labour market – migration, commuting, economic activity rates, increases in other employment and, of course, unemployment. These components are arithmetically related so that it becomes possible to show how large job loss can result in only a small increase in unemployment, or indeed none at all. In the second half of the chapter we look more specifically at unemployment and at hidden unemployment in particular. Given the large rise in economic inactivity among men that the labour market accounts reveal, what is the true level of unemployment in the coalfields?

The UK Coalfields

There are few, if any, more striking examples of job loss in Western Europe than the UK coal industry. Furthermore, given the nature of the coal industry nearly all the burden of adjustment has been thrust upon a few areas and on a specific segment of the workforce – male, predominantly manual workers. Table 5.1 shows the reduction in employment between 1981 and 1994 in British Coal, the state-owned corporation which all but monopolised UK coal production from 1948 until its privatisation at the end of 1994. The causes of the decline in employment need not detain us and have been discussed elsewhere (for example, Townroe and Dabinett 1993) but it is worth noting that the industry's contraction has been a source of major political conflict, notably during a year-long strike in 1984/5 and again in 1992 when further draconian closures were announced.

Table 5.1: Employment in British Coal, 1981–94

	Total British Coal workforce (thousands)	No. of miners (thousands)	No. of collieries
September 1981	279.2	218.8	211
September 1982	266.3	208.0	200
September 1983	246.8	191.7	191
March 1985	221.3	171.4	169
March 1986	179.6	138.5	133
March 1987	141.5	107.7	110
March 1988	117.3	89.0	94
March 1989	105.0	80.1	86
March 1990	85.0	65.4	73
March 1991	73.3	57.3	65
March 1992	58.1	43.8	50
March 1993	44.2	31.7	50
March 1994	18.9	10.8	19

Note: There are no figures for 1984, reflecting the shift from September to March as the recording date for British Coal's statistics.

Source: British Coal Corporation, Annual Reports.

The decline in the UK coal industry is in fact a long-established trend. In the 1920s there were more than 1 million miners, and the 1960s were marked by a particularly large number of pit closures. The 1970s, in contrast, was a period of relative stability for the industry. The period since 1981, as shown in Table 5.1, was one of continuous job loss, with especially large cutbacks in the mid 1980s after the end of the strike and (in proportional terms) after 1992. The significant point is that what was still a very large industry at the start of the 1980s was reduced in the space of not much more than a decade to one with less than 10 per cent of its former workforce.

Although geology dictates that the coal industry is highly localised, there are a number of separate coalfields in the UK. These are shown in Figure 5.1 and listed in Table 5.2. In recent times the most important mining area, accounting for about half the output of the industry, has been the 'central coalfield' covering parts of Yorkshire, Nottinghamshire and North Derbyshire. The famous South Wales coalfield had by the start of the 1980s already been badly affected by earlier closures. So too had the coalfields of Durham

Figure 5.1. UK Coalfields

and Northumberland in North East England, and the scattered coalfields of Central Scotland.

Table 5.2: UK Coalfields

	Population (1981)	Men employed in coal (1981)
Yorkshire*	1,109,000	70,200
South Wales	729,000	27,800
Durham	525,000	22,900
Nottinghamshire*	492,000	41,900
Lancashire	385,000	7,100
North Derbyshire*	299,000	13,900
North Staffordshire	284,000	8,600
Fife/Central	256,000	7,700
North Warwickshire	162,000	6,000
Northumberland	138,000	10,700
South Derbyshire/NW Leicestershire	122,000	9,700
Lothian	116,000	5,100
South Staffordshire	99,000	5,700
Ayrshire	59,000	4,000
Clydesdale	40,000	1,500
Kent	35,000	3,200
North Wales	21,000	1,200
Strathkelvin	17,000	1,500

Source: Census of Population.

* These areas form a continuous mining region generally known as the 'central coalfield'.

For the purpose of this study we defined two categories of coalfield areas. The first of these are the coalfields themselves, shown in Figure 5.1. These are continuous groups of 'wards' – small electoral and statistical units each with around 2–10,000 people – in which at least 10 per cent of the resident males in employment in 1981 were engaged in the energy and water sector (which in these areas overwhelmingly comprises coalmining). This statistical threshold was interpreted flexibly, for example to include some wards that did not meet the 10 per cent hurdle but which were largely or wholly surrounded by other coalfield wards. Also, in the Lancashire and North Staffordshire coalfields, where mining takes place in built-up and diversified industrial areas, some wards with slightly lower dependence on coal were included. In Scotland data availability meant that post-code sectors, which are similar in size to wards, were used to define the areas. We are confident that across the UK as a whole the resulting definition of coalfield areas fits extremely well with local economic geography.

The second category of areas is what we have called 'pit villages'. These are settlements (some rather larger than villages) that form part of the coalfields and comprise wards in which at least 25 per cent of the resident males in employment in 1981 were employed in energy and water. The pit villages are in a sense the heart of the coalfields and invariably have a strong self-identity as 'mining communities'. A pit village need not have its own pit however: in some cases the local mine may have closed much earlier but a high dependence on the industry remained because of men travelling to other nearby mines.

At the start of the 1980s the coalfields included a population of nearly 5 million, or about 8 per cent of the UK total. Pit villages comprised about one-third of the coalfields in population terms, but included about two-thirds of the jobs in coal-mining. The coal industry provided approximately a quarter of all the male jobs located in the coalfields, and not far short of half of those in the pit villages. Net out-commuting from the coalfields to work elsewhere was already well established at this time, reducing the proportion of residents dependent on the coal industry. Nevertheless, it is fair to say that the coalfields in general and pit villages in particular entered the 1980s with a high dependence on coal-mining as a source of jobs for men.

The riddle of massive job loss alongside stable or even falling local unemployment is illustrated in Figures 5.2 and 5.3. The quarterly unemployment rates shown in these graphs are based upon the figures published by the Department of Employment. The number of male residents recorded as unemployed is the number claiming unemployment-related benefits – the so-called 'claimant count' which here and in the rest of the chapter we refer to as 'registered' unemployment. These numbers are produced by the Department of Employment on a ward-by-ward basis (or post-code sector in Scotland). The Department of Employment itself does not calculate unemployment rates for these small areas. The denominator we have used is the number of economically active males (that is, employed plus unemployed) aged 16–64, resident in these same wards in April 1991, from the Census of Population. Population levels change only slowly and 1991 is towards the middle of the period covered by the graphs, so the use of this denominator is defensible. The resulting figures provide an accurate measure of registered unemployment rates in coalfields and pit villages.

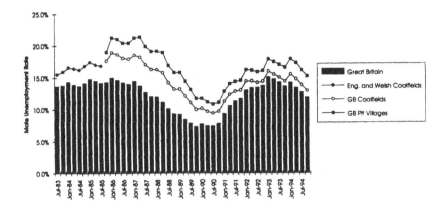

Figure 5.2. Male Registered Unemployment Rates for Coalfields and Pit Villages, 1983–94

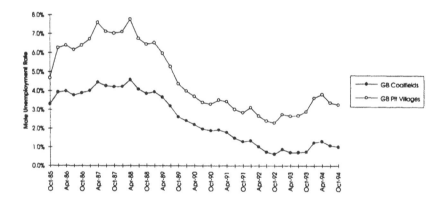

Figure 5.3. Divergence from GB Average Male Unemployment, 1985–94

Throughout the period for which statistics can be produced (since 1983 for England and Wales and since 1985 for Scotland), registered male unemployment rates in the coalfields and pit villages have been above the national (GB) average. The change in local unemployment has also followed the national trend – a decline from peak levels in 1985/6 to a low in 1990, followed by a rise to another peak in early 1993. Throughout the whole period, pit village unemployment has also been higher than that for the coalfields as a whole.

From the point of view of labour market adjustment there are two remarkable features of these figures. First, by mid 1994 registered unemployment rates in the coalfields and pit villages were actually *lower* than in 1985, when the pit closure programme began to accelerate and since which time British Coal shed more than 200,000 jobs. Second, over the same period the difference between registered unemployment rates in the coalfields and the national average *narrowed*.

Figure 5.3 illustrates this last point. In the period up to early 1988, when the post-strike closures were proceeding rapidly, the unemployment differentials between coalfields and pit villages on the one hand and the national average on the other widened a little. There was then a period of more or less continuous convergence up to October 1992 (significantly, the exact start of the most recent wave of closures), followed by some widening of the gap to 1994, more in pit villages than the coalfields as a whole. But in October 1994 the excess over the national average – 1.0 per cent for coalfields and 3.3 per cent for pit villages – was well below the 4–8 per cent gap of the mid-1980s. These trends are shared to a greater or lesser extent by all the individual UK coalfields.

The convergence between coalfield and national unemployment runs contrary to much economic theory. The substantial literature on skill mismatch, exemplified by Layard, Nickell and Jackman (1991), suggests that unemployment should rise in an area of severe job loss from a dominant industry. Skill mismatch – defined as a persistent imbalance in the demand and supply for labour across skill groups – has been put forward by Layard *et al.* as one of the factors responsible for an underlying increase in UK unemployment in the 1980s compared with earlier decades. Skill mismatch should, in theory, have increased particularly sharply in the coalfields because redundant miners are unlikely to have the transferable skills that make them attractive to other employers.

Nor can the apparent convergence between coalfield and national unemployment be explained away by the incidence of job loss elsewhere. During the UK's post-1990 recession, the rate of job loss was higher in the South of England than in the Northern regions where most of the coalfields are located. But the convergence between coalfield and national unemployment began much earlier – in late 1987 or early 1988 – when Southern England was still enjoying a period of strong economic growth. By the time the recession really bit, much of the convergence had already occurred.

The key point is that the jobless figures for the coalfields confirm the importance of labour market adjustments other than rising registered unemployment.

Labour Market Accounts

The labour market flows in an area that mediate between changes in employment and changes in unemployment can be broken down into the following components:

	JOB LOSS IN INDUSTRY 'X'
plus	NATURAL INCREASE IN WORKFORCE
minus	NET OUT-MIGRATION
minus	INCREASE IN NET OUT-COMMUTING
minus	REDUCTION IN LABOUR FORCE PARTICIPATION
minus	INCREASE IN JOBS IN OTHER ACTIVITIES
equals	INCREASE IN UNEMPLOYMENT

This 'labour market account' approach was pioneered in the regional context in the UK by the Cambridge Economic Policy Group (1980, 1982). It has been applied to the UK's inner cities between 1951 and 1981 (Begg, Moore and Rhodes 1986) and with a much greater degree of imputation at the sub-regional scale (Green and Owen 1991; Owen and Green 1989). Its successful application to local areas, without significant imputation, depends on the availability of comprehensive information from the decennial Census of Population.

What we have done is to construct labour market accounts for the UK coalfields for the period 1981–91 using Census of Population data. The 1981–91 period saw about three-quarters of the reduction in employment in the coal industry that occurred between 1981 and 1994. The calculation of the individual components of a labour market account is not a simple process, particularly because of differences of definition and coverage between 1981 and 1991 Censuses, and the need to integrate data from other sources. Full details of the methods used are set out in a separate article (Beatty and Fothergill 1996). Tables 5.3 and 5.4 present labour market accounts for male employment in coalfields and pit villages in England and Wales. (Data are not available to allow similar figures for Scotland to be compiled.) These two tables are particularly important and deserve a full description.

Taking coalfields first, it is striking that over the 1981–91 period a loss of nearly 160,000 jobs in coal was associated with an increase in unemployment, recorded by the Census, of a mere 500 men. Moreover, the employment shortfall arising from the loss of mining jobs was compounded by a natural increase in the workforce (16–64-year-olds) of more than 60,000, or 5 per cent. The high rate of natural increase reflects the large numbers reaching working age in the early 1980s as a result of high birth rates in England and Wales in the middle and late 1960s.

The labour market accounts show that between 1981 and 1991 a reduction in economic activity among men was the single largest response to the surplus of labour in the coalfields. This cut labour supply in these areas by 85,000, or 6.8 per cent. These are additional men of working age who dropped out of either employment or unemployment, and in view of their significance to the overall labour market adjustment process we return later to examine them more closely.

**Table 5.3: Labour Market Accounts for Coalfields,
England and Wales, 1981–91**

		Number of males	As % economically active males aged 16–64 in 1981
	Job loss in coal	159,400	12.8
plus	Natural increase in workforce	62,100	5.0
minus	Net out-migration	59,600	4.8
minus	Increase in net out-commuting	4,500	0.4
minus	Reduction in economically active	84,600	6.8
minus	Increase in non-coal jobs	44,900	3.6
minus	No. on government schemes	27,300	2.2
equals	Increase in unemployment	500	0.04

Source: Census of Population

The second largest response to the surplus of labour was net out-migration. The out-migrants were not necessarily ex-miners, or indeed other unemployed workers. Often they will have been qualified people with jobs who moved elsewhere or young people leaving the area, for example to take up higher education and then not returning. In all, net out-migration reduced the male workforce in the coalfields by nearly 60,000, or 4.8 per cent. By contrast, increased net out-commuting absorbed little of the labour surplus – just 4,500 men. At first sight this is surprising because several UK coalfields are within feasible commuting distance of large industrial cities. Out-commuting from the coalfields was already high in 1981, as we noted earlier.

**Table 5.4: Labour Market Accounts for Pit Villages,
England and Wales, 1981–91**

		Number of males	*As % economically active males aged 16–64 in 1981*
	Job loss in coal	114,600	25.0
plus	Natural increase in workforce	20,900	4.6
minus	Net out-migration	38,000	8.3
minus	Increase in net out-commuting	22,100	4.8
minus	Reduction in economically active	33,500	7.3
minus	Increase in non-coal jobs	22,900	5.0
minus	No. on government schemes	11,300	2.5
equals	Increase in unemployment	7,700	1.7

Source: Census of Population

The relatively small change in net commuting flows may reflect the particular character of the coal industry, which always tended to recruit locally, often through word of mouth and family connections. The loss of jobs in the coal industry therefore probably fell overwhelmingly on coalfield residents and hardly affected in-commuters. By contrast, the new jobs that have been created in the coalfields may be 'open' to a wider range of workers both inside and outside the coalfields, which would boost in-commuting and offset any tendency for ex-miners to seek work outside the coalfields, so reducing the net change.

In the labour market accounts the increase in non-coal employment has been split into two components. One is the employment on government schemes (Youth Training, Employment Training, and so on). In 1981 workers on these schemes were not identified as a separate category but were split among the numbers in employment and in education. In 1991, government schemes accounted for 27,000 people, or just over 2 per cent of the workforce. Genuine new jobs in the coalfields outside the coal industry itself accounted for a larger 45,000 increase, or 3.6 per cent.

Another way of expressing the same figures is that for every 100 'surplus' male workers in the coalfields resulting from loss of coal jobs and the natural increase in the workforce:

- 38 dropped out of economic activity
- 27 became net migrants out of the area
- 20 were absorbed by increases in other employment
- 12 were taken up by government schemes
- 2 became extra net commuters out of the area
- none were added to the unemployed.

Turning to pit villages (Table 5.4) the loss of male jobs in the coal industry – nearly 115,000 – was proportionally a much bigger reduction in local employment than in the coalfields as a whole. The employment shortfall was exacerbated by the natural increase in the workforce. Again, however, the increase in unemployment was very small – just 7,700, or 1.7 per cent of the economically active population. In pit villages, net out-migration – 38,000 – was by a small margin the biggest single labour market adjustment. This out-migration was equivalent to one-in-twelve of the 1981 male workforce. A reduction in economic activity rates – 33,500, or 7.3 per cent of the workforce – was the second largest adjustment. An increase in net out-commuting, an increase in non-coal jobs and, to a lesser extent, government schemes accounted for the remainder of the difference between job loss and the small rise in unemployment.

As before, putting these figures another way, for every 100 'surplus' male workers in pit villages:

- 28 became net migrants out of the area
- 25 dropped out of economic activity
- 17 were absorbed by increases in other employment
- 16 became extra net commuters out of the area
- 8 were taken up by government schemes
- 6 were added to the unemployed.

The precise magnitude of each labour market adjustment is of course specific to the period in question – 1981 to 1991. A period of faster national economic growth, for example, might have encouraged more out-commuting because of the greater availability of alternative jobs and a faster rate of new job creation in the coalfields themselves. Nevertheless, the figures successfully explain the disparity during this period between trends in employment and unemployment, and expose the relative importance of the varied adjustment processes.

The Non-Employed

In the coalfields, as elsewhere, the men of working age without jobs fall into two broad categories. First, there are those who are recorded as unemployed. Second, there are those who are recorded as 'economically inactive', not all of whom can be regarded as unemployed. As both the Department of Employment claimant count figures and the labour market accounts show, on the whole recorded male unemployment in the coalfields has not risen since the early 1980s, despite the massive loss of coal jobs. Recorded unemployment among men in these areas is nevertheless substantial. According to the Census of Population, in April 1991 there were 178,000 unemployed men in the coalfields, representing 13.8 per cent of economically active males. This is slightly more than the Department of Employment's figure for April 1991 – 161,300, or 12.4 per cent – because the Census figure includes some men who were ineligible to claim unemployment-related benefits and were therefore excluded from the Department of Employment's figures.

Predictably, Table 5.5 shows that recorded male unemployment in the coalfields is heavily skewed towards less skilled workers. In 1991, rates of unemployment among unskilled workers were nearly ten times higher than among professionals. This differential is also understated by the figures. About a quarter of the unemployed cannot be classified into a socio-economic group because they have never had a job or because it is so long since they held one. A great many of these men could probably be regarded as 'unskilled', if only because their skills are likely to have waned through disuse. Adding them to the unskilled category would raise the unemployed rate among this group to around 50 per cent.

Table 5.5: Recorded Male Unemployment in the UK Coalfields by Socio-Economic Group, April 1991

Socio-economic group		Unemployed as % of economically active males
I	Professional	2.7
II	Managerial and technical	4.9
III N	Skilled non-manual	7.1
III M	Skilled manual	11.1
IV	Partly skilled	15.6
V	Unskilled	25.1
All Males		**13.8***

*   Includes unemployed not classified into group I–V.

Source: Census of Population

More surprisingly, relatively few of the recorded unemployed in 1991 were ex-miners – or, more accurately, relatively few of the unemployed last worked in the coal industry. Table 5.6 shows that unemployed men whose last job was in the energy sector (including coal) comprised only just over 10 per cent of the total. At first this seems incompatible with the very large loss of coal jobs, or suggests an extraordinarily good rate of re-employment of ex-miners. In fact, since the figures record only the most recent industry of employment they understate unemployment among ex-miners. As Witt (1990) showed, many men leaving the coal industry move into a succession of insecure temporary jobs, for example in the construction industry. Although they may have had 20 or 30 years in the coal industry, once they have worked elsewhere, even for a few weeks, they are no longer recorded as ex-miners. Nevertheless, the industry breakdown of the unemployed does at least show that the problem of unemployment in the coalfields is not exclusively one of ex-miners. It also underlines the importance of taking a wider view of the local economy, because in so far as ex-miners have been successful in finding new work they will often have displaced other local workers.

Table 5.6: Recorded Male Unemployment in the UK Coalfields
by Former Industry, April 1991

Industry of most recent job in last ten years (SIC Division)		% of total male unemployment*
0	Agriculture	1.4
1	Energy and water (inc. coal)	11.7
2	Minerals, chemicals	4.5
3	Metal goods, engineering	11.7
4	Other manufacturing	10.5
5	Construction	19.9
6	Distribution, hotels, catering	14.1
7	Transport and communication	4.9
8	Banking, finance, etc.	4.2
9	Public and other services	13.8
	Not stated	3.5
All Male Unemployed**		**100.0**

*   Includes those on government schemes.
**   Excludes those with no former employment.

Source: Census of Population

In contrast to recorded unemployment, economic inactivity among men has risen sharply. As the labour market accounts showed, this has been the single most important mechanism through which the coalfield labour market has adjusted to the loss of so many jobs. Table 5.7 provides a breakdown of these men. They fall into four categories: those describing themselves as permanently sick, as retired, as students or otherwise as economically inactive (which includes full-time carers, people of independent means and those who have disappeared full-time into the 'black economy'). By 1991 the economically inactive accounted for one in six of 16–64-year-old men in the coalfields, and nearly one in five in pit villages. In both cases, the numbers of inactive males had risen by about two-thirds since 1981. Easily the largest category of economically inactive are the 'permanently sick' accounting for just over half the total in both coalfields and pit villages. By 1991, the 'retired' were the second largest group. The increase in economic inactivity between 1981 and 1991 was also almost all within these two groups.

Table 5.7: Economically Inactive, UK Coalfields

| | % of resident males aged 16–64 | | | |
| | Coalfields | | Pit Villages | |
	1981	1991	1981	1991
Permanently sick	4.8	8.9	5.2	10.1
Retired	1.5	3.6	2.4	4.8
Students	3.8	3.6	3.4	3.2
Other inactive	0.5	0.8	0.4	0.8
ALL INACTIVE	10.6	17.0	11.4	19.0

Source: Census of Population

Neither recorded unemployment nor inactivity are spread evenly across the life cycle. Combined, they reveal a distinctive picture of the rise and fall of participation in paid employment. Figure 5.4, which also includes those on government schemes, shows that in the coalfields in 1991 more than half of 16–19-year-old males and nearly 30 per cent of 20–24-year-olds did not have jobs. Students and those on government schemes accounted for a high proportion of those without work, but recorded unemployment was also significant, particularly for men in their early 20s. Men of prime working age (25–49) had much lower rates of non-employment – less than 20 per cent. The main source of non-employment was recorded unemployment, but permanent sickness was also important, especially among those over 40. Towards the end of men's working lives non-employment again becomes

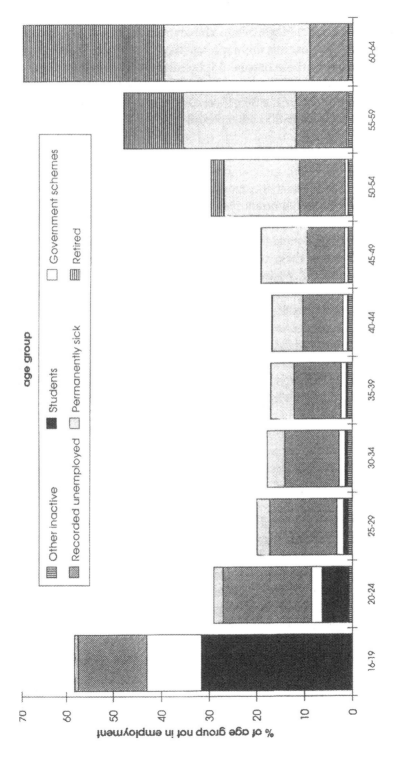

Figure 5.4. Non-Employed Males in the UK Coalfields, April 1991
Source: Census of Population

highly significant. In the coalfields in 1991 only fractionally over half of all 50–64-year-old men actually held a job, and fewer than half in pit villages. For these older groups the form of non-employment shifts radically, however. Recorded unemployment remains important but is overshadowed by permanent sickness and (for those beyond 55) by early retirement. Indeed among all 60–64-year-old men in the coalfields, 30 per cent were recorded as permanently sick and a further 30 per cent as retired. Fewer than 10 per cent of this group were recorded as unemployed.

Hidden Unemployment

This rise in economic inactivity among men in the coalfields and elsewhere is closely related to an important national debate about the validity of the official, registered unemployment figures produced by the Department of Employment. Being no more than the number of people claiming unemployment-related benefits, these registered figures are widely criticised. Wells (1995) and Schmitt and Wadsworth (1994b), for example, have argued that in the UK as a whole the increase in economic inactivity among men is concealing unemployment.

The most frequent criticism of the official figures is that they are vulnerable to changes in the administrative procedures that define a 'claimant'. The changes have been numerous. Gregg (1994) identifies 30 since 1979, the majority of which have reduced registered unemployment. Several of the changes are acknowledged by the Department of Employment to be sufficiently large to have created a discontinuity between early and later figures on the new basis. One of the administrative changes is particularly pertinent to the coalfields: in 1989 ex-miners who were covered by the Redundant Mineworkers Pension Scheme were relieved of the requirement to register for benefits. At a stroke, this reduced registered unemployment by 15,000 according to the Department of Employment (Lawlor 1990) or 26,000 according to the independent Unemployment Unit (Taylor 1989).

Furthermore, there are interactions between different parts of the benefits system so that the numbers claiming unemployment-related benefits are not independent of the availability and level of other state benefits. In particular, Sickness Benefit and Invalidity Benefit can be attractive alternatives for some unemployed claimants because the rate of payment is higher in many circumstances. White and Lakey (1992) found that two-thirds of unemployed men in a 1989 survey who left the register for reasons other than employment began receiving other forms of state benefit. The UK government's Restart counselling and advice initiative for the long-term unemployed, which began in 1986, is widely thought to have moved some of the long-term claimant unemployed on to sickness-related benefits. Conversely the introduction of Incapacity Benefit in April 1995, with its tighter medical rules for eligibility, is expected to push some individuals back on to unemployment-related benefits and thus into the unemployment count.

It has also been argued that the claimant-based unemployment figures fail to take account of the complexity of the labour market. This criticism was strongly supported by the Royal Statistical Society (1995) in its review of UK unemployment statistics. In the real world, individuals move between employment, unemployment and inactivity, and the distinctions between the categories can be blurred. Even when in employment, individuals may be underemployed if their hours of work are less than they would like. On balance, the Royal Statistical Society concluded that the claimant count is an inferior measure of unemployment.

To what extent, therefore, can some of the large numbers of economically inactive men in the coalfields be regarded as unemployed?

There are three reasons for believing that the figures hide substantial numbers of unemployed. The first is the near doubling in the recorded rate of permanent sickness in the coalfields between 1981 and 1991, shown in Table 5.7. This runs contrary to general trends in health. The coal industry itself is notorious as a source of ill-health among older men. However, the declining size of the coal industry over many decades, and its improving safety record, mean that by 1991 fewer men of working age will have been exposed to its injurious effects. This might have been expected to lead to a fall in permanent sickness, not an increase.

The second reason for believing that there is substantial hidden unemployment is a comparison of the incidence of permanent sickness and retirement in coalfield areas with the South East of England and with Great Britain as a whole (Table 5.8). Rates of permanent sickness and early retirement in coalfield areas were well above the national average in 1991, but it is the comparison with the South East that is most revealing because for many years this region has been the UK's most prosperous, and to all intents much of it sustained the elusive goal of full employment between 1986 and 1990. Rates of permanent sickness for men in coalfields and pit villages were between two-and-a-half and three times higher than in the South East. Likewise, the proportion of the male workforce that had taken early retirement was 60 per cent higher in the coalfields and 120 per cent higher in pit villages.

Table 5.8: 'Sick' and 'Retired' Male Workers, April 1991

	Coalfields	Pit Villages	South East	GB
'Permanently sick' aged 16–64	140,300	55,000	185,500	916,300
as % males 16–64	8.9	10.1	3.4	5.2
'Retired' aged 16–64	57,200	26,400	123,600	435,700
as % males 16–64	3.6	4.8	2.2	2.5

Source: Census of Population

The third factor pointing towards hidden unemployment is the incidence of permanent sickness across the different coalfields. Table 5.9 compares rates of permanent sickness and unemployment as recorded by the Census of Population, both expressed as a percentage of resident males aged 16–64. In 1991, rates of permanent sickness varied from around 5 per cent in some of the Midlands coalfields to 13–14 per cent, notably in the large South Wales coalfield. Significantly, the coalfields with the highest recorded

Table 5.9: Recorded Unemployment and Permanent Sickness by Coalfield, April 1991

	Percentage of resident males aged 16–64	
	Unemployed	Permanently sick
Ayrshire	15.6	10.3
Durham	13.2	11.8
Clydesdale	12.7	14.0
South Wales	12.3	13.8
Northumberland	12.1	8.4
Yorkshire	11.8	8.1
Fife/Central	11.7	8.0
Lancashire	11.5	9.7
North Derbyshire	11.0	6.3
Strathkelvin	10.8	9.3
Nottinghamshire	10.1	6.4
Lothian	9.9	6.4
South Staffordshire	9.6	5.7
North Warwickshire	9.5	5.1
Kent	9.1	6.6
North Staffordshire	9.1	7.7
North Wales	8.4	9.8
South Derbyshire/North West Leicestershire	7.1	4.8

Source: Census of Population

unemployment were generally those with the highest rates of permanent sickness. This is consistent with the view that for men who have little chance of finding suitable work, permanent sickness is an alternative to conventional unemployment: the greater the shortage of jobs, the more men are unemployed and the more are diverted into 'permanent sickness' as well.

It is difficult to avoid the conclusion that high levels of permanent sickness and early retirement do indeed hide a large number of additional unemployed people. In areas such as the coalfields where there is a severe shortage of jobs, some workers are realistic enough to recognise that their chances of securing satisfactory paid employment are slim. If they have an ailment, registering as permanently sick is an attractive alternative to long-term unemployment, not least because the sickness-related social security benefits are more generous than Income Support (the means-tested benefit paid to the unemployed who have been out of work for more than a year).

Significantly, in his survey of men made redundant from five collieries in 1992–93, Guy (1994) found that a year later about one-third of the men still without new jobs were registered as 'sick' rather than 'unemployed', despite the fact that until recently they had been holding down demanding jobs in the coal industry. Likewise, if men have a pension from a former employer (such as British Coal) they may opt for early retirement even though their age and health would enable them to take a new job if one were available.

Our view is that the rates of permanent sickness and early retirement that prevailed in the South East of England in 1991 probably represent the levels that can be achieved in a reasonably fully employed economy, and that excesses over this level are a form of hidden unemployment. The 'permanently sick' in the South East will still include some people who are unemployed rather than unfit for work, so even the South East level may still be too high as a benchmark. But this distortion is likely to be offset in the coalfields by a genuinely higher level of real sickness as a result of employment in the coal industry.

In Table 5.10 we have re-calculated coalfield male unemployment rates for April 1991 to allow for this hidden unemployment. The first line of this table shows unemployment measured by the number registered as claimants with the Department of Employment. This is the 'official' figure: 12.4 per cent in the coalfields and 14.0 per cent in pit villages. Real unemployment, as measured in Table 5.10, comprises four categories. The first is the unemployment recorded by the Census of Population. 'Unemployment' in the Census is a self-reported category and, as noted earlier, includes some people who are ineligible to register as claimants. To this we have added those on government schemes (who would almost all take 'proper jobs' if they were available) and the hidden unemployed who are recorded by the Census as permanently sick and retired. The permanently sick and retired unemployed are the excess over the proportions of the male resident population aged 16–64 that are recorded as permanently sick and retired in the South East of England. The inclusion of hidden unemployment radically alters the male unemployment rate to 22.5 per cent in the coalfields and 26.7 per cent in pit villages.

Table 5.10: Registered and Hidden Male Unemployment, April 1991

	Coalfields		Pit Villages	
	No.	% economically active	No.	% economically active
Registered unemployment	**161,300**	**12.4**	**62,000**	**14.0**
Census unemployment	178,300	12.6*	68,800	13.9*
Government schemes	30,400	2.1*	12,200	2.5*
Excess 'sick'	87,700	6.2*	36,700	7.4*
Excess 'early retired'	22,200	1.6*	14,200	2.5*
Real unemployment	**318,500**	**22.5***	**132,000**	**26.7***

* Hidden unemployment added to economically active to calculate rate.

Sources: NOMIS, Census of Population, authors' estimates

Tables 5.11 and 5.12 apply the same methodology to individual coalfields and to pit villages in these coalfields. The statistics are no less alarming. Two large coalfields – Durham and South Wales, with 1.25 million people between them – had estimated rates of real male unemployment in 1991 nudging 30 per cent. Several other coalfields, including Yorkshire, had estimated rates well in excess of 20 per cent. Only two small coalfields in the Midlands could boast real rates of male unemployment of less than 15 per cent. In pit villages the situation is worse. In Ayrshire, South Wales and Durham, real male unemployment is estimated to have been well in excess of 30 per cent in 1991. Only the pit villages in the South Derbyshire/North West Leicestershire coalfield had rates below 20 per cent.

Calculated on the same basis, the increase in national (GB) male unemployment is less dramatic from 10.6 per cent on the official measure to 14.9 per cent for real unemployment. The significant point in this context, however, is that, allowing for hidden unemployment, the gap between rates in coalfield areas and the national average widens considerably, from 1.8 per cent to 7.6 percentage points for the coalfields as a whole, and from 2.4 to 11.8 percentage points for pit villages. In several coalfield areas, our figures indicate that in 1991 the real level of male unemployment was twice the national average and three times the national rate recorded by the Department of Employment.

Table 5.11: Alternative Measures of Coalfield Unemployment, April 1991

| | Percentage of economically active males aged 16–64 | |
	Registered unemployment	Real unemployment
Ayrshire	17.2	30.8
Durham	14.3	28.3
South Wales	14.3	29.2
Clydesdale	14.0	28.7
Northumberland	13.8	24.9
Fife/Central	13.5	21.2
Yorkshire	12.9	22.8
Lancashire	12.7	22.2
Strathkelvin	11.9	20.7
North Derbyshire	11.4	19.7
Nottinghamshire	11.0	18.7
Lothian	11.0	16.8
South Staffordshire	9.6	16.0
North Warwickshire	9.5	14.4
North Staffordshire	9.5	17.3
Kent	9.3	16.2
North Wales	8.6	20.2
South Derbyshire/North West Leicestershire	6.9	13.3
All coalfields	**12.4**	**22.5**
GB	**10.6**	**14.9**

Sources: NOMIS, Census of Population, authors' estimates

Our estimates of unemployment diverge so significantly from the government's figures essentially because the two sets of figures measure different things. Registered unemployment is, as we explained, the number claiming unemployment-related benefits. The claimant count includes some people who are not actively seeking work (for example, because they are waiting to start a new job), but excludes others who are unemployed but ineligible to claim benefits (for example, because their partner's earnings or their savings disqualify them from receipt of means-tested benefits).

The other official source of unemployment statistics is the quarterly Labour Force Survey. This is based on interviews with a large sample of households and uses International Labour Organisation definitions of unemployment. The Labour Force Survey unemployed include those who had

Table 5.12: Alternative Measures of Pit Village Unemployment, April 1991

	Percentage of economically active males aged 16–64	
	Department of Employment registered unemployment	Real unemployment
Ayrshire	20.3	36.1
South Wales	16.7	33.3
Yorkshire	15.1	27.8
Northumberland	15.0	28.1
Durham	14.8	33.9
Fife/Central	13.5	21.8
Lothian	13.1	23.0
North Derbyshire	12.5	23.6
Nottinghamshire	11.9	21.2
South Derbyshire/North West Leicestershire	8.2	15.7
All pit villages	**14.0**	**26.7**
GB	**10.6**	**14.9**

Sources: NOMIS, Census of Population, authors' estimates

actively looked for work in the last four weeks, not all of whom are necessarily claimants. The Survey also regards anyone who has paid work even just for one hour a week as employed rather than unemployed – a more restrictive approach than the claimant count. Unemployment figures from the Labour Force Survey have not been included here for comparative purposes because none are available for small areas. However, during the first half of the 1990s the figures for national unemployment recorded by the claimant count and the Labour Force Survey did not differ significantly, even though the two groups they are counting comprise significantly different people (Department of Employment 1995).

Our measure of 'real unemployment' is quite different. In essence, it counts *those who might reasonably expect to work in a fully employed economy*, whether or not they happen to be active job-seekers or claimants. Many of the men we count as unemployed have probably accepted that, because of the shortage of jobs locally, their remaining years to age 65 will have to be spent on sickness benefits or pension. Those who are ex-miners may have received a lump-sum redundancy payment that combined with social security benefits enables them to enjoy an adequate, though not extravagant, standard of living. These people are not job-seekers in the terms of the Labour Force Survey. Our definition of unemployment also involves specific assumptions, especially regarding the 'sick' and 'retired'. Nevertheless, we regard our figures as a superior measure of unemployment because in areas of chronic job loss the sheer difficulty of finding work encourages many people to give up the struggle. In the UK context there are also powerful interactions between different state benefits, in particular between unemployment-related and sickness-related benefits, that encourage large numbers to drop out of the unemployment claimant count and out of the process of job search. Real unemployment, as defined here, therefore provides a much more reliable guide to the state of coalfield labour markets than the official unemployment statistics. What the estimates of real unemployment do successfully, perhaps, is bridge the gap between the official data and what for some years has been the first-hand experience of unemployment by people living in the coalfields.

Conclusions

The introduction to this chapter speculated whether the failure of local unemployment to rise in response to the massive loss of jobs in the coal industry reflects successful labour market adjustment, or whether much of the resulting unemployment has simply disappeared from view. The labour market accounts succeed in showing how a severe loss of jobs in an area can co-exist with no rise in recorded local unemployment. The accounts provide some evidence of a revival in the coalfields, in the growth of jobs in other sectors of the local economy, which between 1981 and 1991 offset about one in four of the jobs lost from the coal industry itself. The labour market accounts also show that a reduction in labour supply, through net out-migration, is one of the key factors that has held down unemployment.

However, the principal answer must be that unemployment has failed to rise because so much of it has become hidden. Among men of working age in the coalfields there are now substantially more who are 'economically inactive' than there are actually registered as unemployed. Not all these inactive people are hidden unemployed, of course. However, the rise in inactivity and its much higher level in the coalfields than in relatively prosperous regions such as the South East of England point to large numbers of unemployed people among their ranks.

The scale of recorded 'permanent sickness' is especially striking. In the coalfields as a whole in 1991, there were four men of working age who were 'permanently sick' for every five that were recorded as unemployed. At one extreme, in the pit villages of South Wales one in six of all men of working age was 'permanently sick'. Such high levels of permanent sickness are simply not plausible as measures of genuine physical incapacity to work. What we are observing is the interaction of a chronic shortage of jobs and the operation of the social security system. For many men living in coalfield areas it is a logical step to transfer from unemployment to sickness benefits. For men over 50 in particular, who face the greatest difficulty in finding work, the attractions are considerable and the opportunities greatest.

The government might of course seek to weed out those who are not genuinely unfit for work, and with the switch to Incapacity Benefit there is evidence that it intends to do so. The government's hope is that by introducing sterner tests of incapacity it will cut the number of claimants and curb expenditure. Whether it will succeed in reducing the number of claimants remains to be seen. However, our analysis suggests that among men the main effect may be to shift people back to unemployment-related benefits. This would lead to some financial saving, given the different level of benefits, but it would also lead to the political embarrassment of higher unemployment figures and would expose more of the true level of joblessness in places such as the coalfields.

Meanwhile, the combination of registered and hidden unemployment in the coalfields is resulting in what can only be described as a 'revolution' in the pattern of male working life. Increasingly the world of work is becoming the privilege of just a narrow age group, from about 25 to 50. Below the age of 25 the dominant experience is of extended years in education, government make-work schemes and unemployment. Above the age of 50, the dominant experience is of life 'on the sick' and often enforced early retirement. There are signs that the same life cycle is becoming established elsewhere in Britain, but in the coalfields the revolution is particularly far advanced. It is certainly a far cry from the coalfields of yesteryear, when the mining industry provided men with a job from the age of 14 to 64. Few in the coalfields would wish to go back to this era, but it is questionable whether the labour market of the 1990s can be regarded as 'progress'.

Acknowledgements

This chapter presents some of the findings of a research project funded by the Economic and Social Research Council (Contract No: 00221198). Material from Crown Copyright records, made available through the Office of Population Censuses and Surveys, the General Registrar Office (Scotland) and the ESRC Data Archive has been used by permission of the Controller of HM Stationery Office. The authors would also like to thank Andrew Glyn, Graham Gudgin, Ross MacKay, Peter Townroe, John Wells and two anonymous referees who provided comments on an earlier draft of this paper, and the University of Manchester Computer Centre for assistance in accessing Census of Population data.

CHAPTER 6

The Unemployed and the Paid Informal Sector in Europe's Cities and Regions

Colin C. Williams and Jan Windebank

Introduction

The aim of this chapter is to evaluate critically the notion that the unemployed in the European Union (EU) disproportionately participate in, and gain from, paid informal work and thus that many of them enhance their standard of living with such illegal earnings.[1] Having gained currency throughout the 1970s and 1980s (Gutmann 1978; Matthews 1983; Rosanvallon 1980), this perception has become particularly popular at present. The current period of high and prolonged levels of unemployment has been accompanied by media campaigns and public outcries about alleged cases of benefit fraud committed by 'welfare spongers' or 'scroungers' (see Cook 1989; Malone 1994; Pahl 1985). Politicians interested in reducing social security expenditure, moreover, have done little to assess the validity of these claims. Instead such suspicions have been frequently exploited to legitimate reductions in welfare provision for the unemployed and to increase expenditure on policing the system (see OECD 1994, p.204). Neither has it been questioned by much of the recent theoretical academic discourse on employment and welfare. Contemporary analyses of the role of paid informal work in capitalism, for example, view such work simply as another form of peripheral employment conducted by the poor, marginalised and unemployed (Portes and Castells 1989; Portes, Castells and Benton 1989; Sassen-Koob 1984, 1989).

---

1. Illegal in that if discovered by government welfare authorities, unemployed workers receiving income from such paid informal work ('moonlighting') would no longer be eligible to receive state-provided social benefits.

A growing number of studies, however, have found that the employed make up a larger proportion of the paid informal labour force than do the unemployed and that the unemployed actually conduct little paid informal work (Barthe 1988; Foudi, Stankiewicz and Vanecloo 1982; Morris 1990; Pahl 1984; Renooy 1990). This tendency is explained in terms of the unemployed's limited access to the goods and resources necessary for undertaking such work; their smaller and more confined social networks which are less likely to yield opportunities to conduct paid informal work; their lack of skills; their fear of being 'shopped' to the authorities; and the fact that a greater proportion live in areas disrupted by economic restructuring and crisis which do not provide either formal or informal job opportunities (Morris 1994; Pahl 1984; Smith 1986). The negative image of the unemployed as 'villains' rather than 'victims' of economic and labour market restructuring has thus been countered by the suggestion that the paid informal sector accentuates, rather than reduces, the social and spatial inequalities produced by the formal labour market.

The problem is that statistical data and empirical case studies can be mustered to support both viewpoints. In order to bring some clarity to this confusion, the next section of this chapter begins by examining the available evidence, namely the numerous one-off studies of paid informal work which have been conducted on individual localities throughout the EU.[2] By revealing that the paid informal activity of the unemployed varies widely between geographical areas, this chapter thus moves beyond the previously over-simplistic universal generalisations about the unemployed's participation in paid informal work. It argues that the nature and extent of the unemployed's participation is the outcome of the way in which a range of economic, institutional, social and environmental conditions variously combine in different localities. To illustrate this, in the third section we focus on a specific locality in order to show that what is important in explaining the nature and extent of paid informal work in an area is not the existence of certain structural factors *per se*, but rather the ways in which these factors combine to produce particular configurations of paid informal work amongst the unemployed. The result is a finer-grained understanding of the determinants which shape the nature and extent of the unemployed's participation in paid informal work in the EU's cities and regions.

Before commencing, however, it is important to clarify what is meant by paid informal work. As discussed elsewhere (Williams and Windebank

---

2. The only other source of information on paid informal work is macroeconomic data. These cannot be used here because they do not explore who does the work, only the total volume of such work which is taking place (see Williams and Windebank 1995).

1993), the term 'paid informal work' refers to those paid activities that are hidden from the state for tax, social security or labour law purposes, but which are legal in all other respects. Thus purely financial fraud as well as criminal activities where the goods and services themselves are illegal are excluded, so that only those activities in which the resulting goods and services are legal but their production and distribution involves some illegality constitute paid informal work. Throughout this chapter, moreover, a distinction is made between 'individual' and 'organised' paid informal work. Individual paid informal work is activity undertaken on a personal and independent basis. It ranges from casual one-off cash-in-hand jobs, such as helping a friend or neighbour repair a washing machine or do some plumbing, to the concealment of a major proportion, if not all, of their earnings by the self-employed. Organised paid informal work, on the other hand, is that work undertaken as an employee either for companies which operate wholly 'underground' or for formal companies which employ some staff on a paid informal basis. Although financial considerations are of course important in deciding to engage in either type of paid informal work, participants often feel greater autonomy, flexibility and control when conducting individual paid informal work, whilst organised paid informal work is frequently perceived as exploitative and undertaken more out of necessity than choice. Organised and individual paid informal work, moreover, overlap in limited ways, especially when sub-contracted self-employed labour is used by companies. They should thus be perceived as polar opposites on a spectrum of types of paid informal work.

To What Extent are the Unemployed Engaged in Paid Informal Work?

It is helpful to examine the locality studies conducted in Northern and Southern EU nations separately, since macroeconomic studies have suggested some significant differences between these two broad regions (Commission of the European Communities 1991; Dallago 1991). Such macroeconomic data, however, are unable to distinguish who is doing this paid informal work (Williams and Windebank 1995). For that, it is necessary to examine the one-off case studies of individual localities.

Northern EU nations

A large number of the studies undertaken in Northern EU nations reveal that the unemployed engage in little paid informal work, that they are less likely to undertake paid informal work than the employed, and that areas with higher levels of unemployment are characterised by less paid informal work than those with lower unemployment rates. In the Netherlands, Van Geuns, Mevissen and Renooy (1987) studied six contrasting localities and found that the higher the level of unemployment in an area, the less paid informal work takes place. In all six localities, moreover, the unemployed were generally found not to be participating in such work. This same result is found for the Netherlands by van Eck and Kazemier (1985). It is also echoed in studies carried out in France (Barthe 1988; Cornuel and Duriez 1985; Foudi *et al.* 1982; Tievant 1982), Germany (Glatzer and Berger 1988; Hellberger and Schwarze 1987) and in Britain (Economist Intelligence Unit 1982; Morris 1994; Pahl 1984; Warde 1990).

However, the evidence is not unequivocal. Other studies suggest that similar levels of paid informal work are to be found amongst the employed and unemployed. For example, Mogensen (1985) shows that, in Denmark, the frequency of positive responses concerning whether people engage in paid informal work is identical for employed and unemployed persons. Wenig (1990) arrives at the same conclusion for Germany, where the proportions of the employed and unemployed undertaking such work were identical (9.3 per cent). Yet other locality studies, in contrast, reveal that the unemployed engage in more paid informal work than the employed. For example, Leonard (1994) and Howe (1988) discover this to be the case in Belfast, whilst Pestieau (1984) and, more recently, Kesteloot and Meert (1994) identify similar tendencies in Belgium.

The conclusion to be drawn from this contradictory evidence in Northern EU nations is that the unemployed should not be treated as a homogeneous whole as regards paid informal work. There is a need to distinguish between not only the unemployed's experience in different localities but also between the unemployed within any locality. Thus there appears to be significant differences between the experiences of the long- and short-term unemployed. In Germany, for example, Wenig (1990) finds that whilst 16.7 per cent of the temporarily unemployed engage in paid informal work, only 5.8 per cent of the permanently unemployed conduct such work. Morris (1990) comes to a similar conclusion in Britain, as do Engberson *et al.* (1993) in the Netherlands. For cities and regions of Northern EU nations, therefore, we cannot make generalisations about the extent to which the unemployed as a group participate in paid informal work. Instead their participation appears to differ between the long- and short-term unemployed in all localities where this variable has been studied, and apparently between differing regions and localities. Findings also suggest that some populations of the unemployed appear to undertake mostly individual paid informal work whilst others engage more in organised paid informal work which is exploitative in character (Barthelemy 1990; Leonard 1994).

Southern EU nations

Locality studies in Southern EU nations reveal similar apparently contradictory findings. On the one hand, some show that the unemployed are less likely to engage in paid informal work than the employed. In Spain, the Ministry of the Economy estimates that 29 per cent of those in employment also have a paid informal job (in Hadjimichalis and Vaiou 1989), whilst Lobo (1990) finds that just 12 per cent of those claiming unemployment benefit perform such work. Benton's (1990) study of the Spanish labour market also reveals that 65.7 per cent of all paid informal workers have a formal job, whilst just 5.2 per cent are 'doing the double', that is, working in the paid informal sector whilst receiving social security. The remaining 30 per cent of paid informal workers, we must assume, are those not entitled to benefit who engage in paid informal work as a means of survival. In Italy, similarly, the majority of studies conclude that it is the employed rather than the unemployed who constitute the vast bulk of the paid informal labour force (Mingione 1991; Mingione and Morlicchio 1993).

Other studies, however, assert that the unemployed undertake more paid informal work than the employed, or at least that this is the case so far as organised paid informal work is concerned (Lobo 1990; Miguelez and Recio 1986). In Greece, for example, Hadjimichalis and Vaiou (1989) and Leontidou (1993) identify the proliferation of paid informal work, especially in its organised form, in the tourist and coastal areas, and argue that it is often the unemployed who undertake such work, particularly in the summer period.

Studies in Southern EU nations, moreover, distinguish between the unemployed who are claiming benefits and those who are not when discussing participation in paid informal work, in contrast to Northern EU studies which differentiate between the long- and short-term unemployed. The reason for this difference, as Reissert (1994) reveals, is that a much lower percentage of the total unemployed in Southern EU states receive unemployment compensation benefits compared with Northern EU nations, due to the unavailability of permanent social benefits. The outcome is a major qualitative difference in the experience of unemployment for those receiving benefit and those socially excluded from such assistance. Meanwhile, the social divisions of unemployment in those Northern EU nations with universal social benefits are more between those who consider themselves between jobs and those viewing themselves, and being perceived by others, as more permanently excluded from employment.

In sum, these locality studies in Northern and Southern EU nations reveal that the unemployed appear to engage in paid informal work more than the employed in some localities but not in others. Equally, in some localities, certain populations of the unemployed make more use of the informal sector than others. Moreover, the type of work which they undertake seems to differ across localities. In some areas, they are more likely to engage in organised paid informal work, whilst in others they are more likely to participate in individual paid informal work. The next section attempts to explain such spatial variations.

Explaining Spatial Variations in the Unemployed's Participation in Paid Informal Work

From a review of these one-off locality studies, it is clear that explanations for the nature and extent of the unemployed's participation in paid informal work have to be sought through an analysis of the ways in which a range of economic, social, institutional and environmental conditions combine in a locality to produce a particular configuration of paid informal work so far as the unemployed are concerned (see Table 6.1). However, it is not the existence of a specific condition on its own which causes a particular configuration of paid informal work amongst the unemployed in a locality, but rather it is the way in which various conditions combine to determine whether an area is conducive or not to the unemployed's participation in paid informal work. To illustrate this, we consider the example of a working-class housing estate in Catholic West Belfast studied by Leonard (1994).

Table 6.1: Regulators of the Unemployed's Participation in Paid Informal Work

Economic regulators
- Level of unemployment
- Duration of unemployment
- Structural economic conditions

Social regulators
- Socio-economic mix of area
- Social cohesiveness of population
- Existence of shared 'political' values
- Local cultural traditions, social mores and moralities

Institutional regulators
- Availability of welfare benefits
- Taxation levels
- Labour law
- Effectiveness of enforcement of rules and taxation regulations

Environmental regulators
- Social isolation of area
- Access to formal goods and services

Explaining the configuration of paid informal work: a case study of West Belfast

In the area of West Belfast, characterised by widespread long-term unemployment, Leonard (1994) found that paid informal work was rife and that much of it was undertaken by the unemployed (see Table 6.2). Of the 93 married couples questioned, none of the dual earner couples engaged in paid informal work, but of the couples in which both were unemployed, 49 per cent participated in 'organised' and 58 per cent in 'individual' paid informal work (Leonard 1994, p.195). Amongst the 57 single, divorced and widowed respondents, similarly, none of the employed but 15 per cent of the unemployed engaged in organised paid informal work, whilst 33 per cent of the employed compared with 8 per cent of the unemployed engaged in individual paid informal work (Leonard 1994, p.196). On the whole, therefore, the unemployed participated in paid informal work on this estate more than the employed, and the work which they undertook was of both the individual and organised kind. Couples in which both were unemployed undertook slightly more individual than organised paid informal work, but single, divorced and widowed respondents who were unemployed were slightly more likely to conduct organised than individual paid informal work.

Table 6.2: Social Distribution of Paid Informal Work in Belfast

Household composition	% Engaging in paid informal work
Married couples (N=93)	
Husband and wife formally employed (N=10)	0
Husband or wife formally employed	0
Husband unemployed and wife housewife (n=12)	49
Husband and wife retired (n=12)	8
Single, divorced and widowed respondents (N=57)	
Formally employed (N=6)	0
Housewife (N=22)	4
Unemployed (N=13)	15
Retired (N=16)	0

Source: Derived from Leonard 1994, Table 9.1

What are the conditions, therefore, that have caused such a configuration? On the economic side, the high level and long duration of unemployment has been an important factor on this West Belfast estate. This is because unemployment here is a product of endemic economic crisis, rather than merely the temporary result of cyclical downturns. This is not only due to global economic restructuring, but also to what have been seen until recently as the seemingly intractable political problems which beset Northern Ireland.

With little likelihood of finding employment in the near future or beyond, the unemployed have thus sought paid informal work, reinforcing Gallie's (1985, p.522) assertion that, 'the most probable location of the growth of widespread informal work will be in areas of catastrophic economic collapse where the possibility of re-insertion into normal economic activity appears particularly remote'. However, this condition, although necessary, is not sufficient in itself to bring about the unemployed's participation in paid informal work in an area. Indeed in many areas which suffer from high levels of very long-term unemployment, for example Hartlepool (Morris 1994), the unemployed tend not to engage in paid informal work. Moreover, in some areas with lower unemployment levels and less long-term unemployment, such as Amsterdam (Renooy 1990), the unemployed's participation in paid informal work appears to be as, or indeed more, extensive as that in more deprived areas. So the level and duration of unemployment have different impacts in different areas due to the host of additional social, environmental and institutional characteristics which prevail in these contrasting locations.

Indeed the social conditions which prevail on the West Belfast estate are an important determinant of the unemployed's participation in such work. First, there is the nature of local social networks. In areas where social networks are created mainly through the work-place, unemployment causes a contraction of social contacts and thus of opportunities for hearing about paid informal possibilities (Barthe 1988; Foudi *et al.* 1982; Morris 1990). In West Belfast, however, there are strong alternative social networks, not based upon the work-place, in the form of extensive kinship and friendship networks. These are products of the social and spatial isolation of the estate, the lack of in- and out-migration and the social homogeneity of the local population. The result is that the population is not dependent upon the work-place for hearing about opportunities for paid informal work. Hence the deprivation and high unemployment which would otherwise reduce opportunities for paid informal work are mitigated by dense social networks. Social networks, however, are only communications channels which can put the unemployed in touch with work opportunities. If no such opportunities exist, then obviously dense social networks are of no value: they have nothing to communicate.

A second social condition influencing the unemployed's participation is the socio-economic mix of the area. Most studies reveal that it is when an area unites people with high incomes but little free time with others who have low incomes but much free time, that the unemployed engage in greater amounts of paid informal work (Barthelemy 1990; De Klerk and Vijgen 1985; Pestieau 1984; Renooy 1990; Sassen 1991; Terhorst and Van de Ven

1985). The West Belfast estate, however, is a socially homogeneous area which, in this instance, aids and abets paid informal work because the common deprivation shared by most residents makes the undertaking of such work as a means of survival an acceptable activity, as do the 'political' values shared by the population of the estate, discussed further below. Due to the widespread deprivation of the locality, however, prices of, and incomes from, paid informal work are fixed at a level somewhat lower than the formal sector so as to allow exchange to take place. Although the income from paid informal work may not allow many purchases to be made outside this economy, it does provide the means to 'buy back' in a reciprocal manner other paid informal goods and services. In other deprived, socially homogeneous localities, however, the unemployed undertake little paid informal work since there are few opportunities to undertake such employment (Coffield, Borrill and Marshall 1983; Morris 1993). Hence socio-economic mix is an important determinant of whether the unemployed in a locality conduct paid informal work, but the nature of its influence is a product of the way in which it interacts with other factors in the area.

A third social characteristic which is of major importance in shaping the extent of paid informal work on this estate relates to local cultural traditions and the consequent social norms and moralities. The unemployed in this locality demonstrate little fear about being caught 'doing the double'. This is not the case elsewhere in the Northern EU nations (see, for example, Wenig 1990). On the West Belfast estate, however, the situation is perhaps different. Here, there is less fear of detection because the local social mores are not conducive to reporting such behaviour. In Catholic West Belfast, as Howe (1988) has highlighted, there is a greater moral acceptance of working whilst claiming benefits than in Protestant East Belfast, in part because the legitimacy of the state is not recognised in the former area. When the state is not even recognised as a valid organ amongst a proportion of the population and a 'shadow' state is in operation, it is little surprise to find people, whether employed or not, engaging in paid informal work.

It is not only the 'republican issue', however, which makes the unemployed's participation in paid informal work socially acceptable. Other studies show that such conducive social mores can also result from the widespread deprivation, social isolation and/or the social cohesiveness of the population (Barthelemy 1991; Legrain 1982; Weber 1989). In such areas, paid informal work is perceived as an acceptable part of community life rather than as tax or social security fraud, and is undertaken as much for social as for economic reasons. The monetary aspect of the activity is suppressed in the minds of those engaged in it, and thus so is its illegality. As such, it can be seen as a last bastion of civil society. Noble and Turner

(1985, p.4) discovered a similar situation in a small Scottish lowlands town where many frequently justified their paid informal work, which they recognised as wrong, in terms of the injustices perpetrated on them. The establishment of the welfare state, for instance, meant a move away from self-provisioning of health care and other welfare services, with money from rates, taxes and national insurance being passed, along with responsibility, to government agencies. This facilitated the view that it is the duty of the state, or indeed society as a whole, to provide people with what they need (and desire). For some, this encourages the belief that if society fails to fulfil its side of the bargain or discriminates against certain groups who feel hard done-by, which is blatantly the case for the population of this Belfast estate, then they are justified in contravening their part of the agreement. Pressures of a materialist culture are an added spur to such activity. The unemployed on the West Belfast estate, therefore, lack the fear of losing their benefits and thus have a similar attitude towards paid informal work as the unemployed in countries with little or no access to permanent state benefits, who are less reserved about engaging in paid informal work as a survival strategy (Del Boca and Forte 1982) because they have little or nothing to lose if caught, unlike those eligible to claim more generous benefits in some Northern EU nations. The unemployed also have the social networks and the social cohesiveness in their population to facilitate their participation in paid informal work.

Besides the social characteristics of this Belfast estate influencing the unemployed's paid informal work, there are also institutional factors. That is, it is not only the way in which rules and regulations are interpreted and enforced by the population itself, but also by the state, which sways the extent of paid informal work. In some areas of Southern EU nations, for example in Italy, lax enforcement of state rules and regulations is often deliberately promoted to help the unemployed engage in paid informal work (Portes and Castells 1989; Sassen-Koob 1989; Warren 1994). In Northern EU nations, however, measures to catch any unemployed engaging in paid informal work are strictly enforced (Pahl 1990; Wenig 1990).[3] The problem is that there are particular difficulties in detecting and monitoring benefit fraud on this estate and more subtle forms of investigation have had to be

3. There has been a widespread trend in Europe in recent years towards matching administrative records such as social security, and tax and work contract files with unemployment benefit data, in order to detect 'concealed' work by beneficiaries more reliably (see OECD 1994, pp.201–12). In the UK, the government has even resorted to a public advertisement campaign to encourage people to inform the social security service of suspected benefit fraudsters, especially those who may be 'moonlighting' (that is, undertaking casual and informal paid work whilst claiming unemployment compensation).

introduced (Leonard 1994, p.194). The social cohesion of the estate, nevertheless, allows the usual institutional constraints which prevent the unemployed from engaging in paid informal work to be negated.

Finally, the nature of the physical environment can influence the unemployed's participation in paid informal work. It is the relative isolation of the West Belfast estate and the poor access to formal services which have led to many forms of paid informal work developing, such as 'house shops' and 'community bakers'. Such work provides access to goods and services which would not otherwise be available, therefore ameliorating deprivation, even if not providing a complete survival strategy for the unemployed. Legrain (1982) finds the same in France, as does Renooy (1990) amongst the coalfield communities in the Netherlands.

It is not only the extent of the unemployed's participation in paid informal work which is influenced by economic, social, institutional and environmental factors, but also the degree to which it is individual or organised in character. On the West Belfast estate, the unemployed are as likely to engage in organised as individual paid informal work, thus appearing to have equal opportunities for both categories of employment. The inhabitants of this estate use their dense kinship and friendship networks to hear about opportunities for organised informal work and to exchange individual paid informal services. This contrasts with other areas where recruitment for organised paid informal work takes place through an employment-based social network system, thereby excluding the unemployed (Pahl 1984). In the more isolated and socially cohesive areas of Belfast, friends, neighbours and relatives already in employment or paid informal work recruit the unemployed to join them. These individuals act as intermediaries between formal and informal employers and recruits. However, Leonard's (1994) study reveals that such recruitment strategies lead to a polarisation between those households which can gain access to this organised paid informal work, and, indeed, individual work, and those which cannot.

It is important, moreover, that the unemployed in West Belfast are not treated as homogeneous when examining their participation in paid informal work. Leonard's study reveals that, similarly to the formal labour market, some households have access to work on the paid informal labour market whilst others are excluded even from this form of work. Of the 45 married couples where both were unemployed, Leonard (1994, p.196) highlights how neither partner engaged in paid informal work in 51 per cent of the couples, one partner in 31 per cent and both partners in 18 per cent. Those couples in which both conducted paid informal work, moreover, tended to undertake the better paid work in this sphere, such as running the 'house shops', rather than poorer paid activities such as 'scavenging' for empty cans for sale as scrap metal. Even in the realm of informal work, then, there appears to be 'work-rich' and 'work-poor' households.

Conclusions

Examining the evidence from the one-off studies of paid informal work in particular localities, which is the only evidence available, this chapter has argued that whether or not the unemployed engage in paid informal work, and whether their participation is likely to be of the individual or organised kind, varies across localities and regions. To explain these spatial variations, we have not listed a range of factors which automatically lead to greater amounts of paid informal work by either the unemployed or employed in individual or organised paid informal work. Rather, as the case study of a West Belfast estate highlights, it is the way in which a variety of economic, social, institutional and environmental conditions *combine* in a locality which produces a particular configuration of paid informal work in that area. However, the intention here is not to counter the previously universal conceptions about the participation of the unemployed in paid informal work with the idiographic conclusion that economic, social, institutional and environmental factors combine in particular ways in particular localities to produce unique local configurations. Instead it is to argue that a finer-grained understanding of the spatial variations in the unemployed's participation in paid informal work is necessary. Examining the findings of both the study of West Belfast and the other locality studies undertaken throughout the EU, it can be tentatively asserted that whether or not the unemployed are using the paid informal sector to 'get by' economically in particular cities and regions is dependent upon the supply of informal labour, the demand for informal goods and services and the 'institutional' structure of the locality, in terms of both the structure of networks which can organise informal work and the extent of sanctions against informal work. It is the variation in these factors and how they interact with each other which reduce or increase the likelihood of the unemployed's participation in paid informal work. In West Belfast, for instance, under 'institutional' conditions of dense social networks, low sanctions and extreme isolation, the more conventional relationship between demand and supply (that is, that greater social mix is required for the participation of the unemployed) does not hold.

The challenge for those attempting to understand geographical variations in the unemployed's participation in paid informal work is to begin to develop a typology of the unemployed's role in paid informal work under different local 'regimes' in which the demand and supply of paid informal labour are variously mediated by local 'institutional' structures. What is certain, however, is that the previously over-simplistic and generalised statements about the participation of the unemployed in paid informal work will no longer suffice, and neither will the over-simplistic political solutions and reactions which are derived from such generalisations. Much more careful and considered analysis is required about the unemployed's participation in paid informal work than has so far been the case.

Acknowledgements

Earlier versions of this paper were presented to the 1995 Regional Studies Association European Conference in Gothenburg and the 1994 ESRC Urban and Regional Economics Seminar Group meeting in Leeds. The authors would like to thank the participants for their useful feedback and comments.

CHAPTER 7

Gender as a Form of Social Exclusion
Gender Inequality in the Regions of Europe
Diane Perrons

Introduction

The term 'social exclusion' is often used to refer to the unemployed, single parents and those in intense poverty (see Green 1995). This chapter focuses on gender as a form of social exclusion and specifically on gender inequality in employment in the regions of the European Union. Women workers experience social exclusion in a broad sense because they are disproportionately confined to the lower levels of paid employment, to insecure jobs and those with little opportunity for advancement (Neathey and Hurstfield 1995; Rodgers and Rodgers 1989). During the 1980s and 1990s there have been a number of important changes in the system of economic and social regulation within which regional economies develop. Explanations for this vary. References are made to the changing regime of accumulation: from Fordism to post-Fordism, to processes of globalisation or to the effects of austerity policies implemented to meet the convergence criteria for economic integration, or, indeed, to various different combinations and interrelationships between these developments. Whatever the explanation, the main underlying characteristic has been slower overall economic growth, at least in comparison with the boom years of the 1950s and 1960s (Dunford and Perrons 1994), and this slower growth has been associated with increasing inequality at a variety of levels, especially in the UK (Glyn and Miliband 1994; Rowntree Foundation 1995). In relation to the European regions, although some areas have prospered, development has been uneven. Moreover, the experience of the relatively prosperous regions has differed according to whether they are part of a growing or declining economy overall (Benko and Lipietz, cited by Dunford and Fielding 1994). Even in the more prosperous regions, forms of social polarisation and exclusion are found, and these have also been shown to have a gendered dimension (Perrons 1995b; McDowell and Court 1994; Sassen 1991).

Within this more general recessionary climate, one common feature has been the increase in female labour force participation, which has reduced social exclusion in the sense that more women are participating in the employment sphere (Rubery and Fagan 1993). However, although some women are visibly present in the upper echelons of employment, in general women are employed in subordinate roles. This second form of exclusion, although disproportionately experienced by women, will not be entirely gender-specific in the less developed regions, because of the more limited range of job opportunities found there. The different degrees of participation in paid work and the associated levels of remuneration have implications for women's traditional social role. But if ideas about this role or its objective nature change as a consequence of shifts in the form and content of domestic work, then both the possibilities for, and effects of, women's paid employment on gender roles will also vary. For example, there have been significant changes in family size and structure, in ideas about raising children and in the technology of domestic labour, although there has been little change in the domestic division of labour. There are also variations in the extent of publicly provided care and in the provision of 'marketised' domestic services. Thus economic change, the evolving forms and degrees of involvement in paid work, and changes in patterns and processes of social reproduction, all contribute to explaining regionally differentiated gender roles.

In this chapter, however, emphasis is placed on identifying the comparative patterns of gender inequality in employment and a further objective is to explore the usefulness of official statistics on these inequalities at the regional level in Europe. Exclusion from official statistics is itself another form of social exclusion. Until statistics with a gender dimension are more widely collected and collated, then it will be difficult to measure the precise extent of women's exclusion within the labour market. In this respect the European REGIO database provides only limited detail on the gender division of labour and the gender structure of unemployment. Many writers have methodological reservations about what can be deduced from quantitative analyses based on official statistics, even if they were more suited to the issues and priorities of research on women. Indeed the paucity of statistics by gender has contributed to the rise of 'feminist methodologies' based on qualitative and ethnographic research (MacDonald 1995). However, qualitative and quantitative research methods are complementary rather than substitutes (Glucksmann 1994). Just as there are problems with quantitative research, case studies based on in-depth interviews are problematical. While qualitative studies provide interesting insights into the experiences of particular people and may contribute to identifying mechanisms and processes of change where more quantitative-based research may only provide general associations, such methods are similarly not free from questions about their epistemological status (Maynard 1994). In particular, there are problems of interpretation,[1] of how to resolve conflicting accounts and of deciding how representative the different cases are. Comparative qualitative work poses even more problems (Ungerson 1996). Moreover, it would be difficult to produce an overview of gender inequality in employment in Europe from a series of case studies of individuals, and yet such an overview, however imperfect, is nevertheless likely to be a necessary prerequisite for the development of progressive policies for women.

I begin by briefly summarising explanations of national differences in gender inequality in employment in Europe. My main objective, however, is to explore regional variations and to consider whether women are excluded by the nature of local economic opportunities available or by the prevailing customs and expectations of women's role in society, and further to consider the interrelation between these economic and social factors.

National Variations in Gender Inequality in Employment in Europe

Gender inequality in employment is a universal phenomenon and yet there are significant national and regional variations. Many explanations have been developed to explain national differences. Some focus on general employment regulations and how these indirectly produce different degrees of gender inequality. Others introduce a feminist perspective into the welfare regimes approach of Gosta Esping-Andersen, emphasising the importance of different gender roles between countries (Esping-Andersen 1990; Lane 1993; Leibfried and Ostner 1991; Lewis 1992; for a review of some of these approaches, see Duncan 1996 and Sainsbury 1994). However, other researchers have become rather disenchanted with the way in which these perspectives have led to repeated and different categorisations of countries and have either tried to integrate welfare regimes with regulatory frameworks

---

1. Within postmodern discourse, where some of the critiques of quantitative research derive, all reporting of experience is considered to be 'culturally and discursively constituted'. In other words, peoples' lives are 'culturally embedded' so that their descriptions of them are both a construction of the events that have taken place together with an interpretation of them (Maynard 1994). A second problem derives from the reflexivity between the researcher and the researched – the impact of answering or being heard may reconstitute the experience being recounted, and furthermore the interpretation made by the interviewer will similarly be shaped by their own biography. Both need to be considered. As Mary Maynard (1994, p.23) points out, it is simply not possible to record women 'speaking for themselves'.

or returned to linking gender issues more generally with largely economic variables such as globalisation, marketisation and European integration (Gonas 1995). Nevertheless, there seems to be some consensus that women experience greater equality in societies with more regulated employment structures and more advanced welfare systems than they do in liberal market regimes (Perrons 1995a; Rubery 1992b; Whitehouse 1992). However, even in the more progressive social-democratic societies, gender segregation in employment remains at a high level (Meulders, Plasman and Vander Stricht 1993) and in discussions of the comparative performances of different countries, or, indeed, regions, it is important not to lose sight of the fact that gender inequality remains widespread (Rubery 1996).[2]

Some of the approaches above can be applied to the sub-national, regional level. Social welfare policies such as maternity leave and parental leave tend to be similar across regions within nation states, although there are instances when the policies are the same in principle but the practice across regions differs. For example, the actual level of child care provision may vary significantly across regions within a given territory, even though in principle the state supports such provision (Duncan 1991). However, other processes such as globalisation and economic integration will have differential effects between regions, as will macroeconomic policies introduced in response to these supra-national processes. Some regional economies will expand as a consequence of their position and status within the global economy, while others will contract as their industries are eliminated by more competitive firms in the more advanced regions. Regional restructuring in response to these developments will affect the kinds of jobs available to women and men (Lindley 1992).

Thus if the objective is to explain regional – that is, sub-national variations in gender inequality, then any approach based solely on welfare regimes and regulatory frameworks will require some modification (Peck 1994). Some perspectives which make explicit reference to the role of gender relations are reviewed below.

---

2.   The diversity, or, indeed, polarisation, between women should also not be overlooked. There is evidence for both the polarisation between women's incomes in the UK (Bruegel and Perrons 1996) and for a convergence between more highly educated women across Europe, while major differences remain between countries for women with few qualifications (Rubery 1996).

Regional Variations in Gender Inequality in Employment in Europe: Some Theoretical Issues

Historical approaches

Regionally and locally differentiated employment patterns and gender roles have been attributed to the continuation and accumulation of patterns from the past and are linked either to regional industrial structures (McDowell and Massey 1984; Walby 1984) or to regional social cultures (Sackmann and Haüssermann 1994). In both cases in areas where women have had a history of paid employment they continue to experience high levels of female labour force participation even though the original activities have long since declined.[3] For example, in their study of regional differences in Italy, Cortesi and Marengo (1992) emphasise the role of cultural factors in accounting for the higher female activity and employment rate which characterises the north of the country. Family values emphasising the role of wife and mother are stronger in the south, and attitudes of female subservience prevail there. These beliefs tend to, 'hold back, and sometimes imprison women within the four walls of the home'. Nevertheless, 'in areas where a manufacturing industry develops which favours female labour – as for instance, the tobacco industry in the Salentine peninsular – women are able to overcome social constraints and actively move into employment' (Cortesi and Marengo 1992, p.10).[4] However, in these accounts of regionally differentiated gender relations, even though reference is made to the intersection of family and economic relationships and of patriarchy and capitalism, the initiator of change seems to arise from changes in the local, national or global economy, not from gender. What is less clear, however, is whether involvement in paid work fundamentally changes gender relations. Indeed in the Italian case it is argued that women are emancipated *from* the home but not *within* the home (Bettio and Villa 1996).

---

3. Elsewhere, however, the lack of industrial tradition among female workers has been attractive to inward investment. In these areas the ensuing combination of reduced employment for men and increased employment for women has challenged the prevailing gender order (McDowell and Massey 1984). However, the extent of the change may be debatable. Given the relatively low pay offered in the new 'female jobs' it could be argued that although the form of patriarchy has changed, patriarchal structures remain in place.

4. Other writers have linked this domestic division of labour to a more extended social division of labour in which women's role in the domestic sphere underpins both the division of labour between market work and work on family farms and also sustains social reproduction in societies where welfare services are underdeveloped (Vinay 1985). It is thus not a purely cultural phenomenon but a means of adaptation to a particular pattern of regional development.

Gender contracts

A similar point could be made about the gender contract approach (Pfau-Effinger 1994). Gender contracts refer to the socio-cultural consensus which develops about the respective roles of women and men (see Duncan 1996). Having come into existence, gender contracts are slow to change. However, it is less clear how particular gender contracts come into being or how they change, except by reference to specific histories in which processes of economic change seem to play a major role. So again, the dynamic behind gender inequality remains elusive (Perrons 1995b). To provide an explanation, mechanisms of change need to be identified. Reference to the interplay between gender relations and economic structures and specific histories is not sufficient in this respect.

Forms and degrees of patriarchy

A further perspective, using the concept of patriarchy, has been developed by Sylvia Walby (1994).[5] Allowing both the form and degree of the different elements of patriarchy to vary allows for both diversity and change within and between regions; that is, it allows for the structuring of past events without a prescription for the future, although the mechanisms of change still need to be identified in order to provide a satisfactory account.

While explanations need to be rooted in particular social, economic and political settings in order to avoid overly abstract theorisation, histories themselves are not explanations. As a consequence, explanations which seek to highlight the significance of gender relations need to derive theoretical concepts which can be used to explore the mechanisms of change within particular settings, analogous to the various concepts that have been used to analyse capitalist economies. Otherwise it is hard to avoid a fairly materialist conclusion, namely that the economic structure is paramount and gender regimes develop in a supportive way. In a sense this may require the reopening of the debate between the single system and dual systems in the feminist literature of the early 1980s (see Cockburn 1991). However, the 'gender order' model developed below provides some means of establishing a framework within which the cumulative relations between gender roles, sex stereotyping and economic change can be considered.

---

5. Patriarchy refers to, 'a system of social structures and practices in which men dominate, oppress and exploit women' (Walby 1990, p.20).

The 'gender order' of employment

This model was developed originally to identify the costs to both the economy and women of unequal employment opportunities in the UK (Bruegel and Perrons 1995). It specifies how cumulative interactions between labour market processes, household decisions and state policies lock the UK into a particular gender order which is beneficial neither to women nor the economy nor even to some men in the long term (see also McDowell 1991). This model can also be applied to account for the apparent stability of regional patterns of gender inequality in employment and for the fact that involvement in paid work may have a limited impact on gender roles.

As with any model of cumulative and circular causation, the analysis can be entered at any point (see Figure 7.1). Starting from the household division of labour, competitive market processes exacerbate inequality between women and men in the labour market through both different training levels and different reward structures which then feed back to rationalise and reinforce the initial household division of labour. In the case of the UK, because men are assumed to be breadwinners, partial wages are considered to be sufficient for women.[6] Given the prevailing social security system, women's low pay reinforces the dual earner/no earner division between households which is in fact a further important form of social exclusion, as it is usually economically irrational for low paid female partners of unemployed men to remain in employment (Morris 1990). However, given the increasingly deregularised employment structure, the poor conditions of female work are now spreading to areas traditionally occupied by men (Gregg and Wadsworth 1994), although the continuing gender wage gap suggests that this is not taking place as rapidly as would be expected in a perfect labour market and that even in impoverished working conditions men still seem to colonise the better niches.[7] This model of gender relations is then linked to the similarly self-reinforcing patterns of under-investment and under-skilling of labour which have characterised the UK economy either because low wages inhibit investment or because low skills have made such investment problematical. Together, then, the gender order and the under-

---

6. This assumption still seems to hold despite the actual decline of the 'traditional household'. The gender wage gap seems to be remarkably resilient to rising male unemployment and male inactivity (Bruegel and Perrons 1995).

7. Linda McDowell argues that increasing numbers of men, 'are employed in the peripheral labour market too, on terms and conditions that were traditionally regarded as female' (McDowell 1991, p.408). However, even when a sector is characterised by low pay and insecure conditions, such as contract cleaning, male workers, often with the tacit support of managers, appropriate the better conditions (Allen and Henry 1995). So although challenged by new forms of work, some kind of patriarchal power remains.

skilling/under-investment cycles reinforce the development of a low wage, low skilled, low investment economy which offers few prospects for the majority of workers, either men or women (Bruegel and Perrons 1995).

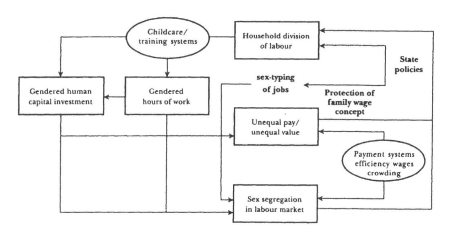

Figure 7.1. The Gender Order Model

Source: Bruegel and Perrons 1995

To unlock the 'gender order', some external intervention such as training or public provision of care, or a radical re-evaluation of social skills is required which could then initiate a more progressive series of events that would increase women's participation and pay. This in turn would enable society to move away from the low wage equilibrium which the existing 'gender order' supports. At the regional level this may arise from the location of some new economic activity, as, for example, in the Italian case referred to above. However, it is questionable whether participation alone would be sufficient to produce change. The quality, pay and social and spatial organisation of the employment are also important (McDowell and Massey 1984).[8] The

---

8. In the domestic sphere, full-time workers do only half the number of hours as part-time workers and yet neither capitalism nor men seem to be harmed as a consequence (McDowell 1991). However, caring responsibilities for children and the elderly remain firmly in women's hands and even relatively short withdrawals from the labour market can have long-term effects on women's lifetime earnings (Joshi and Davies 1993). Perhaps what has happened has been some substitution of domestic work by paid work which has been eased in some cases by forms of state provision, by marketised services made possible by low female wages (Gregson and Lowe 1994) and, in some cases, by changes in domestic technology and super-Fordist modes of consumption provision – not the shopping mall of the post-modernists, but the superstores which are responsible for an increasing proportion of consumer expenditure.

model suggests, therefore, that the prevailing gender order is not immutable, but that the scale of the policies would have to be profound in order to transform household decision-making and gender roles. This approach does not overlook the fact that some women have moved into higher level and higher paid managerial and professional jobs, and as a consequence women's earnings have increased in recent years (Humphries and Rubery 1992; Perrons 1995b). But more detailed analysis suggests that these women are more likely to be without children and in the professions rather than management where the male model of working continues!9•,andthussuch moves may be partial solutions for individual women rather than a means of unlocking the gender order for society as a whole. I now examine regional variations in the patterns of participation in employment more explicitly.

Regional Variations in Gender Inequality in Employment in Europe: Some Empirical Measures

Employment data by gender at the regional level in Europe are limited. There are few data on segregation and none on earnings, so it is difficult to compare employment quality. Using different measures of participation extracted or calculated from the REGIO database, some idea can nevertheless be obtained about the universality, diversity and changes in gender inequality across the regions of Europe and some tentative conclusions can be drawn about the conceptualisation of changing gender roles.

Activity rates

Activity rates measure the percentage of the population of working age which is economically active, that is, employed and unemployed (and seeking work). Female activity rates are generally higher in more developed regions. Regions with female activity rates of less than 33 per cent are almost exclusively in the southern periphery of the EU. Female activity rates may be low because of low labour demand, longer periods of education or early retirement, that is, not specifically because of gender issues. To identify gender differences, the female:male activity rate ratio (fa/ma) is mapped in Figure 7.2. This map shows the universality of gender inequality, but also that significant regional

---

9. Women's representation in management is nowhere near as significant as in professional jobs, where work is much more focused on clients and based on women's individual professional expertise. As a consequence, the work is both adaptable to flexible hours and part-time work and does not require women to be part of any organisational structure with power or control over others (Crompton 1994). The processes of male power within the organisation therefore remain unchallenged.

variations exist. Regions with low female activity rates also tend to have low *fa/ma* rates.[10] In many of the poorest regions, female activity rates are low in comparison with women elsewhere in the EU and in relation to men in the same region, that is, women seem to be excluded from labour market participation by the lack of economic opportunities and by cultural/patriarchal traditions.[11] The highest levels of gender inequality are found in Voreio Aigaio and Notio Aigaio (Greece), Sicilia, Puglia and Campania (Italy) and Castilla la Mancha (Spain), where female activity rates are less than 45 per cent of the male rate. Denmark,[12] Mecklenburg-Vorpommern, Brandenburg and Magdeburg in the north of the former GDR are in the highest quintile

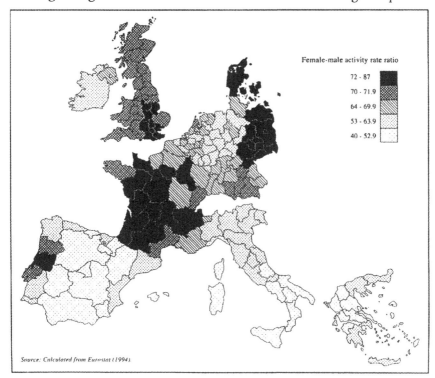

Figure 7.2. Female/Male Activity Ratios, 1994

---

10. Twenty-eight of the 30 regions in the lowest quintile of female activity rates were also present in the lowest quintile of the female: male activity rates, giving a high value on the Spearman's rank correlation coefficient.
11. Official statistics understate female paid work where a large informal sector exists, for example Greece (Stratigaki and Vaiou 1994), but this lack of formal recognition is itself a form of exclusion in addition to the poorer terms and conditions in which informal work is generally carried out.
12. The regions of Denmark have the same values as there is no breakdown by NUTS2.

of female activity rates. So too is Oberfranken in Southern Germany which, together with Niederbayern and Schwaben, is more highly placed than Chemnitz, a region of the former GDR. Other regions with high female activity rates are the Ile de France, South East England, Scotland and the East and West Midlands. However, there are some differences between the regions in the top quintile of female activity rates and the top quintile of the fa/ma ratio. Denmark and former GDR regions are present in both cases; however, many French regions are in the top quintile of fa/ma ratio but not on female activity rates, while for many of the British regions the reverse is the case.

Highly placed French regions vary in character. For example, Limousin, a rural and mountainous area, has the highest fa/ma ratio (80%) in France and ranks tenth in the EU. However, its female activity rate (46%) is fairly low in comparison with other French regions. In this case, although gender inequality exists, women and men both suffer from the limited employment opportunities available in the region.[13] The Ile de France by contrast has the highest female activity rate (54%) in France but a lower gender ratio (77%), indicating that there are more opportunities for everyone but that men are more involved than women. The northern regions of Portugal also have high fa/ma ratios as indeed does Madeira which is by far the highest placed island, reflecting the traditionally high rates of female participation in Portugal, partly deriving from necessity during the colonial wars and also perhaps from the relatively low level of economic well-being which both enforces and facilitates participation in paid work as a consequence of the relatively low cost of paid domestic workers.[14] However, the north–south divide within Portugal on both of these rates probably reflects the different patterns of land ownership, with the 'minifundia' system in the north generating high levels of formal female labour force participation in agriculture, in contrast to the 'latifundia' system in the south where more often only men are formally included in the labour force. Even so, the activity rates in the southern regions of Portugal are significantly higher than those in the rest of the Mediterranean region. However, as the French example demonstrates, the fa/ma ratio can reflect different combinations of female and male activity rates. Some of

---

13. In the case of Limousin both the economic structure based heavily on agriculture and the ageing population structure may be responsible for the relatively low activity rates for both women and men.

14. In the case of Madeira, there is a lace-making industry organised through networks of sub-contractors and the increasing importance of tourism in which females are strongly represented.

the different determinations of gender inequality are examined more fully by differentiating activity rates by age.

Activity rates by age[15]

Regional variations in activity rates by age are much higher for women than men. In general the size of the gender gap increases with age. For the age group 14–24, gender differences for all regions are less varied than differences between men[16] indicating the importance of variations in economic opportunities, different ways of recording people in training and young people without jobs, that is, factors largely unrelated to gender. On average both female and male activity rates have declined slightly since 1983 and the gender gap has also narrowed. Gender inequality is highest in the less developed regions but in many cases these are also the regions where change has been quite rapid. For example, the gender ratio in Basilicata increased from 57 per cent to 75 per cent between 1983 and 1992. In 19 of the 183 regions, the female activity rate exceeded the male rate. However, this is not necessarily a sign of women's relative advantage because the lower male rate may be due to men receiving greater amounts of training which would enhance their relative labour market status in the long run.

Regional variations are higher for subsequent age groups,[17] probably reflecting variations in the gender differentiated response to child care. Figure 7.3 shows differences by age for a selection of regions reflecting different welfare regime types. Nearly all regions experience the largest fall in the *fa/ma* ratio in the 25–34 age category. Eastern German regions have high *fa/ma* ratios and have fairly flat age participation profiles (similar to Denmark). In Southern Germany, in Oberbayern for example, *fa/ma* ratios are lower but the age profile is still relatively flat. Emilia Romagna in north east Italy also has a relatively high *fa/ma* ratio in the 25–34 age group but inequality then increases with age, similar to other Italian regions. In France the more developed regions such as the Ile de France, Rhone Alpes, Centre and the Pays de la Loire have above average *fa/ma* ratios, the latter two

---

15. Analysis of activity rates by age is important as age can be used as a proxy for motherhood. However, other approaches also emphasise the importance of cohort analysis linking people's life chances to the economic and social events prevailing as they pass through their life cycle (Aufhauser 1995).

16. From 1992 this age category became 15–24. The coefficient of variation for *fa/ma* was 7.9 per cent while for men it was 23 per cent in 1992.

17. For the 25–34 age group the coefficient of variation is 14.3 per cent for the *fa/ma* and only 1.7 per cent for the male activity rate in 1992, indicating that the main source of dispersion is in the female activity rates.

regions having acquired new industries with a high proportion of female labour in recent years, as does the more sparsely populated and more mountainous area of Limousin. The lowest quintile for the 25–34 group *fa/ma* ratio is dominated by regions from the southern periphery, although Wales, West Nederland and Overijssel also follow this pattern. Another interesting point is that many UK regions fall below the EU average for this age range.

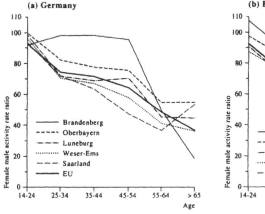

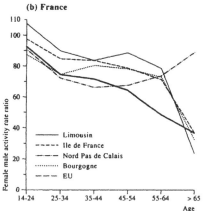

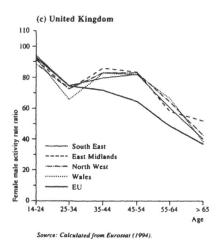

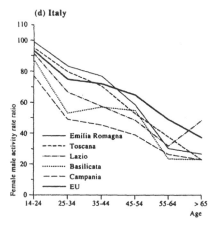

Source: Calculated from Eurostat (1994).

Figure 7.3. Female/Male Activity Rate by Age, 1994

For the 35–44 age group, although the majority of European regions have experienced decline, the British regions (excepting Northern Ireland) have all experienced increases, particularly Wales (although as indicated above Wales had a very low rate in the 25–34 age group). This is also the case for some regions in southern Italy (for example, Basilicata), Kriti and Peleponnisos in Greece, West Nederland and Friesland, and a few largely rural French regions. For the UK regions, the upturn is particularly striking and probably indicates women returning to part-time employment,[18] although these women tend to be relatively disadvantaged in terms of occupational status and pension rights compared with those, for example, in Denmark and France where they are more likely to continue in paid work.

Although large, the gender difference for prime age workers (ages 25–54) has narrowed during the 1980s in all but four Southern regions of the EU. However, there are substantial regional variations around these figures which arise from different permutations of change in female and male activity rates. Emphasis is placed on the 25–34 age group because it is in this age range that gender differences emerge sharply and can have lasting impact. The changes for 1987–92 are given in Figure 7.4.[19] This shows that male activity rates have declined slightly (-1.4%) while there have been positive increases of a greater magnitude in *fa/ma* ratios. In the top quintile of *fa/ma* ratio, every country with the exception of Greece, Denmark and Luxembourg, has at least one region represented. Although many of these regions have above average declines in the male activity rate these are small in relation to the size of the increases in female activity rates (8% on average between 1987 and 1992; 17% between 1983 and 1992). Just over half of the Spanish regions are present in the top quintile, including Extremadura, Castilla-la-Mancha and Andalucia, and more developed regions such as Comunidad Valenciana. At the opposite end of the distribution, 11 regions had declining *fa/ma* ratios, but 8 of these regions also had declines in the male activity rate, indicating economic change rather than changes in gender relations. The regions with large declines on both rates are Basilicata (-15% on *fa/ma* and -5% on the male activity rate) and Campania (-8% and -10%, respectively). The biggest outlier is Berlin, where the large increase in the male activity rate may reflect a gender imbalance in inward migration.

---

18. These data are cross-sectional so it is not possible to trace the labour market behaviour over the life cycle of particular age cohorts, but given the closeness of these particular age categories this is a reasonable assumption.
19. For the period 1983–92 with Portugal, Spain and most of the Greek regions missing, the distribution of the regions between these categories is very similar. However, there was no case in which male rates increased and female rates declined and the rate of increase in the female activity rate was always greater than the decline in the male rate.

(a) Influence of male activity rate changes

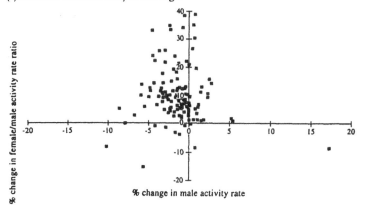

(b) Influence of female activity rate changes

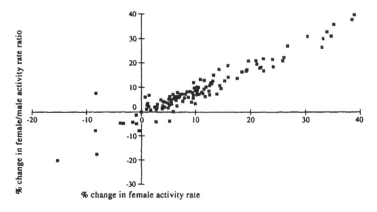

(c) Gender differences in activity rate changes

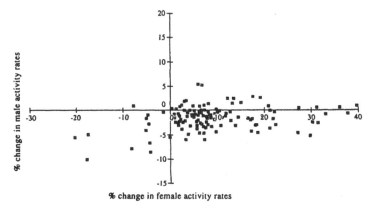

Figure 7.4 Changes in Female/Male Activity Rates
Source: Calculated from Eurostat (1994)

In many cases the greatest rates of change have taken place in regions where the initial *fa/ ma* ratio and female activity rate were low, indicating a tendency towards convergence. To clarify the way in which changes in the *fa/ ma* ratio may arise from different rates of change in male and female activity rates, Figure 7.4 (c) plots these rates of change separately, effectively producing four quadrants. Only one region has declines in female activity rate and increases in the male rate: Bourgogne in France. Nearly 8 per cent of regions had declines in both male and female activity rates. Denmark and Emilia Romagna were in this category, but in each case the decline was small, being from a comparatively high initial level. However, other regions, mainly from southern Italy – Basilicata and Campania – had declines from comparatively low initial starting positions. Twenty-eight per cent of the regions had increases in both rates. These regions were in Spain and in Northern countries including Germany, Belgium, the Netherlands, France and the UK, but in general these increases were fairly small. However, in the vast majority of the regions (68%) female activity rates had increased and male rates had declined.

From this analysis and from the data as a whole, two points stand out clearly. First, gender inequality exists in all regions of the EU and these differences are highest in the 25–34 age group, which can probably be linked to the gender-differentiated response to the care of children. Second, however, for any of the child-rearing age groups, women are more likely to be recorded as being part of the working population in 1992 than they were in 1987 or in 1983, and the extent of the change has been especially rapid in regions where the initial levels of female activity were low, for example in the Southern periphery but also in many regions of the Netherlands. In some rural regions the gender ratio in activity rates has narrowed dramatically, while in those areas where the female working population was already high, for example in Denmark, little change has occurred.

Clearly such diverse patterns need to be explained in terms of detailed analysis of the economic and cultural changes in particular regions. Nevertheless there are some common trends in the direction, magnitude and speed of change that make it difficult to sustain explanations set solely in terms of regional cultures. It is unlikely that these would change so quickly and simultaneously across the regions of Europe. Perhaps it is more reasonable to link changes in activity rates to changing economic opportunities, and in particular to the restructuring of European economies towards service industries together with the gender stereotyping of jobs, and to suggest that whether labour force participation subsequently leads to more significant changes in gender roles will depend on the extent and quality of employment as proposed by the 'gender order' model. Many of the newly created jobs in

(a) Female employees to total employees ratio

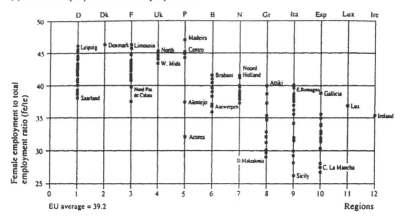

(b) Female full time employment to total employment ratio

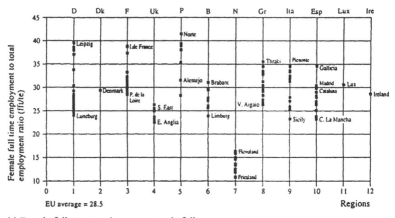

(c) Female full time employment to male full time ratio

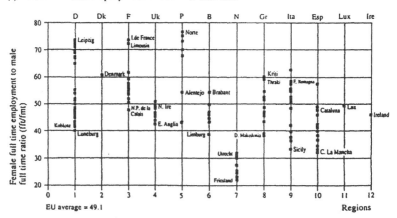

Figure 7.5. Employees in Employment

Source: Calculated form Eurostat (1994)

the service sector are precarious and this is especially so in the economically lagging regions, either traditional agricultural regions or regions experiencing industrial decline (Rodriguez-Pose 1994). In these areas, high status occupations are often missing, in contrast to the core regions where both extremes of the occupational distribution are to be found. Both the precarious nature and low pay associated with these jobs probably limit the role of paid employment in modernising gender relations.

People in employment

Activity rates provide no indication of the extent of labour force participation which is necessary in order to examine the implications of paid work on gender roles. REGIO contains data on people in employment by gender and by full-time and part-time categories but not by age. From these statistics a number of measures have been derived which give some indication of the scale of female involvement in paid work (see Figure 7.5).

FEMALE EMPLOYMENT TO TOTAL EMPLOYMENT (fe/te)

In 1992, the proportion of the total employed (full-time and part-time) accounted for by women (fe/te) varied from just over one-quarter to just under one-half. In general the regional variations are similar to the variation in overall activity rates. High female to male ratios are found in Denmark, Eastern Germany and the UK, especially in the North, Wales and Yorkshire and Humberside, although all UK regions have above average rates. Low ratios are predominantly located in the Southern periphery, for example in Sicilia, but again the Portuguese regions, especially those in the north, follow a different pattern. An indication of the extent of women's involvement in paid work is provided by differentiating between full-time and part-time employment.

FEMALE FULL-TIME TO TOTAL EMPLOYMENT (fft/te)

For example, using the ratio of female full-time to total employment (fft/te) as a measure of gender equality, the Dutch regions have the lowest levels and are 10 percentage points lower than the next lowest region. While national differences seem to be important in the Dutch and British cases, other countries display remarkable regional variations. For example in Spain, Madrid is well above average, while Extremadura lies at the opposite end of the distribution. Similarly, in Italy, Piemonte and Emilia Romagna in the north have high rates, while in Sicilia the fft/te ratio is low. However, as the proportion of jobs provided on a full-time and part-time basis varies between countries and regions, the ratio of female full-time employment to male full-time employment (fft/mft) should also be examined.

FEMALE FULL-TIME EMPLOYMENT TO MALE FULL-TIME EMPLOYMENT *(fft/mft)*
Norte and Centro in Portugal (75%) have the highest *fft/mft* values, followed
by the Ile de France and Limousin, and then the East German regions of Leipzig
and Magdeburg. Also well above average are the Greek regions of Kriti and
Thraki. On this measure the centre periphery pattern is much less evident,
probably reflecting the lack of a tradition of part-time work in the peripheral
regions. At the lower end of the spectrum are the Dutch regions and regions
in Western Germany such as Luneburg and Koblenz. On both measures
involving full-time work there is a higher degree of dispersion between
regions than for female employment as a whole. In fact, while *fe/te* is highly
correlated with *fft/mft* there is no correlation between *fe/te* and *fft/te*.[20]

There have been considerable changes on each of these measures over
time. For the period 1981–91 all but 6 of the 132 regions[21] experienced an
increase in *fe/te* ratios. This pattern is repeated for a wider range of regions
between 1987 and 1992. In only 12 out of 154 cases did female employment
decline, and in four of these the male decline was greater. These changes
probably reflect the general restructuring of economies throughout the EU,
expressed both by the decline of employment in traditional manufacturing
sectors (parts of which have been characterised by male employment) and
by the growth of services, which again in many but not all cases has been
associated with increases in female employment. There is no clear common
pattern to the regions where *fe/te* ratios have declined, but many of the
regions with low rates of increase already had high levels of female
employment. This, together with the high levels of growth in regions where
the initial value of *fe/te* was low – such as in the Netherlands, Belgium and
parts of Italy, together with Spain, where 14 of the 17 regions experienced
above average increases – indicates some convergence in feminisation trends
but also that a universal barrier to total equality remains.

Nevertheless variations between regions also exist. For example, the *fe/te*
ratio increased by 14 per cent in Sardegna which contrasts significantly with
the fall of 4 per cent in Basilicata (see Table 7.1). The rapidity of the change
and the fact that both these regions are in southern Italy suggest that
economic rather than cultural factors were responsible. In Basilicata women
are increasingly over represented in the agricultural sector but the overall
total amount of employment in this sector is decreasing. In Sardegna,

---

20. The coefficients of variation were 11 per cent for females in employment to total in
employment, and between 21 per cent and 22 per cent in the other two cases. Correlation
coefficients between *fe/te* and *fft/mft* were 0.5 and 0.1 between *fe/te* and *fft/te*.
21. For this period data are not available for Spain, Portugal, the former GDR regions and most
of Greece.

however, although the proportion of female employees in the agricultural sector also increased sharply, albeit from a relatively low base, women are more highly concentrated in and represent a higher proportion of employees in the expanding service sector, perhaps as a consequence of the increase in tourism. Thus it is the different distribution of women between the sectors and their differential growth rates that seem to be important in accounting for the different changes in female employment, especially as other aspects of employment such as the full-time and part-time composition are similar. However, to explain the gendered division of labour between sectors and between different occupations within sectors, both socio-economic and cultural factors may be important. In Basilicata, female agricultural workers are concentrated in an area of intensive farming on the coastal strip. There are short seasons of intensive work, which elsewhere has been deemed to be

Table 7.1: The Diversity of Employment Change
in Two Southern Italian Regions

	Basilicata			Sardegna		
	Agriculture	Industry	Services	Agriculture	Industry	Services
% share of female workers	33.1	10.5	56.4	10.9	6.4	82.59
Female share of employment 1992(%)	56.5	12.5	36.4	20.3	8.5	43.2
Full-time	48.1	11.3	33.4	14.9	6.7	39.5
Part-time	8.4	1.23	3.0	5.5	1.3	3.8
% Change in sectoral totals, 1983–92	-42.9	7.2	29.7	-15.3	-5.9	7.1
% Change in female sectoral share	2.2	28.5	1.8	69	-1.47	11.48
Change in female share of total employment, 1983–92	net loss of -4% (1992 share 31.6)			net gain of 14% (1992 share 29.3)		

Source: Eurostat (1994)

particularly appropriate for 'women's nimble fingers'.[22] In Sardegna, by contrast, agriculture is mainly pastoral. Care of the animals often involves staying overnight in the countryside and is deemed to be a male task. Thus in one sense it is the economic and even physical factors that determine the nature of employment, but it is the sex-typing of jobs which has shaped the resulting gender distribution of work.

While feminisation has been common to most regions, its form varies, with different implications for gender roles. Some regions have experienced increases on each of the (in)equality measures, especially in Spain and the UK. However, elsewhere there have been large increases in fe/te but declines in fft/te and fft/mft, for example in Groningen, Limburg and Overijssel and Noord Holland (which contains Amsterdam), although other Dutch regions such as Drenthe have had increases on each of the measures. In Southern Germany, Neiderbayern and Oberpfalz have had sharp declines in fft/te and fft/mft, as have some French regions such as Nord Pas de Calais and Haute Normandie. In these cases more women are participating in the labour market but in a way which poses a minimum challenge to the established gender regime, and if these changes are due to women moving out of full-time employment then traditional gender roles may be strengthened rather than weakened as a consequence. The immediate factors promoting these changes are probably as attributable to changing employment levels in sectors where female employees are concentrated as much as with different choices in the gendered division of domestic and paid work. However, more detailed regional analyses would be necessary to identify both the specific processes involved and the implications of these changes.

For all regions there is a positive correlation (0.5) between fe/te and the female part-time: full-time ratio (see also Figure 7.6). However, these measures also highlight some of the difficulties of comparative research in the sense that the same category of data can have different connotations for different countries. This is particularly the case for the full-time/part-time distinction, which not only is defined differently in different countries but the associated attributes also vary (Perrons 1995a). For example, part-time work can be a progressive way of integrating paid work with other activities (Platenga 1994) or a form of inferior work with few opportunities for advancement (Simkin and Hillage 1992). Thus in the case of the Netherlands,

---

22. However, if employed for 51 days or more unemployment benefit can be claimed for any period without work in that year – so although these workers may only work for short intensive periods they could either appear as full-time workers or as unemployed in the statistics. The employment statistics can therefore be highly volatile and depend crucially on the timing of the survey and the precise wording of the questions.

part-time work has been demanded by feminists and has been supported by
the unions and the state as part of an emancipation policy designed to bring
about a more even distribution of paid and unpaid work between women
and men. As a consequence, the terms and conditions of part-time work are
said to be relatively good (Pfau-Effinger 1995). This example raises important questions about the role of culture and tradition in shaping not only
gender roles but also the task of caring and the more general allocation of
time between paid work and other activities in contemporary societies.[23] In
particular, why is it that these demands have been made in the Netherlands
while in other societies feminists have been pressing for the more equal

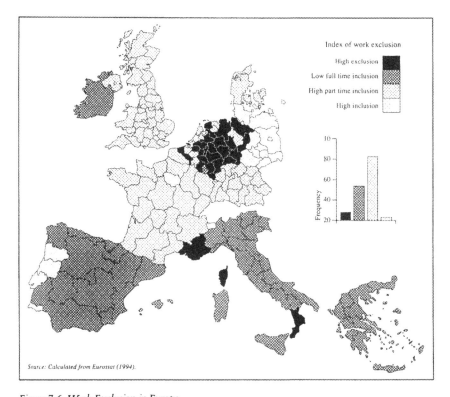

Figure 7.6. Work Exclusion in Europe

23. A parallel debate was initiated by the Mitterand government in France in the early 1980s in
the context of rising unemployment (the 'temps choisi' policy). Workers were able to choose
working hours in tranches of 10 per cent, ranging from 50 per cent to 90 per cent of a
standard day (Gregory and O'Reilly 1996).

integration of women into standard forms of employment?[24] One explanation rests with the way in which different gender arrangements have arisen
in different national contexts (Pfau-Effinger 1995), but the diversity between
women within different national systems by region, ethnicity and social class,
as well as the available economic opportunities, also needs to be taken into
consideration.

Variations in the extent of full-time work are also important because they
will necessitate some adjustment to traditional social roles – for example,
more caring facilities may have to be provided by the state, the private sector
or by men, or there may be changes in domestic technology or in family
tasks that permit or promote shifts in the division of labour within households. Moreover, the extent of domestic responsibilities varies through the
life cycle, and before any conclusions can be inferred from measures of labour
force participation about changing gender roles some differentiation by age
is required. In the context of London, for example, it is clear that the women
who have moved into the higher echelons of employment are young with
few child-caring responsibilities. It is not yet clear how they would adapt to
any such responsibilities in the future (Bruegel et al. 1995). Thus more
research on the interrelated nature of some of these changes is required in
different regional contexts. Two further measures which again try to measure
the extent of women's exclusion are gender inequality in the unemployment
rate and the employment rate.

Unemployment rates

Unemployment statistics are relatively more complete and are generally
available by gender at the NUTS3 level. However, the interpretation of
unemployment statistics is complex, as measures of unemployment are often
inextricably interlinked with the question of social benefits. Thus inactivity
is in some ways a better measure of exclusion. However, the official statistics
indicate that gender inequality in unemployment is wide and for many
regions has been increasing to the disadvantage of women. Thus, with the
exception of the UK and eastern Denmark, for the over 25 age group the
female unemployment rate exceeds the male unemployment rate in all
regions. One of the striking features is the high comparative level of female

---

24. This difference is attributed to the long tradition of a caring society together with high levels
of material affluence that enabled the division of labour between male breadwinners and
female home-makers to be realised by a higher proportion of the population in the
Netherlands, in contrast to Germany, where working-class women were unable to share in
this 'bourgeois ideal'. Also important were the different social constructions of childhood
between the two countries (Pfau-Effinger 1995).

unemployment in Italy. For all Italian regions for which there were data in 1993, the lowest level of gender inequality was in Campania, where women were 2.4 times more likely to be unemployed than men and in the far north eastern region of Friuli-Venezia-Giulia women are 6 times more likely to be unemployed. Similarly, gender inequality in unemployment is also very high in much of Spain. However, over the period 1983–93, while there has also been a deterioration in the extent of gender inequality on this measure in central Spain, there has been some relative improvement for some of the Italian regions, especially Liguria, Campania and Sicilia. Elsewhere, particularly in Germany, there has been an improvement in the relative position of women, although in absolute terms overall unemployment has increased.

What is perhaps more surprising is that in contrast to activity rates, where there is greater equality among young people, gender inequality in unemployment, although lower on average than for subsequent age groups, is considerable and young women are at a marked disadvantage. In the case of Italy the greatest gender imbalance occurs in some of the relatively more prosperous regions. Young women in Toscana, for example, are 2.5 times more likely to be unemployed than men, in Lombardia 1.75 times and in Piemonte 1.5 times more likely. The lowest level of gender inequality is in Campania, where women are only slightly more likely to be unemployed. Other regions where young women suffer disproportionately from unemployment are in the rural areas of France and Portugal. Regions where women experience lower levels of unemployment than men are predominantly in Britain and Germany.

Employment rate

The employment rate is defined here as the ratio of people in employment to the population as a whole, and provides a measure of the extent of formal paid work. Unfortunately there are no data by age on people in employment, so that the demographic structure of the employment rate cannot be taken into account. For example, the overall employment rate would be expected to be low if there were a high proportion of young or elderly people. However, it is possible to differentiate by gender, and thus the relative levels of women's participation in, or exclusion from, paid employment can be measured. The employment rate is also low where 'inactivity' arises from unemployment, early retirement and ill-health or where home-making is seen as a full-time role.

The distribution of regions on this measure again reveals a centre-periphery pattern, similar to the activity rate measure. There is a positive correlation between the female and male employment rates which probably reflects population structures and policies in relation to schooling and retirement, and also indicates that opportunities for both women and men are shaped by the overall economic and labour market environment. There is also a high positive correlation between the female employment rate and the female/male employment rate gender ratio (0.94) and a much lower degree of correlation between the male employment rate and the gender ratio (0.4), meaning that there is greater diversity in the female than in the male employment rate across the regions.[25] This suggests that there are regional differences in the ways in which women are incorporated into the labour market.[26] In absolute terms, in the lowest quintile only half as many women as men are actually in employment, with only one-third in the lowest region, Sicilia. These regions are exclusively in Spain, Greece and southern Italy, together with Corse and the Acores. At the opposite end of the distribution is Denmark, with 80 per cent as many women as men in employment, followed by many of the British regions, the Ile de France, Limousin and a few regions from the former GDR. However, this measure does not distinguish between full-time and part-time work and thus does not really provide a very good measure of the extent of exclusion from paid work or the need for adjustment to social roles. Combining this measure with measures of the full-time: part-time ratio allows a paid work exclusion index to be calculated (see Figure 7.6).

Paid work exclusion

Figure 7.6 maps this paid work exclusion index.[27] Women in about one-fifth of the EU regions have a low level of involvement in paid work. Both the

---

25. The respective coefficients of variation are 9 per cent for the male rate, 23 per cent for the female rate and 19 per cent for the gender ratio.
26. One striking difference is the comparatively low proportion of women in the service sector in the Southern countries. In the case of Italy, for example, while both the service sector as a share of total employment and women's share of the service sector have both been increasing, only in three regions (Piemonte, Valle d'Aosta and Trentino) does women's share exceed 50 per cent. Thus there can be no simple association between the sectoral composition of employment and women's participation.
27. Each region is given a score ranging from 1 to 4 on the basis of their relative position on the female full-time: part-time ratio and the female: male employment rate ratio: 1 = high inclusion – above average on both measures; 2 = high part-time inclusion – above average on the gender ratio but below average on the full-time: part-time ratio; 3 = low full-time inclusion – above average on the full-time: part-time ratio but below average on the gender ratio; and 4 = high exclusion above average on both measures. The intermediate values 2 and

employment rate gender ratio and the female full-time/part-time ratio are below the EU average. These regions are predominantly located in the more rural areas of the Netherlands and the formerly heavy industrial regions of Belgium and in the West of Germany. The two French regions of Provence and Corse also fall in this category, as does Calabria in Italy. Regions where women are highly involved in paid work are all the mainland regions of Portugal, regions in the former GDR, Limousin and the Ile de France, and the Valle D'Aosta in Italy. In contrast, the UK regions together with Denmark and regions in Northern and Southern Germany have above average levels of gender equality in terms of participation in paid work but the full-time/part-time ratios are below average, indicating that their involvement is partial. Conversely Italy, with the exception of Valle d'Aosta, and Spain and Greece have a greater degree of relative female exclusion from paid work, but the women who are in paid work are more likely to be full-time employees. The implications of these different degrees of involvement on gender roles will also vary with the quality of the work involved.

Conclusion: Feminisation of Employment and Social Exclusion

Both the universality of gender inequality and the diversity in its form and degree have been illustrated by a variety of measures. While the changes have been diverse, some common patterns have been identified which have important policy implications.

During the 1980s and early 1990s, women became more involved in paid work and there is a positive correlation between economic growth and women's participation.[28] Although women's paid work may often be monotonous and low paid, it does provide an income and a means of engaging in public life. Efforts therefore need to be made to ensure that any detrimental effects of further economic integration in Europe are offset by comparable increases in Structural Funds and policies for social cohesion as it is women who suffer disproportionately from unemployment in many regions.

---

3 are more difficult to interpret. For example, although there are significant variations between countries, part-time workers are often excluded from higher status jobs and the limited pay means that their paid work is often combined with fairly traditional gender roles. What is more, if only a small proportion of women are engaged in full-time paid work the extent of social adjustment that is required may be limited.

28. Correlations between the female: male employment rate ratio and GDP are positive. Similarly, positive correlations exist between increases in female full-time workers as a percentage of the female total and female full-time workers as a percentage of all workers and increases in GDP. What this suggests is that women's exclusion from paid work falls in the more developed regions, although the direction of the relationship has not been established.

However, it is also clear from studies in the UK that economic growth is not a complete remedy, as gender inequality (measured on a more composite index) seems to be higher in the more developed regions (Bruegel and Perrons 1996; Perrons 1995b). Sectoral data from REGIO also suggest that the form of women's inclusion is often secondary, with women's entry into particular spheres occurring at the moment when they are being deserted by men – for example, as agricultural employment declines overall, women's share of the total increases. Moreover, although women are concentrated in the service sector, which is expanding, this is often associated with part-time work.

The evidence presented here indicates that rapid changes in participation in paid work can take place, but it is far from clear whether this involvement leads to more general changes in gender equality. Thus it is questionable whether participation in paid work alone is a useful criterion on which to base a categorisation of gender roles. As the gender order model suggests, the quality of employment is crucial. Where unequal pay and segregation remain, participation in paid work is entirely compatible with a subordinate role in the household and in the work-place. Thus before any optimistic conclusions can be drawn about gender diminishing as a form of exclusion, measures of employment quality, especially earnings, need to be collected at this level. Referring to the results of national studies, however, it is clear that gender inequality is lower where employment is more regulated and thus the social policies of the EU should be supported in order to reduce gender inequality.

At the regional level, patterns of gender inequality in employment are diverse and more detailed studies are necessary to identify the processes involved. In particular, the relationship between gender relations and the structures of regional economies needs to be clarified. For example, are gender relations a cause of regional socio-economic change or are they simply an outcome of such processes? If it is argued that gender relations and forms of economic restructuring take place in an interactive way then the mechanisms of interaction need to be clearly specified and the role played by gender relations identified. Perhaps only regional case studies of households can really illuminate these issues, but even so such studies would benefit from an awareness of the overall trends taking place in the EU which have been presented in this chapter.

More research is clearly needed on employment inequality and also on the connections between employment and other forms of gender inequality across the regions if policies are to be devised which remove gender as a form of social exclusion. These policies would need to address the question of economic and social cohesion – not only meaning differential regional growth – as evidence suggests that regional growth can have gender-differentiated outcomes but social cohesion in its wider sense. This wider definition would include equal opportunities between women and men and equivalence in social rewards for different forms of work. Beyond employment, however, opportunities for engaging in the public sphere more generally – for example in politics, where the representation of women would need to be increased; in the media, which would need to portray positive images and lifestyles of women and men; and in the street, where women must be enabled to walk without fear – would all need to be considered if gender as a form of exclusion is to be overcome.

Acknowledgement

I would like to acknowledge the help received from Mina Moshkeri with the diagrams in this chapter.

CHAPTER 8

Female Employment and Changes in the Share of Women's Earnings in Total Family Income in Great Britain

Susan Harkness, Stephen Machin and Jane Waldfogel

Eighty per cent of people in Wages Council industries live in households with at least one other source of income.

Department of Employment Press Notice, 5 November 1992

If I want to create employment, should I target full-time men who are on the dole and may never get a job, or should I encourage low paid part-time employment for mostly middle-class women?

John Prescott, 24 June 1994

Introduction

In recent decades women have dramatically improved their labour market position. Women now account for almost half of all employees and 36 per cent of full-time workers (compared with 38% and 30%, respectively in 1971)[1] and, although women still earn less on average than men, the gap between male and female earnings has been closing (see Harkness 1996). The New Earnings Survey reports a rise in the ratio of median female to male earnings for full-time employees from 65 per cent in 1970 to 73 per cent in 1976 and 80 per cent in 1994. These changes have however been

---

1. *Source: New Earnings Survey*

accompanied by a decline in the labour market position of less skilled men. Over the same period there was a sharp decline in male employment (see Gregg and Wadsworth 1994) and a rapid rise in male wage inequality (documented for the UK by, amongst others, Gosling, Machin and Meghir 1994; Gregg and Machin 1994; Machin 1996 and Schmitt 1995).

Typically, household inequality and poverty have been assumed to be strongly linked to male wage inequality, male low pay and male unemployment, while the relationship with women's earnings and employment has been assumed to be weak. As such, men have been seen as 'breadwinners' while women have been seen as working only for 'pin money'. It was with such reasoning that the government argued that the abolition of the Wages Council at the end of 1993 would have little impact on poverty. At the time of abolition it was suggested that the minimum rates of pay set by the Council did little to alleviate poverty because the majority of workers covered lived with a second earner (and, of course, the majority of workers covered were women). In this chapter we assess how accurate this view of women's earnings is by examining the impact of women's earnings on family inequality and poverty and how this relationship has changed over time.

Orthodox economic theory typically models a married woman's employment decision as a function of her husband's earnings and the wage that she can command. *Ceteris paribus*, the faster the rate of increase of a woman's partner's earnings the lower the probability that she will seek employment herself. On this basis, we would expect that as male wage inequality increases, women married to low wage men would raise their labour force participation by more than those married to high wage men, in response to their partners' declining relative earnings position. Thus changes in female employment would be expected to act as a countervailing force in reducing the effect of rising male wage inequality on family income inequality. Using descriptive material we provide an account of changes in female employment across the family income distribution and we find that this is indeed what occurred between the late 1970s and early 1990s. However, although our evidence is consistent with an explanation such as that given above, there may be other reasons too for observing such a change. Other factors, including the narrowing of the gender earnings gap and cultural changes which have increased the acceptability of women working, are also likely to have contributed towards increased female employment since the late 1970s.

The structure of this chapter is as follows. First, we look at attitudinal evidence from the Women and Employment Survey, British Social Attitudes Survey and British Household Panel Survey on the dependence of women on their own earnings and on their reasons for working. We use this qualitative data to assess how important women perceive their earnings as being to their own and their families' welfare. In the next section we go on to examine changes in employment and in the employment structure of families amongst couples aged 24 to 55 using quantitative data from the General Household Survey. We then examine how these changes in employment have affected the composition of family income.

Having assessed how women's contribution to the family budget has changed, we examine the link between female earnings and family income inequality and poverty, and how this relationship has changed over time. Finally, we break our analysis down by region to examine regional differences in female employment and composition of family income. This is of particular interest because we may expect the factors that influence female employment to differ in low and high income regions. Our objective is to see if there is any evidence in support of the view that women's earnings are unimportant because they have little impact on family poverty or household inequality. It should be noted, however, that even if we find any evidence in support of this view there are many more reasons for rejecting the 'pin money' hypothesis. For example, where income is not fairly shared within households it is desirable in itself to raise women's independent income. Further, changing family structures, and in particular the rising number of single mothers, mean that women do not always have a potential 'breadwinning' partner. While we do not look at changes in the employment and earnings position of single women in this chapter, it should be noted that the proportion of women aged 24 to 55 who were single increased from 27 to 32 per cent between 1979/81 and 1989/91 (for further information on changes in the earnings position of single women, see Harkness, Machin and Waldfogel 1995). Finally, rising male unemployment means that an increasing number of women are married to men who are not 'breadwinners'. While the design of the benefit system combined with low pay amongst women has prevented many women married to unemployed men from entering the labour force (see Gregg and Wadsworth 1996), and while many families in which only the woman works are poor, a great many more families would be in poverty without these women's earnings.

Survey Evidence on the Importance of Women's Earnings

Several surveys provide useful qualitative information on the importance of women's earnings in the family budget. This section of the chapter reviews the survey evidence from the Women and Employment Survey (1980), British Social Attitudes Surveys (1984 and 1991) and British Household Panel Survey (1991).

Table 8.1: Survey Evidence from the Women and Employment Survey

(a) Financial dependence on work, all working women (n = 3354)

	Definitely True	Partly True	Not True
I couldn't manage unless I was earning	0.43	0.27	0.30
I don't need to work for the money	0.11	0.25	0.64
If I lost my job, I'd look for another right away	0.66	0.18	0.16
It wouldn't bother me if I lost my job and couldn't find another	0.12	0.19	0.69

(b) Main reason for working, all working women (n = 3354)

	Proportion of all working women
Working is the most normal thing to do	0.03
Need money for basic essentials such as food, rent or mortgage	0.35
To earn money to buy extras	0.20
To earn money of my own	0.14
For the company of other people	0.07
Enjoy working	0.14
To follow my career	0.05
To help with husband's job or business	0.01
Other reasons	0.01

(c) How well working married women would manage financially if not working (n = 2435)

	Proportion of all working married women
Get by alright	0.46
Have to give up a lot	0.40
Not be able to manage at all	0.14

Note: Women and Employment Survey data as described in Martin and Roberts (1984). Sources for panels (a), (b) and (c) are Tables 6.1, 6.11 and 8.16 of Martin and Roberts (1984), respectively.
Source: Women and Employment Survey

The Women and Employment Survey was an interview-based survey carried out in 1980 of 5588 women of working age (16–59) in Britain.[2] Sixty-three per cent of the women surveyed were working, and of these 35 per cent worked full-time and 28 per cent part-time. This survey asked these women questions about their financial dependence on their own earnings. Their responses, which were reported in Martin and Roberts (1984), are shown in Table 8.1. Looking first at panel (a), where women were asked about their financial dependence on their work, it is clear that a high proportion of working women were very reliant on their own earnings. Seventy per cent said that it was definitely or partly true that they would not be able to manage without this money, and 64 per cent said that it was definitely not true that they did not need the money from work. Similarly, 84 per cent of women said it was definitely or partly true that if they lost their job they would look for another one straight away, while 69 per cent said it was not true that it would not bother them if they lost their job and couldn't find another.

In panel (b) responses to questions about women's main reasons for working are reported. Over one-third of women said that they worked in order to earn money to pay for essentials, such as food, the rent or the mortgage. So far the responses we have reported to these questions have been for all working women. In panel (c) we display the responses of married working women only to questions about their financial dependence on their earnings. Over one-half of married working women (54%) said that they would have to give up a lot or could not manage at all if they were not working. The answers to all three sets of questions suggest that working women and their families are very dependent on their earnings.

In 1984 and 1991, female respondents to the British Social Attitudes Survey were asked what their main reason for working was. Responses to these questions are reported in Table 8.2 for women in work. The most frequent response given by women for working was that they worked to buy essentials: in 1984 50 per cent of all working women said their main reason for working was to buy essentials, while in 1991 44 per cent gave this response. Amongst married women, as we might expect, the proportion giving their main reason for working as to earn money to pay for essentials falls, although the drop is not substantial and it remains the most common reason given for working. In 1984 and 1991 46 and 43 per cent, respectively gave this as their main reason for working. Where a married woman's partner was not in employment she was, however, much more likely to say she was working mainly to pay for essentials (70% in 1984 and 59% in 1991).

---

2. See Martin and Roberts (1984) for more details on the survey.

Table 8.2: Working Women's Main Reasons for Working:
Evidence from the British Social Attitudes Survey, 1984 and 1991

	All	Married	Married, partner works	Married, partner doesn't work	Single
1984					
Working is the normal thing to do	0.02	0.00	0.00	0.00	0.05
To earn money for essentials	0.50	0.46	0.42	0.70	0.57
To earn money for extras	0.16	0.23	0.25	0.07	0.01
To earn own money	0.09	0.06	0.06	0.06	0.13
For the company of others	0.02	0.03	0.02	0.04	0.01
Enjoy working	0.13	0.13	0.14	0.13	0.11
To follow career	0.08	0.06	0.07	0.00	0.10
Change from kids	0.01	0.02	0.02	0.00	0.01
Other/Don't know	0.01	0.01	0.01	0.00	0.01
Sample Size	336	223	195	28	112
1991					
Working is the normal thing to do	0.03	0.02	0.02	0.00	0.04
To earn money for essentials	0.44	0.43	0.41	0.59	0.44
To earn money for extras	0.15	0.19	0.20	0.19	0.05
To earn own money	0.11	0.08	0.08	0.05	0.18
For the company of others	0.04	0.04	0.05	0.00	0.03
Enjoy working	0.14	0.15	0.16	0.11	0.13
To follow career	0.08	0.06	0.06	0.03	0.13
Change from kids	0.02	0.02	0.02	0.01	0.01
Other/Don't know	0.01	0.01	0.01	0.01	0.01
Sample Size	786	517	460	57	268

Analogously, in 1984 the proportion of married women in employment stating that their main reason for working was to earn money for extras was 25 per cent. This proportion was much lower amongst both single women and married women whose partners were not in employment. By 1991 the proportion of women with a partner at work who said they were working mainly to pay for extras had fallen to 20 per cent. Again, this survey evidence provides little support for the idea that women typically work for pin money.

Our results from the 1991 British Household Panel Survey reinforce our conclusions from the previous two surveys. As before, the most important reason for working given by women in employment was to earn money to pay for essentials. Table 8.3 shows that three times more women said that their main reason for working was to earn money for essentials than said it was to earn money for extras. Results from the British Household Panel Survey are very similar to those reported in Table 8.2 from the British Social Attitudes Survey once account is taken for differences in family structures.

**Table 8.3: Working Women's Main Reasons for Working:
Evidence from the British Household Panel Survey, 1991**

	All	Married	Married, partner works	Married, partner doesn't work	Single
Working is the normal thing to do	0.02	0.02	0.02	0.03	0.04
To earn money for essentials	0.42	0.40	0.40	0.52	0.47
To earn money for extras	0.14	0.17	0.18	0.10	0.04
To earn own money	0.13	0.11	0.10	0.12	0.18
For the company of others	0.04	0.05	0.06	0.02	0.02
Enjoy working	0.04	0.15	0.15	0.15	0.12
To follow career	0.08	0.06	0.07	0.03	0.13
Other/Don't know	0.02	0.03	0.02	0.03	0.13
Sample Size	2487	1781	1490	177	706

All our qualitative data sources thus indicate that women's earnings are an important component of family income, with the most common response given by working women when asked about their main reason for working being that they required the money in order to pay for family essentials (such as the mortgage, the rent or food). While this evidence gives us some grounds on which to reject the 'pin money' hypothesis (that is, the idea that women work for extras and that their earnings are not a very important determinant of family welfare), the subjective nature of the questions asked means that we do not want to draw too strong a conclusion from these results alone. Instead, by supplementing this evidence with further (complementary) evidence on the contribution of women's earnings to the family budget and on the impact of women's earnings on inequality and poverty, we hope to be able to draw stronger conclusions. The rest of this chapter uses a large British household-level data set (the General Household Survey) to quantify the importance of women's earnings in the family budget and to assess how their importance has changed over time.

Employment of Married and Cohabiting Men and Women and Family Structures

Since the late 1970s the proportion of women in employment has grown rapidly, while in contrast the proportion of husbands who are working has shown a steady decline. Table 8.4 reports employment rates for married and cohabiting men and women only, aged 24 to 55, from 1979 to 1991. For this group the gap between male and female employment rates halved over the period, with female employment rates rising by 12 percentage points to 68 per cent. The majority of this increase (10 percentage points) was due to an increase in full-time employment, while just 2 percentage points resulted from part-time employment. As a result we find that between 1979 and 1991 the proportion of married women working full-time rose rapidly from 24 per cent to 34 per cent, while the proportion working part-time increased from 32 to 34 per cent. In marked contrast there was a sharp decline in the employment of married and cohabiting men over the period. In 1979, 95 per cent of married or cohabiting men worked but by 1991 this had fallen to 87 per cent.

Table 8.4: Employment of Married and Cohabiting Men and Women aged 24–55, 1979–91

	'79	'80	'81	'82	'83	'84	'85	'86	'88	'87	'89	'90	'91	Change
% men employed	96	94	90	88	89	88	88	88	89	91	91	90	87	-9
% women employed	56	57	53	57	61	60	61	63	67	75	72	73	68	+12
% women employed full-time	24	24	22	24	27	26	27	29	30	38	34	36	34	+10
% women employed part-time	32	33	31	33	34	34	34	34	37	38	38	36	34	+2
% working women employed full-time	43	42	42	42	44	43	45	46	45	50	47	50	50	+7

Source: General Household Survey

In order to remove the effects of short-term fluctuations in employment and to boost our sample sizes, we pooled the years 1979–81 and 1989–91 to examine changes in family structure by employment status. This change is reported in Table 8.5. It is clear that by 1989–91 dual earner families were the most common family type, there being three times more families where both husband and wife went out to work than where there was a single male breadwinner. This is a significant change since 1979–81, when the number of dual earner families exceeded the number of male breadwinner families by just 30 per cent.

Table 8.5: Family Type by Employment Status

	1979–81	1989–91	Change
Dual Earner	53.1	67.0	+13.9
Male Breadwinner	40.3	22.6	-17.7
Female Breadwinner	2.1	4.1	+1.9
No Earner	4.5	6.4	+1.9

Source: General Household Survey

Between 1979–81 and 1989–91 female employment grew by 16 percentage points. This is reflected in a 14 percentage point increase in the number of dual earner families, and a 2 percentage point increase in female breadwinner families. Meanwhile, a 4 percentage point drop in male employment led to the number of male breadwinner families falling by more than the increase in dual earner families. Both the number of female breadwinner and no-earner families grew by 2 percentage points over the decade, to account for 4 per cent and 6 per cent of all families, respectively in 1989–91.

The Composition of Family Income and Earnings Shares

Table 8.6 shows average family income, male and female earnings, and male and female budget shares, in 1979–81 and 1989–91. Over the period, women increased their average earnings contribution to the family budget by 92 per cent, four times faster than the rate of increase of the average male earnings contribution. This has resulted in a fundamental change in the composition of family income. Over the decade the average male share of the family budget dropped substantially, to account for just three-fifths of the family budget in 1989–91. Meanwhile, the average female share rose steadily, accounting for over one-fifth of family income in 1989–91.

Table 8.6: Income, Earnings and Earnings Shares

	1979–81	1989–91	Change
Real Monthly Income	1387	2019	+632
Average Male Monthly Earnings	1030	1271	+241
Average Female Monthly Earnings	238	457	+219
Male Share	73	61	-12
Female Share	15	21	+6

Note: All prices are in 1991 pounds (£).
Source: General Household Survey

Much of the change in the female budget share can be attributed to changes in female employment rates. In Table 8.7 average income and earning shares by family type are reported. In 1989–91 the average woman employed full-time brought home over two-fifths of the family budget, which is little different from her earnings share in 1979–81. The average woman working part-time contributed an average of 20 per cent to the family budget in 1989–91, which again is little different from her earnings share a decade ago. While the share of the average full- or part-time working woman in the family budget may have altered little over the decade, this disguises a change in the variance of women's earnings shares across families. For example, in 1989–91 more than one in five married or cohabiting women contributed more to the family budget than their partner, compared with only one in fifteen women in 1979–81.

Table 8.7: Income, Earnings and Shares by Family Type

Dual Earners	1979–81	1989–91	Change
Real Monthly Income	1560.0	2252.0	+692.0
Male Share	68.5	62.5	-6.0
Female Share	26.6	27.9	+1.3
Dual Earners: Women Work Full-time	*1979–81*	*1989–91*	*Change*
Real Monthly Income	1773.0	2520.0	+747.0
Male Share	58.5	53.7	-4.8
Female Share	38.6	39.1	+0.5
Dual Earners: Women Work Part-time	*1979–81*	*1989–91*	*Change*
Real Monthly Income	1406.0	2010.0	+612.0
Male Share	75.8	70.1	-5.5
Female Share	17.8	18.6	+0.4
Male Breadwinner	*1979–81*	*1989–91*	*Change*
Real Monthly Income	1287.0	1874.0	+587.0
Male Share	90.6	85.2	-5.4
Female Breadwinner	*1979–81*	*1989–91*	*Change*
Real Monthly Income	802.0	1149.0	+347.0
Female Share	57.0	52.1	-4.9

Source: General Household Survey

Over the decade, the average contribution of men to the family budget has fallen rapidly, from 73 per cent in 1979–81 to 61 per cent in 1989–91 (see Table 8.8). This change is in part a result of falling male and rising female employment, which has led to a shift in family structures towards those where the man's average budget share is lower. However, unlike the change in the female share, the average male share has also fallen within family types. In families where both partners work, the average man's share of the family budget fell from 69 per cent to 63 per cent over the decade (and this fall occurred both in families where the woman worked full- or part-time), while in male breadwinner families the average male share fell from 91 to 85 per cent.

Table 8.8: Decomposition of the Change in Male and Female Shares

	1979–81	1989–91	Change in Share	Change within group	Change between group
Female Share	15.3	20.8	5.5	0.7	4.8
Male Share	72.8	61.1	-11.7	-5.3	-6.4

Note: Decomposition of changes within married/cohabiting couples based on changes within and between four family types: dual earner households, male breadwinner families, female breadwinner families and households with no earners.
Source: General Household Survey

Decomposing the change in female share across four family types (dual earner, male breadwinner, female breadwinner and no earner), we find that of the 5.5 percentage point rise in the female share, 0.7 percentage points of the rise were due to a rise in the female share within each family type, and 4.8 percentage points were due to changing family structures. Rising female (and falling male) employment therefore accounted for 90 per cent of the rise in the female share. Decomposing the change in male share across the same four family types, of the 11.7 percentage point fall in the male share, 5.3 percentage points of the fall were due to a fall in the male earnings share within each family type, and 6.4 percentage points were due to a change in the structure of families. Only just over half of the fall in the male share can therefore be attributed to changes in employment patterns, the rest of the decline being a result of a fall in the average male share within each family type.

Dual earner families have an income significantly greater than other families. In 1989–91 families in which there was a single male breadwinner had an average income equal to only 83 per cent of that in families with two earners. However, families with a single female earner fared significantly worse, with an average income equal to only 51 per cent of that in dual earner families. Thus low pay amongst women meant that those families headed by a female breadwinner had an income 40 per cent lower than if the family was headed by a man. Yet these families are still significantly better off than no-earner families, with an income almost double that of no-earner families.

Female Earnings, Income Inequality and Poverty

In order to assess the impact of changes in female employment on family income inequality, we examined changes in rates of female employment across the family income distribution. Table 8.9 shows rates of employment for those in the top 50 per cent and the bottom 50 per cent of the family income distribution. For those in the top half of the distribution, employment rates were high in both periods (72% in 1979–81 and 83% in 1989–91), while for women in the bottom half of the distribution employment rates were significantly lower (39 and 59% in 1979–81 and 1989–91, respectively). However, of most interest to us is the change in employment rates over the decade. It is clear that for women in the bottom half of the distribution, employment grew much faster (by 20 percentage points) than for women in the top half of the distribution (whose employment increased by only 11 percentage points).

Table 8.9: Employment Rates in the Bottom 50 per cent and Top 50 per cent of the Income Distribution, 1979–81 to 1989–91

	1979–81		1989–91		
	Male Employment	Female Employment	Male Employment	Female Employment	Change Female Employment
Bottom 50%	87.4	38.9	80.6	59.4	+20.5
Top 50%	99.4	71.5	98.6	82.7	+11.2

Source: General Household Survey

Breaking this analysis down further, we examined changes in female employment by family income decile. Figure 8.1 illustrates rates of female employment by family income decile in 1979–81 and 1989–91. It is clear that women from high income families had relatively high rates of employment in 1979–81. However, although their rates of employment increased over the decade, the rate of increase was much slower than for women in low and middle income families. This is illustrated in Figure 8.2 which shows

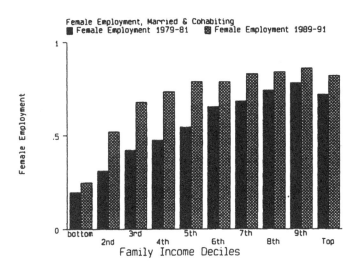

Figure 8.1. Female Employment by Family Income Deciles
Source: General Household Survey

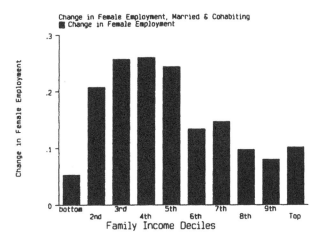

Figure 8.2. Change in Female Employment by Decile
Source: General Household Survey

the *change* in female employment between 1979–81 and 1989–91 by income decile. There is one exception, however: women in the very lowest income decile, who have not managed to increase their employment rates over the decade. Many of these women have a partner who is out of work, and the design of the benefit system has made it difficult for these women to enter the labour market.

Assessing the impact of female earnings on family income inequality, we found first that female earnings had an equalising impact on the overall distribution of family income, and second that the equalising impact was greater in 1989–91 than a decade previously. Table 8.10 shows the impact of women's earnings on family income inequality in 1979–81 and 1989–91. Family inequality grew over the decade, as indicated by the rise in the dispersion of family income ($V(y)$ = squared coefficient of variation of family income) from 0.236 to 0.424. $V(y_1)$ indicates how great the dispersion of family income would have been without women's earnings. It is apparent that in both periods family income would have been more unequally distributed without women's earnings. Moreover, the equalising impact of women's earnings was greater in 1989–91 than a decade previously. The last row of Table 8.10 indicates that in 1979–81 women's earnings reduced the dispersion of family income by 18 per cent, but by 1989–91 the equalising impact had risen to 34 per cent. This was a result of a 20 per cent reduction in the dispersion of female earnings across all families (that is, including zero earnings) resulting from changes in patterns of female labour force participation, and occurred in spite of increased female wage inequality.

Table 8.10: The Impact of Women's Earnings on Family Income Inequality

	1979–81	*1989–91*
V(y)	0.236	0.424
v(y1)	0.279	0.568
[(V(y) - V(y1)]/V(y)	-0.183	-0.340

Source: General Household Survey

Table 8.11 gives an indication of how important women's earnings are for preventing poverty. In 1989–91 1 in 12 families in our sample were in poverty. However, without women's earnings up to 50 per cent more families would have been classified as poor. Families with a single male breadwinner were far more likely to be poor than those in which there were two earners. In 1989–91 fewer than 1 in 100 families in which both partners worked faced poverty, compared with 1 in 20 families where there was a single male breadwinner. Moreover, the probability of a 'male breadwinner' family being in poverty was ten times greater in 1989–91 than a decade previously. What

Table 8.11: The Impact of Wives' Earnings on Family Poverty

1979–81	Actual % in poverty	Predicted % in poverty without female earnings	Predicted % increase in poverty
All married and cohabiting couple families	3.58	5.28	1.70
Dual Earner families	0.00	0.63	0.63
Families where the man only works	0.60	0.60	-
Families where the woman only works	14.72	80.37	65.65
No-Earner Families	67.05	67.05	-

1989–91	Actual % in poverty	Predicted % in poverty without female earnings	Predicted % increase in poverty
All married and cohabiting couple families	7.91	12.26	4.35
Dual Earner families	0.56	4.44	3.88
Families where the man only works	5.28	5.28	-
Families where the woman only works	30.82	74.10	43.28
No-Earner Families	80.17	80.17	-

Note: Poverty is defined as below half mean equivalised income.
Source: General Household Survey

is most striking, however, is the difference in poverty rates between families supported by a male and female breadwinner. In 1989–91 low pay amongst women meant that families supported by a female breadwinner were six times more likely to be poor than those which were supported by a man.

Regional Differences

The General Household Survey allows us to perform the same analysis for the ten standard regions of Great Britain.[3] It is evident that female employ-

---

3. Namely, the South East, East Anglia, South West, North West, East Midlands, West Midlands, Scotland, Yorkshire and Humberside, Wales and the North. Data are not available for Northern Ireland.

ment has increased across all regions over the past decade: this is illustrated in Figure 8.3, which shows levels of female employment by region in 1979–81 and 1989–91. Regions are plotted on the X-axis in descending order of average income. From this we can see that in 1989–91 there appeared to be distinct patterns of female employment and family structures (by employment status) across the low, middle and high income regions of the UK, suggesting that pressures on women to work – and perhaps employment opportunities – differ by region. In Table 8.12 we report average incomes, employment rates and family structures (by employment type) for each region in 1989–91.

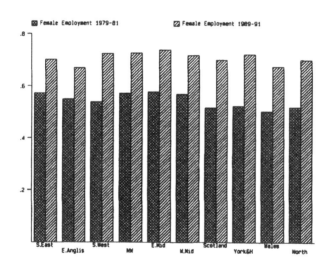

Figure 8.3. Female Employment Rates by Region, 1979–81 and 1989–91
Source: General Household Survey

In East Anglia, the second highest income region of the ten surveyed, significantly more families are supported by a single male breadwinner (28% of families) than the national average (23%). High income and high rates of male employment suggest that married women are less likely to go out to work as a result of financial necessity in East Anglia than in other regions. East Anglia has the lowest rate of female employment in the country (4% below average, at 67%). In the South East, the highest income region in the UK, an identical trend is observed.

Table 8.12: Income, Family Structure and Employment by Region, 1989–91

	Income	Dual Earner	Percentage Male Bread-winner	Female Bread-winner	No earner	Female employ-ment	Male employ-ment
South East	2432	67.2	25.5	3.0	4.3	70.2	92.7
East Anglia	2028	65.1	28.0	1.8	5.1	66.9	93.1
South West	1933	68.2	23.1	4.3	4.4	72.5	91.4
North West	1906	68.6	20.2	4.1	7.2	72.6	88.8
East Midlands	1898	70.7	21.0	3.1	5.2	73.8	91.7
West Midlands	1882	68.4	21.6	3.3	6.7	71.8	90.0
Scotland	1808	65.0	22.9	5.0	7.1	70.0	87.8
Yorkshire – Humberside	1790	67.7	19.4	4.5	8.4	72.2	87.2
Wales	1737	60.9	21.1	6.6	11.4	67.5	82.0
North	1686	62.2	19.6	8.0	10.2	70.2	81.7

Source: General Household Survey

In the middle income region of the East Midlands, there are more dual earner families than in any other region. In 71 per cent of families both husband and wife go out to work (4% above the national average), and female employment is higher than in any other region. While the rate of male employment is the third highest, male earnings are below average. High rates of male employment, combined with relatively low earnings, appear to provide a strong incentive for women to work. The North West, also a middle income region, shows similar employment and earnings relationships.

In contrast, Wales has the second lowest level of family income of the regions surveyed. It also has the lowest number of dual earning families (6% below the national average, at 61%) and significantly more non-earner families (11%, compared with an average of 6%). Male and female employment and earnings shares are lower than anywhere else in Britain, except the North. With only 82 per cent of married men in work, women too are less likely to work than women in other regions of the country. Again, the North of England, the lowest income region of Britain, shows a similar pattern.

Table 8.13 shows differences in poverty, and the impact of women's earnings on keeping families out of poverty, by region in 1989–91. The table is ranked by income, with the highest income regions at the top and the lowest income regions at the bottom. It is no surprise that poverty rates increase as income falls (for a general analysis of regional income inequalities and the regional incidence of poverty, see Martin 1995). In the North, 1 in 7 families are in poverty compared with 1 in 20 families in the South East.

Further, in spite of low female rates of participation in the North, women's employment plays a greater role in keeping families out of poverty. In the North, poverty would have increased by 7 per cent without women's earnings, compared with 3 per cent in the South East.

Table 8.13: Poverty by Region, 1989–91

	Actual % in poverty	% who would be poor without women's earnings	Difference
South East	4.8	7.8	+3.0
East Anglia	6.9	10.5	+3.6
South West	6.8	11.9	+5.1
North West	8.9	13.4	+4.5
East Midlands	7.6	10.9	+3.3
West Midlands	9.2	12.5	+3.3
Scotland	9.2	15.6	+6.4
Yorkshire – Humberside	8.9	14.0	+5.1
Wales	13.1	19.4	+6.3
North	13.0	20.2	+7.2

Note: Families in poverty are defined as those with below half average income, account being taken for differences in family structure and size.

Source: General Household Survey

Conclusions and Policy Implications

The assumption that men earn the 'bread' while women earn 'pin money' continues to underlie many of Britain's employment and welfare policies. This is in spite of evidence that women's earnings are playing an increasingly important role in the family budget (while the male earnings make up a diminishing share of family income). While women's earnings now account for a greater proportion of the family budget than a decade ago, we have shown that this increase has been mostly a result of increased female employment, and not of an increase in the average earnings contributions of full-time female employees. Changes in female employment have occurred most markedly amongst women from low and middle income families. However, women in the poorest families have failed to increase their rates of employment over the decade. These women often have a partner who is out of work, and low pay amongst women combined with the design of the benefit system, have discouraged these women from entering into the labour market.

A formal assessment of the impact of female earnings on family income inequality reveals that female earnings reduced the distribution of family income (amongst families in our sample) in both 1979–81 and 1989–91, and that this equalising effect has increased over the decade. However, employment rates amongst women in the bottom half of the family income distribution still remain lower than those for better-off women. The regional analysis confirms our suspicion that low pay and male unemployment are important factors in reducing the incentive for women to take up employment, so that regional and local labour market conditions would seem to play a significant role in enabling or constraining female employment and earnings, and hence the incidence of family poverty. In addition to reducing the inequality of family income, women's earnings have played an important role in reducing poverty levels amongst married and cohabiting couples. Rates of poverty have doubled over the decade, but without increased female employment the number of families in poverty would be significantly higher today. Again, low pay amongst women means that one in three families headed by a single female earner are poor, a poverty rate six times higher than amongst families headed by a single male breadwinner.

These findings imply that raising employment amongst women in the bottom half of the distribution would have a beneficial impact on reducing the distribution of family income, and on reducing family poverty. Three factors stand out as having a particularly prohibitive impact on raising female employment at the bottom of the income distribution: low pay amongst women, the design of the benefit system, and inadequate provision of child care. Given the potential benefits for the distribution of family income and reduction in poverty, appropriate policy measures for raising female participation in the bottom half of the family income distribution could include the introduction of a minimum wage, legislation to provide equal pay and benefits for part-time work, and 'family-friendly' initiatives (such as the provision of child care) to enable families to balance work and family responsibilities.

CHAPTER 9

Poverty, Inequality and Exclusion in the Contemporary City

Paul Lawless and Yvonne Smith

The Political and Policy Context

Questions of urban poverty and social exclusion have again re-emerged as central issues in contemporary debate. For those with long enough memories there is a sense of *déjà vu* in this. The 1960s and early 1970s witnessed a veritable outpouring of academic and polemical material triggered by the American War on Poverty (Marris and Rein 1974) and to a lesser extent the emergence of a specifically inner city dimension to social inequality within the United Kingdom (Edwards and Batley 1978). But although common themes characterise both contemporary and historical discourse, the scale of social exclusion currently evident in many larger towns and cities has undoubtedly fostered a new and more immediate sense of urgency throughout the developed world. This seems to have occurred for a number of reasons.

First, there tends to be a general assumption that however difficult the position may be for many in the major cities and conurbations, the worst is yet to come: the problem is ahead of us. Currently there are at least 35 million unemployed in the OECD countries alone. Unemployment cannot be equated with social exclusion – but it can act as a useful surrogate. What is especially disturbing in this context is that there is little to suggest that current socio-economic trends and policies will moderate this scale of unemployment to any significant extent. Indeed some processes are likely to accentuate the problem: jobless economic growth; the incorporation of Eastern Europe within the European Union; the privatisation of public utilities; the longer-term effects of GATT on some traditional industries; and rationalisation amongst service sectors such as finance and banking. These, and other, processes indicate that unemployment has already impinged upon, and will continue to affect, groups such as skilled blue collar workers and those working in a wide range of both high and low value added services in ways which would not have occurred in the 1960s and early 1970s (see Dunkerley 1996).

Second, this widening composition of unemployment has been associated with a new spatial patterning of social distress. In the North American context there is evidence that the concentration of poverty and neighbour-hood distress within the inner cities actually worsened in the 1980s (Kasarda 1993). But in much of Europe, processes such as continuing urbanisation in some southern cities (Cheshire and Hay 1989) and immigration from the Mediterranean rim, have helped drive the construction of new suburban social housing projects which may well now be the location of the most acute manifestations of social exclusion.

And third, it is clear too that the apparent worsening and spatial re-patterning of poverty has, not surprisingly, occurred at a time when the wider issues of poverty and inequality have been subject to much more obvious academic and political airing. In the American context the scale and dynamics of urban poverty have been the focus of intense discussion (Cisneros 1993; Murray 1984; Wilson 1987), some of which has in turn been assimilated into the British context (Lee 1994; Murray 1984). Policy and political communities have similarly contributed to wider discussion surrounding urban poverty. Governments have attempted to evaluate the overall impact of intervention on urban communities (for example, Depart-ment of the Environment 1994). Interestingly, perhaps the most intense political debate on the issue has been expressed by a range of inter-govern-mental organisations. The OECD, for example, has helped pull together experience on aspects of urban regeneration (Community Development Foundation/OECD 1993). Moreover, the European Union has made a number of interventions in the area, including its Poverty programmes. It has also introduced specific initiatives designed to enhance social integration and cohesion through social policy (Commission of the European Communities 1993a) and to incorporate unemployment-related issues into the wider consideration of macroeconomic policy, as exemplified in the White Paper *Growth, Competitiveness, Employment* (Commission of the European Communi-ties 1994). The tenor of much of this thinking is expanded in the Green Paper on European Social Policy: 'no democratic state or union of states can function without efforts towards economic cohesion and solidarity between poor and rich regions and between fortunate and disadvantaged social groups' (Commission of the European Communities 1993b, p.21).

Definition and Causation

Controversy surrounding questions of definition and causation have been central to issues of urban poverty and social exclusion. Four perspectives will be considered here, although it should be stressed that this is very much a generalised overview of the problem and these interpretations are not mutually exclusive. One explanation would locate social exclusion within wider processes of global economic change (Harloe, Pickvance and Urry 1990; Harvey 1989). Trends such as globalisation, flexible specialisation, down-sizing, and technological innovation and adaptation may collectively conspire to accentuate the scale and intensity of urban unemployment. Many of those made unemployed or made subject to considerable reductions in income will in turn be affected by other dysfunctions such that some have identified a new multi-deprived 'class' (Dahrendorf 1987). Social exclusion in this perspective is thus very much rooted in the relationship between social division and economic restructuring (Hamnett 1994; Van Klempen 1994).

A second related interpretation would perceive social exclusion, at least in part, as a response to inadequate welfare provision. This 'reformist' position would argue that a general diminution in resources available through the welfare state, combined with a more overtly bureaucratic welfare system, has tended to marginalise groups in society. In the UK, this process has been fuelled by a number of associated socio-economic trends. These include a range of social policies effected by anti-collectivist Conservative governments, changing lifestyles such as the increase in single parent families, and severe economic recessions which have imposed additional strains on the welfare system. Some commentators see the interrelationship between changes within the economy and pressures on welfare as leading to the emergence of the 'new poor' (Room 1990). Further developments of this broad approach emphasise the role of the household in defining social division. Pahl's (1984) work, for instance, highlights the growing distinction between households which possess multiple wage earners and those in which members are unemployed (that is job rich and 'job poor' households).

A third approach to social exclusion would embrace what can broadly be seen as an institutional perspective. At one level this can be seen to include problems of physical dislocation caused by the construction of suburban social housing which is locationally divorced from jobs and social infrastructure. More profoundly, others would point to the ways in which institutions governing, say, housing markets can lead to the creation of a spatially divided society characterised by both rich enclaves and areas with high concentrations of marginalised groups (Winchester and White 1988).

Fourth, and most controversially, there are cultural perspectives developed by commentators such as Murray (1984, 1990). He has identified an underclass ostensibly characterised by specific moral and behavioural traits emerging out of an expansion of welfare dependency. This process is apparently reflected, *inter alia*, in increasing crime, long-term unemployment and a substantial increase in single parent families. Murray's views have been given considerable attention in the popular press. The approach has, however, been subject to intense criticism. It appears to play down structural economic change, it ignores inter-generational discontinuities in disadvantage (Heath 1992), and it fails to address issues of inequality (Walker 1990). Crucially, too, it equates poverty with the emergence of an underclass when many of the poor do not exhibit 'pathological' behaviour and some of those adopting unorthodox lifestyles are not poor.

Although issues surrounding social exclusion have been the subject of increasing comment, this has not always been paralleled by appropriate empirical study. At one level, for example, it is clear that there is a spatial dimension to social exclusion, in that manifestations of inequality are often most apparent at the local level (Morris 1987; Pinch and Storey 1991). However, relatively little area-based research into social exclusion has been published. This chapter seeks to contribute to rectifying this paucity of place-based analysis. It examines aspects of social exclusion within two local urban areas: Kelvin/Thorpe in Sheffield and Bell Farm in York. Some of the major economic characteristics of each of these urban areas are developed below.

The Sheffield and York Economies in the Post-1980 Period: A Brief Overview

During the 1980s, the Sheffield economy experienced considerable changes as a range of national, global and regional processes adversely affected the local labour market. In brief, the city witnessed a substantial decline in its traditional manufacturing base of steel and engineering. These sectors were undermined through the collective impact of factors such as acute recessions at the beginning and end of the decade, the privatisation of British Steel, over-capacity in steel throughout the European Community and fierce global competition. These processes promoted a marked restructuring of the local economy. More than 10 per cent of the city's jobs were lost in the 1980s, of which 35,000 were in traditional manufacturing sectors. Whilst some increases occurred in finance and business services, the city finds itself increasingly dominated by its major regional competitor, Leeds. In the decade 1981 to 1991, employment in finance and business services rose by 73 per cent in Leeds, but by only 40 per cent in Sheffield. By mid 1995 the city's official unemployment rate of 10.3 per cent was substantially higher than the equivalent national rate of 8.1 per cent. On the other hand, the expansion of the service sector has offered some increased opportunities for female employment. By 1993 women comprised 48.3 per cent of the workforce in Sheffield (Sheffield City Council 1993a). However, in line with national trends, this was largely in part-time, low paid jobs. Partly as a result of these adverse economic trends, the city council identified more than 72,000 people as living in areas of poverty in 1993 (Sheffield City Council 1993b).

In common with Sheffield, York's economy also experienced substantial change during the 1980s. As a result of national processes such as deterioration in the balance of payments and low investment in the manufacturing sector, York experienced a de-industrialisation which was more acute than that experienced nationally (Stafford 1990). This steep deterioration in York's manufacturing base is partly explained by the decline of the food sector. In 1984 this accounted for 17.3 per cent of employment in York, but only 2.3 per cent nationally. By 1987 these figures had fallen to 14.6 per cent and 2 per cent, respectively. However, the service sector is an increasingly important element in the local economy, particularly Distribution, Hotels, Catering and Repairs, which together accounted for 23 per cent of York's employment in 1991, by which time the food sector had declined to 13 per cent (York City Council 1995).

As a result of these and other processes, several features have come to characterise the city's labour force. First, employment in York has tended to concentrate in industries which demand low skills and offer low pay. Second, part-time jobs in York have increased, such that by 1987 approximately 29 per cent of employment in the city was part-time. As might be expected, much of this is performed by women, who are six times more likely to be so employed than are men (Stafford 1990). Third, unemployment within the city rose during the 1980s, although by the mid 1990s it closely paralleled national figures. However, 52 per cent of claimants have endured long-term unemployment (that is, of more than a year), and 28 per cent of the jobless are under 24 years old, a problem particularly affecting young women.

Kelvin/Thorpe and Bell Farm Estates:
Key Characteristics and Research Methods

Kelvin/Thorpe consists of two adjoining housing estates, located about 2 km to the north west of Sheffield city centre, which were built in the late 1960s and early 1970s. The area is almost entirely made up of local authority (public sector) housing and displays the full range of 'inner city' problems associated with major public sector housing projects. The economic, physical and social problems associated with Kelvin prompted the city authority to announce that the flats were to be demolished by 1995. At the time of this research, however, Kelvin consisted of 944 multi-storey, deck-access flats which were consistently regarded as one of the least attractive public sector housing estates in the city. Social indicators disclosed that those living on the block suffered from acute poverty: 80 per cent of children attending school were eligible for free school meals, 59 per cent of families received income support, and 84 per cent of households did not have access to a car. It was also subject to concentrations of individuals suffering from factors relating to poverty, such as ill-health and mental illness (Sheffield City Council 1993b). The Thorpe estate comprises almost 2000 dwellings in multi-storey developments, low rise flats and maisonettes. Whilst similarly identified by the local authority as an area of poverty, this is not as obvious as is the case for Kelvin. Even so, 44 per cent of individuals in Thorpe received income support in 1993 (Sheffield City Council 1993b).

Bell Farm is a relatively small estate, comprising 364 homes, situated to the north east of York. Although it occupies a fairly central position in the city, it has become an isolated public sector enclave in the midst of an owner-occupied suburb. Built in the 1930s, it comprises cottage-style accommodation, grouped around two main streets and a series of cul-de-sacs. For many decades Bell Farm was perceived as a problem estate, perhaps because its original tenants were former slum dwellers. Various factors, including the changing status of council housing since the 1950s and a process of encroaching residualisation, did little to dispel this image. In response to these increasing difficulties, the local council launched an Estate Action Programme in Bell Farm in 1992. This initiative was designed to effect repairs and improvements to both properties and the local environment, as well as fully involving residents in the overall regeneration scheme (Cole and Smith 1995).

One difficulty facing the local council was distinguishing between 'the real and imaginary problems' existing on Bell Farm (York City Council 1990). Census data for 1991, for example, suggest that the estate suffered from the effects of concentrated social and economic disadvantage. Some 69 per cent of households did not own a car, compared with a city-wide figure of 43 per cent; about 15 per cent of households were headed by a lone parent, compared with 4 per cent for York; and 23 per cent of the population were aged under ten. Bell Farm did not, however, appear to constitute an area of severe deprivation in relation to many other urban localities throughout the country. Even so, in the context of a relatively affluent city, its socio-economic problems were perceived by the city council as a cause for concern.

This chapter draws upon empirical data arising from micro studies on these two local authority housing estates. It should be stressed that these studies had specific objectives and were not primarily designed to reflect on broader issues of social exclusion. Nevertheless, they provide a valuable insight into the processes of social exclusion operating at the local level. Various data collection methods were utilised. First, detailed quantitative skill surveys were conducted in both areas during 1992/3. These sought to capture socio-economic characteristics including educational and job-related qualifications, employment aspirations, training needs, and barriers to employment and training. In Kelvin/Thorpe interviews were held with 441 individuals, or 19 per cent of the population. In Bell Farm, a smaller estate, 356 interviews were completed, representing some 46 per cent of the population. To supplement these statistical data a number of qualitative interviews were also undertaken. In Kelvin/Thorpe 20 were conducted with the disabled and women returners, as these groups appeared particularly disadvantaged in the job market. In Bell Farm interviews were intended to explore a range of socio-economic issues relating to the regeneration of a moderately deprived local authority housing estate. Thirty hour-long interviews took place with members of various social groups on the estate.

The Local Labour Market and Poverty

Many residents of Kelvin/Thorpe and Bell Farm experience at least one problem in common: manifestations of social and economic deprivation. Not surprisingly, high concentrations of the unemployed are found in both areas. Unemployment within Kelvin/Thorpe was experienced by 46 per cent of individuals (Lawless, Smith and Short 1993) compared with 10 per cent for Sheffield as a whole. Similarly, 41 per cent of residents in Bell Farm stated that they were unemployed in 1993 at a time when the equivalent figure for York as a whole was 6.9 per cent. In total 69 per cent of the population in Kelvin/Thorpe and 64 per cent in Bell Farm were economically inactive at the time the two surveys were conducted. In Kelvin/Thorpe 52 per cent of men were unemployed, three times higher than the city average. Female unemployment, at 38 per cent, was six times higher.

As Table 9.1 demonstrates, only 30 per cent of residents in Kelvin/Thorpe, and 33 per cent in Bell Farm were actually in work at the time of the surveys. Not unexpectedly, the majority of those in full-time employment in both areas were men. Conversely, 81 per cent of women in Kelvin/Thorpe and 91 per cent of those in Bell Farm were employed on a part-time basis. Most of the economically active in both areas worked in relatively unskilled or semi-skilled jobs. For example, 38 per cent of men in

Bell Farm work as machine operatives, and 31 per cent of residents on the estate are employed as shop assistants, food preparation workers or cleaners. In Kelvin/Thorpe, 12 per cent are employed as cleaners. As Table 9.2 suggests, one implication of this employment structure is low income. In Bell Farm, only 10 per cent of the employed work in jobs which produce higher than average wages (Centre for Regional Economic and Social Research 1993).

Table 9.1: Employment Status (%)

	Kelvin/Thorpe, 1992/93	Bell Farm, 1992/93
Full-time employed	21	23
Part-time employed	8	9
Self-employed	1	1
Unemployed	47	41
Inactive	23	22

Note: Percentages may not add up to 100 due to rounding.

Source: Bell Farm Skills Survey (1993)
Kelvin/Thorpe Skills Survey (1993)

Table 9.2: Employed by Occupational Group and Average Weekly Earnings

SOC Group	Kelvin/Thorpe (%)	Bell Farm (%)	Average Earnings (£)
Managers	6	4	438
Professional	5	0	428
Associate Professional and Technical	8	6	354
Clerical/Secretarial	10	9	222
Craft and Related	12	9	278
Personal/Protective	17	15	241
Selling	6	9	243
Machine Operatives	14	23	255
Other Elementary Occupations	22	24	220

Note: Percentages may not add up to 100 due to rounding.

Sources: Additional Information: 1992 New Earnings Survey
Bell Farm Skills Survey (1993)
Kelvin/Thorpe Skills Survey (1993)

A Structural Cause of Unemployment: Demand-Side Deficiency

How can this level of unemployment, low economic activity and poverty be explained? One factor frequently identified as being of major significance in explaining unemployment is demand deficiency. There may not be enough jobs to go round in the local labour market (Layard and Nickell 1985). This assertion appears to be supported by the evidence presented in Tables 9.3 and 9.4. Table 9.3 relates jobs of respondents living in Kelvin/Thorpe to employment change in Sheffield in 1981–91. Only 48 per cent of the employed living in Kelvin/Thorpe work in industrial sectors which expanded during the 1980s. This is slightly higher than for the city as a whole. But fully 43 per cent work in 'other services', a sector characterised by low wages, poor conditions and relatively limited growth. Likewise, as is indicated in Table 9.4, only one-quarter of Kelvin/Thorpe's unemployed last worked in one of Sheffield's expanding sectors. Unemployment in Kelvin/Thorpe is largely the result of an over-concentration of individuals, employed and unemployed, in sectors which offer only limited, generally declining, job opportunities.

Table 9.3: Employment by Industry (%)

Division	Kelvin/Thorpe	Sheffield	% Change Sheffield 1981–91
Energy/Water	1	1	-51
Steel/Chemicals	5	3	-73
Engineering	7	14	-32
Other Manufacturing	9	6	-19
Construction	14	5	-13
Distribution/Catering	14	21	0
Transport/Communication	2	6	-5
Finance/Business Services	5	10	+39
Other Services	43	34	+9

Note: Percentages may not add up to 100 due to rounding.

Sources: Additional Information: Census of Employment (NOMIS)
Bell Farm Skills Survey (1993)
Kelvin/Thorpe Skills Survey (1993)

A similar picture emerges in relation to occupation. The highest proportion of the unemployed in Bell Farm, 38 per cent, were previously employed in the retail sector. However, this sector only comprises 13 per cent of the jobs in York's labour market. In relation to occupational sectors, as Table 9.5 indicates, 39 per cent of the unemployed previously worked in Other Elementary Occupations, which comprise only 10 per cent of jobs in York.

Table 9.4: Unemployment by Previous Industry (%)

Division	Kelvin/Thorpe	Sheffield	Sheffield 1981 Unemployed
Energy/Water	0	1	-51
Metal/Manufacturers, etc.	8	3	-73
Engineering	8	14	-32
Other Manufacturing	11	6	-19
Construction	15	5	-13
Distribution/Catering	28	21	-13
Transport/Communications	6	6	-5
Finance/Business Services	4	10	+39
Other Services	20	34	+9

Note: Percentages may not add up to 100 due to rounding.

Sources: Additional Information: Census of Employment (NOMIS)
        Bell Farm Skills Survey (1993)
        Kelvin/Thorpe Skills Survey (1993)

Table 9.5: Previous Occupational Sector of Unemployed in Bell Farm (%)

SOC Group	Unemployed, Bell Farm	Employed, York 1991
Managerial	2	13
Professional	1	9
Associate Professional and Technical	0	9
Clerical/Secretarial	6	18
Craft and Related	14	14
Personal/Protective	16	8
Selling	9	9
Machine Operatives	14	10
Other Elementary Occupations	38	10

Note: Percentages may not add up to 100 due to rounding.

Sources: Additional Information: Census of Employment (NOMIS)
        Bell Farm Skills Survey (1993)
        Kelvin/Thorpe Skills Survey (1993)

Mediating Structural Change: The Estate Dimension

Unemployment and declining jobs appear to be strongly associated with an accentuating mismatch between employment opportunities available in local labour markets and the types of job sought, and skills offered by, residents on the two estates. There is a further dimension to the equation. A range of other factors interact with, and may accentuate, the broader structural imperative. Issues of education and training are likely to be relevant here. In Kelvin/Thorpe, for example, highest employment levels were found to relate to intermediate, not high, educational qualifications. However, space permits an examination of only two themes here: on the demand side, employer stigmatisation and, on the supply side, issues surrounding the household and unemployment.

The stigmatisation of an estate: employer discrimination

Economic analyses concerning discrimination in the labour market tend to explain stigmatisation in terms of its functionality for capital (for example, Loveridge 1987). Neo-classical theorists argue that discrimination is a rational response to market forces. Employers may discriminate against both racial minority groups and women in order to maximise profits (Phelps 1980). As past experience leads employers to believe that individuals from these social groups are unreliable, withholding jobs is regarded as rational and cost-effective. Similarly, both neo-Marxist writers (Braverman 1974) and dual labour market theorists consider that segregation of the workforce has occurred in response to restructuring in Western capitalist economies. Whilst discrimination may be 'functional' for the labour market, its maintenance relies upon the assumptions of employers, which may be 'damaging to its victims' (Phelps 1980).

Social discrimination generally tends to be associated with obvious physical or biological differences (Loveridge 1987), such as gender or race. Discrimination may also occur, however, where 'differences' are not so apparent (Lee 1987). This section will examine a form of stigma which is not easily observable and which has received limited attention from commentators: namely, discrimination associated with *residence*. This type of stigma tends to be associated with problem local authority housing estates (Damer 1992). It is thus not surprising to discover that both Kelvin/Thorpe and Bell Farm share this characteristic. Both areas have a negative reputation and residents are consequently perceived in a detrimental light. One Bell Farm resident said: 'As soon as you say you live on Bell Farm, you're some sort of deranged monster...a criminal, can't look after your children, you're in the pub all day...'. This form of discrimination may impact on individuals' lives in many respects. It may, for example, limit their social life or ability to gain credit (Cole and Smith 1995; Lawless *et al.* 1993).

Evidence from both Kelvin/Thorpe and Bell Farm suggests that employers may possess discriminatory attitudes towards individuals living on stigmatised estates which affect labour market participation. For example, when asked to cite barriers to employment, 51 per cent of respondents in the Bell Farm survey mentioned employer prejudice. It can be argued that this response is a convenient excuse for individuals who have been unsuccessful in obtaining employment. The existence of residential prejudice, however, was also mentioned by professionals working on these estates, who might be expected to possess a more reflective position. Certainly residents living on both estates display a strong conviction with regard to employer discrimination. As one resident said when asked whether he considered that the reputation of Kelvin influenced employers: 'It's got a very bad reputation. It's always had a bad name. I've been living on there for nearly seven years, and to me, as soon as you mention Kelvin Flats you've got no chance of getting anything'. Residents frequently describe strategies devised to circumvent employer prejudice. For example, false addresses are used on application forms. One resident spoke of her experience in this manner:

> As soon as I have written a letter [of application] and I have written where I live, I have not heard from them. And also when I have been for interviews, these people say 'well'! I never put Kelvin Flats on my letters of application [now], because I know I won't hear anything. So I have gone to an interview to give them the opportunity to see me first, rather than judging what sort of person I am from where I live. Their faces dropped. I look for it and I have seen it, their face drops when you say I live at Kelvin.

Evidence from both Kelvin and Bell Farm suggests that the media are instrumental in reinforcing a negative reputation, a finding confirmed by Damer (1992). Local press reports in both Sheffield and York appear sensationalist, emphasising criminal behaviour, destruction, misery and neglect. It might be assumed that the press will report any local authority estate in the same manner. However, a comparison between press reports of Bell Farm and similar estates in York indicates that this is not always the case (Cole and Smith 1993). Whilst articles concerning other public sector estates were varied in tone, Bell Farm appeared to be subject to largely detrimental coverage. 'Notorious' was the most common adjective used to describe the area. Stigma may of course be further reinforced by institutional factors associated with housing policies. It is possible that housing policies create 'ghettos' of marginalised groups, because high priority cases are offered houses in the least popular estates (Morris 1994a).

The household: supply-side constraints to employment

The relationship between the household and employment is relevant here for at least two reasons. First, housing estates such as Kelvin/Thorpe and Bell Farm are not homogeneous entities. Estates consist of varying groups such as older households, dual adult families with dependent children, single adults with no dependants and single adults with dependants. Second, despite recent attempts to study the household and its relationship to the labour market, the household has received limited attention within the traditional urban literature (Pratt and Hanson 1991). Evidence from this research allows for commentary on two particular household types: older households and dual adult households with dependants.

It is often assumed that participation in the labour market declines with age, especially after the age of retirement. This is not necessarily the case. Older people, particularly those living in local authority tenure, may have no private pensions and hence may be solely dependent on benefit (Oppenheim 1993). They may wish to work in order to supplement their income. This may be especially relevant in cases such as Bell Farm where 24 per cent of households consist of those aged over 60. Older households are less common in Kelvin/Thorpe. Nevertheless, 22 per cent of the population on the estate was made up of those aged over 50.

Older workers may encounter severe difficulties in obtaining employment. This may often be because demand for their skills has declined. The Kelvin/Thorpe study, however, highlights another significant barrier to employment in relation to older workers: sickness or invalidity, and disability. Thus 22 per cent of men aged over 50 and a further 20 per cent aged over 60 claimed that their main reason for being unemployed was due to sickness or invalidity. The figures for women were even higher. About one-third of women aged over 50 stated that their main reason for not working was sickness or invalidity, whilst a further 22 per cent said that their unemployment was caused by disability. A link between old age and a decline in physical well-being is to be expected. It is possible, however, that this comparatively high incidence of sickness/invalidity and disability may relate to other factors such as socio-economic deprivation experienced by these individuals. The disparity between levels of male and female ill-health may be explained with reference to women's role in the household. Women caring for children at home in unhealthy housing conditions may suffer more ill-health than men who are out at work (Oppenheim 1993). Alternatively, women may put the needs of others within the family before their own when resources are limited (Glendinning and Millar 1991).

The role of women may be of particular significance in at least one other context: dual households with dependants. Female wages are an important source of income for many households and will obviously be of particular significance where male partners are unemployed. The labour market participation of women living on these estates is, however, relatively low. For example, only 30 per cent of women in Kelvin/Thorpe are employed, compared with 59 per cent for Sheffield as a whole. It might be argued that women in dual adult households, particularly those caring for dependants, would not wish to obtain employment. This was not the case. In Kelvin/Thorpe fully 52 per cent of women at home wanted to work immediately and very few did not want to work at all.

Whilst both men and women experience difficulties in obtaining employment due to the structural features discussed earlier, women may also encounter barriers associated with their role as primary carers of dependants. It may be, for example, that women experience a conflict of responsibility between remaining at home to care for the family and obtaining jobs (Land 1978). This conflict is reinforced by the state, which does not provide adequate support for working mothers. Child care provision in state nurseries has declined since the 1950s and parents are taxed if they use nurseries subsidised by employers (Brannen and Moss 1991). Child care for the under-fives was identified as a barrier to employment by 56 per cent of women with child care responsibilities living on Kelvin/Thorpe. Similarly, almost half of women in Bell Farm considered that the cost of child care was a factor which reduced job opportunities. Bearing in mind the low wages which most women in Bell Farm might expect to receive, this is hardly surprising.

Women living with men who are unemployed may also encounter further difficulties. It has been argued (Martin and Roberts 1984; Metcalf and Leighton 1989) that the social security system discourages women living with unemployed men from participating in paid work. The system disregards a relatively small proportion of a wife's earnings before the family benefit is reduced. Thus the level of earnings required by a woman to make employment profitable is raised. Women might consider working and disclaiming benefit, but in the case of women in Kelvin/Thorpe and Bell Farm, earnings may be insufficient to support the household. One respondent from Kelvin/Thorpe, who lives with her unemployed husband, illustrates the difficulties faced by many women in her position:

> I can't work while he's on social. Well I could work but it's not worth us while really, not the wages that you get paid for my type of job. So I mean that's not an option, not at all for him [her husband] to stay at home and look after the kids. I mean, he'd be very willing to, we've spoken about it, but I wouldn't be able to find a job that would be worthwhile doing that. If I'm reading the papers and I get to the [job] section, well I look more for Joe [husband] than me. But I do look at the ones that I could do. You know, I think, I could do that. But then I look at the salary per annum and it's like £4000 or something and I

think, well you know, I can't feed our Ben [their young son] on that, never mind about the rest.

This inability of mothers to obtain employment may, of course, affect the life chances of all members of a household. This is especially so with regard to single parents, who comprised 36 per cent of economically inactive women in Kelvin/Thorpe and 33 per cent of households in Bell Farm.

A Concluding Comment

The evidence from these 'micro studies' confirms, to an extent, what might be seen as conventional currency with regard to urban unemployment: that the main cause is structural. Demand deficiencies in the local economy provide the central rationale around which the urban social exclusion debate must revolve, although much of that debate will of necessity concentrate on broader UK, and European, macroeconomic policies. Whilst broader economic change may play a significant role in causing social exclusion, this chapter has also suggested that a variety of other mutually reinforcing factors may collectively combine to create barriers to participation in the labour market. Other commentators have also indicated that a constellation of factors may contribute towards a process of social exclusion (McGregor and McConnachie 1995). This chapter has examined just two of these issues: employer discrimination and constraints to labour market participation associated with the household.

Earlier in this chapter, it was suggested that a variety of theoretical perspectives could be employed when analysing the causes of social exclusion. The issues explored here indicate the desirability of locating social exclusion within a pluralistic theoretical context. Clearly, issues of demand deficiencies in the local economy link to those theoretical perspectives which perceive social exclusion as emerging out of the processes of global economic restructuring. This work also suggests, however, that it is necessary to consider an approach to labour market exclusion which also incorporates theoretical perspectives which interpret social exclusion as a response to inadequate welfare provision and as the outcome of localised institutional forces.

When considering policy issues, there is not a lot that local communities or their elected representatives can do about demand deficiency in the economy. Nevertheless, for those working at the local level there are policies which can be pursued. None of these will 'solve' the problems of unemployment, but they can help moderate its generalised effects. On the demand side, there may be scope for community enterprise initiatives and local investment through housing and environmental improvements. On the supply side, decentralised and customised training, a closer involvement of employers in the needs of their immediate neighbourhoods, encouraging locals to use all available labour recruitment channels, enhanced facilities for basic education and anti-poverty programmes may all prove worthwhile. It is, of course, possible to integrate supply and demand considerations in terms of policy development. The Estate Action Programme in Bell Farm illustrates an holistic approach to economic regeneration. The results of the skill survey were publicised to employers to promote positive perceptions of residents' skills. An attempt was also made by residents to reinforce this positive image by developing a closer relationship with the local press, and an outreach worker was employed to work with households to encourage training and determine employment requirements. It is difficult, however, to imagine that these kinds of initiative will have much of an impact in the most disadvantaged of urban communities. For many of the socially excluded, real change will only come through the espousal of alternative political and economic parameters on the part of national government.

CHAPTER 10

Glasgow: A Tale of Two Cities?
Disadvantage and Exclusion on the European Periphery
Mike Danson and Gerry Mooney

Introduction

From having one of the most developed industrialised economies in the world at the start of this century, Scotland has experienced an almost uninterrupted relative decline. In the period since the mid 1970s, there has been a fundamental transformation of the economy, with the disappearance of many of the traditional industries and a growth in the branch plants of the high-tech and information technology sectors (Danson 1991). While the North Sea Oil and Gas sector has given a fillip to the underlying depression of the northern and eastern regions of Scotland, the industrial heartland has continued to suffer throughout the last two decades. Studies by Cheshire (1990) and Lever (1993) amongst others have catalogued the decline of the Glasgow economy in the context of a 'Europe of the regions', with the conurbation placed in the bottom decile of EU functional regions (metropolitan areas) by 1988. Many of the changes that have accompanied these economic processes have impacted heavily on the social and physical environment of the industrial towns of central Scotland. Several regeneration packages to arrest decline were introduced by public development agencies in response to this depressed status. Generally seen as a 'comparatively early response to perceived problems' (Cheshire 1990, p.330), these programmes were associated with a 'remarkable improvement' in the city's position, appearing to suggest that Glasgow had been the sixth most successful European city over the period 1971–88 in terms of a set of economic and social indicators of urban problems. Against this apparent success, Keeble, Owens and Thompson (1982) have argued that peripheral European cities, such as Glasgow, will fall further behind the average because of their limited regional accessibility and economic potential, while Mayer (1992) and

Perrons (1992) have suggested, respectively, that new institutions are critical in maintaining even this position and that inequalities and regional imbalances are in fact likely to increase over time. Whether the improvement in the relative economic position of the city is sustainable, therefore, is of wider policy significance to metropolitan areas in lagging regions throughout the European Union.

These local developments capture one of the predominant issues in the 'urban studies' literature in recent years: the impact of global economic change on urban social and spatial structures (see, for example, Castells 1994; Fainstein, Gordon and Harloe 1992; Sassen 1991). One of the central questions concerns the new social and spatial structures which are developing in these urban areas. For some theorists (Sassen 1991) it is the urban arena which serves as the focus of new patterns of social and economic inequality and of growing polarisation. A number of disparate arguments come together in relation to this: first that economic and social change has led to the creation of various marginalised groups, or at best has further excluded and peripheralised sections of the population long considered disadvantaged, many of whom are located in run-down urban areas. Little else serves to encapsulate this idea better than the notion of an urban 'underclass'. Second, that within urban areas growing social and economic 'polarisation' is accompanied by a corresponding reorganisation of the urban spatial structure. And third, that the newly emerging 'post-industrial' cities contain within them groups who have 'lost out' as the cities are transformed. This in turn has given rise to the idea of a 'dual city' or 'dualising city'.

Although Castells has argued that the dual city image has long been a classic theme of urban studies (Castells 1989), in recent years the dual city metaphor has become a popular means in academic and media circles of describing urban spatial change and the growing divide between rich and poor, or included and excluded. In both British and American literature, the dual city is seen primarily in terms of declining and impoverished inner city districts (or ghettos) contrasted with more affluent middle-class districts located in suburban areas. While acknowledging that processes of gentrification are evident in some city centres, the prevailing image is one which highlights the inner city or central urban areas as home to the poor, the marginalised or the new 'underclass'. Images of, to quote Berry (1985, p.71), 'islands of renewal in seas of decay' are widely interpreted as highlighting growing polarisation within the contemporary city.

While these models of an urban dualism are considerably more developed (and popular) in American literature, there are some indications that the concept is becoming a convenient tool for describing the contemporary urban landscape in Britain. This chapter considers the applicability and usefulness of this dual city notion in the context of the decline and 'regeneration' of Glasgow in recent years. It focuses on Glasgow for three main reasons: of all British cities it has been widely regarded as *the* model of urban renewal and regeneration; second, and closely related to this, is the idea that Glasgow is now a modern 'post-industrial' centre. Third, in Glasgow ideas of a dual city take a different spatial form from those depicted in the majority of studies: while a distinction is still drawn between affluent and poor areas, or between the 'affluent city' and the 'deprived city', for the most part the 'deprived city' is defined as the large local authority housing estates located on the city's edge. This is not to argue that spatial divisions are a new feature of cities such as Glasgow. As in many other British cities, historically spatial divisions have long existed between different parts, often taking the form of an east- versus west-end divide. In the Glasgow context such divisions were accentuated in the post-war period by the rapid development of the large peripheral estates, and in many accounts of Glasgow's regeneration in recent years it is these estates which represent *the* 'problem' areas of modern Glasgow (see, for example, Keating 1988, 1989; Pacione 1986, 1990, 1993). In this respect the example of Glasgow is much closer to the experience of several French cities, where recent studies have focused attention on economic exclusion and spatial segregation in the urban periphery (Silver 1993). Within the French context, however, issues of racism and immigration are often emphasised in discussions of urban polarisation (Donzel 1993).

The Idea of a Dual City

It was noted previously that the use of dualisms in urban studies is not a new phenomenon. From Plato – in *The Republic* – to Gareth Stedman-Jones (1971) and beyond, it is possible to trace the concept of 'two cities' and divisions in society. However, the notion has been applied in recent years with a renewed vigour. A number of interconnected developments are responsible for this. The uneven impact on urban areas of national and global processes of economic change, as measured in terms of 'de-industrialisation' and 'tertiarisation', is widely regarded as increasing the economic and social marginalisation of particular social groups and the abandonment of much of the urban industrial landscape. In the American literature in particular (Mollenkopf and Castells 1991; Sassen 1991; Savitch 1988), this process has been interpreted in the framework of a post-industrial transition. Sassen has further emphasised the impact of processes of work casualisation on the social structure of 'global cities', which she interprets as leading to increased social and economic polarisation (Sassen 1991). For many, the growth of poverty over the past two decades or so has become a major characteristic of urban landscapes. Anglin and Holcomb (1992), Katz (1989) and Auger (1993) have argued that, in the US at least, there is an increasing 'urbanisation of poverty' which, for Auger, is the product of the combination of uneven economic decline and government policies which have drastically reduced the scope and level of services for disadvantaged groups in American cities.

Economic transformation and the growing incidence of poverty in urban areas have been accompanied by, or have given rise to, a growing spatial polarisation whereby 'affluent' and 'marginalised' or 'excluded' localities exist side by side. 'Gentrification' and 'displacement' are discussed by Sharpe and Wallock (1989), with some illuminating description of the limited impacts of tourism-led regeneration in Baltimore being apposite to the Glasgow case (Hula 1990):

> Baltimore may complete a pattern, already visible, of a 'double-dough-nut' of concentric rings. The centre would contain a business, cultural and entertainment centre that remained strong because it served the whole metropolitan area, and attractive housing for the well-to-do. The centre would be ringed by the decaying and much more populous neighbourhoods of poor and dependent, very largely black. These in turn would be surrounded by middle- and upper-income suburbs, very largely white. (p.209)

The dual city idea has increasingly entered debates about urban polarisation in Europe, for example in investigations of poverty in Amsterdam (Van Kempen 1994) and in Hamburg (Dangschat 1994), with both studies questioning its usefulness. In Britain it is the residents of run-down inner city districts and large local authority housing estates who are seen as excluded from urban regeneration, particularly in the central business districts, and from the benefits accruing to more affluent middle-class localities. MacGregor (1994) has recently argued that these areas have become central not only to much of the contemporary discussion of social and spatial polarisation, but to the very language of urban poverty itself. For Robson (1989), these processes of polarisation suggest that the future for Britain's urban centres is bleak, with ghettos accommodating an urban underclass trapped in its own subcultures.

The Urban Underclass

As with ideas of a dual city, the underclass debate is more developed in American social science and social commentary than in British academic discourse. But the ideas which inform the underclass debate in the US are all too familiar in Britain (Morris 1994b). In both societies there are similar arguments that the new underclass is a product of long-term social and economic change (Wilson 1987). Further, there are also common themes in respect of claims about the negative and debilitating effects of prolonged welfare 'dependency', long-term unemployment and exclusion from the formal labour market. While in Britain attention has also been drawn to the alleged criminality and moral degeneracy of the underclass (Dahrendorf 1987; Murray 1990, 1994) – and for that matter of much of the poor in general – such ideas are more widespread and popular in US studies and research. It is a theme, though, all too readily taken up by the media on both sides of the Atlantic.

It is the issue of the spatial concentration of the underclass which connects most clearly with images and representations of a dual city. Kasarda and Littman have argued that, over the past two decades, poverty has become an increasing fact of life for many of the residents of American central cities (Kasarda 1990; Littman 1991). Further, Katz has suggested that poor blacks are increasingly concentrated within central districts (Katz 1989), echoing Wilson's argument that these areas are becoming home to 'the truly disadvantaged' (Wilson 1987).

The resulting image, then, is one which portrays an increasingly divided city: a relatively affluent and increasingly suburbanised white (and growing black) middle class on the one hand and a poor black underclass, economically and socially isolated and trapped in the central city ghettos. Sassen argues that global cities historically have had a significant concentration of poor people, but the extent of their spatial segregation and economic segmentation has become more marked in recent times (Sassen 1991). The dominant perspective suggests that economic and social change are producing an increasingly isolated mass of poor people, cut off from processes of economic growth. The outcome is the creation of two cities in a shared geographical context: one for the rich and one for the poor; for 'the haves' and 'the have nots': a city doing 'well' and one doing 'poorly' and a dramatically widening gulf between the two.

In Britain the language of the underclass debate has largely been imported from the United States, with ideas of an underclass central to many arguments about increasing social polarisation (Pinch 1993). Nevertheless, the notion of an underclass has been widely attacked on both sides of the Atlantic, with critics focusing in particular on definitional problems and the lack of any solid evidence to support claims of its existence (Bagguley and Mann 1992; Gans 1990; Morris 1993, 1994b).

Economic Background

Built upon the Empire, the Clydeside economy was not only affected more harshly than most by the decline of British influence this century, but also continued to feel the impact on the development of the city, conurbation and Scottish economies well beyond the inter-war period (Danson 1991). With the extensions to the built environment in the 1930s, the old tenement slums of the working class were abandoned by the labour aristocracy as they fled to the garden estates being constructed within the city boundaries (Damer 1990). These developments, however, rather than creating a polarised dual city, were of little significance in the overall scheme of the conurbation; city, region and nation were becoming clearly more working class *vis-à-vis* England than at any time since the First World War (Payne 1977).

In the post-Second World War era, the Scottish experience was of continuing relative decline, with the introduction of foreign capital to promote external ownership and control as the alternative to indigenous planning and development. The degeneration of Glasgow and its economic hinterland continued apace, with an amelioration of the forces of full-scale run-down through the establishment of the new towns and commuting suburbs around the conurbation. Out-migration from the region was accompanied by a suburbanisation of the mobile and skilled, while the traditional old industrial areas around Clydeside continued to wither and decline as their native industries were nationalised, taken over and closed (Lever and Moore 1986). New enterprises tended to be attracted to the greenfield outer areas, reinforcing these processes of relative deprivation in terms of job and life opportunities (Danson 1982). By way of contrast, the decentralisation of the remaining population away from the congested core to the peripheral estates around Glasgow was not matched by the movement of employment. These were to be dormitory townships for the historic industrial centres of the inner city and its immediate environs, though the idea of maintaining a large population within the city was deemed necessary to attract new manufacturing industries to Glasgow.

Faced with a declining city-region (97% of the most deprived areas in Britain were to be found on Clydeside (Census of Population 1971, OPCS)), the newly created Scottish Development Agency and local governments of the mid 1970s introduced a comprehensive set of proposals to reverse the social and economic deterioration of Glasgow's inner city with the Glasgow Eastern Area Renewal project (Donnison and Middleton 1987; Lever and Moore 1986). The perceived 'success' of this approach was followed progressively in the early 1980s by projects to redevelop the older industrial towns of Clydeside, and then to rejuvenate the city as a post-industrial metropolitan centre. Restructuring of industries and industrial quarters, wholesale clearances, demolitions and redevelopments of businesses, housing and communities, gentrification and 'imagineering' were the day-to-day phrases of change; the Garden Festival, City of Culture, Merchant City, Royal Concert Hall were the symbolic flagships. The last 15 years have seen the battle lines drawn between the modernisers, promoting the plethora of schemes to re-create Glasgow in their own image, and the militants, asking questions of whose Glasgow and whose image is being promoted. Commentators have joined this debate in increasing intensity, with academics playing a supporting role to the main cast.

Glasgow's outer estates were a product of slum clearance programmes and the need to address the acute housing shortages of the 1930s, 1940s and 1950s. Starting with the Pollok estate (or 'scheme') in the mid 1930s, for the next 25 years the city built a series of large public sector estates in each of its four corners. The biggest estates, at Castlemilk, Drumchapel, Easterhouse and Pollok, were the main recipients of the slum clearance population who were rehoused within the city, with significant numbers of people rehoused in New Towns and elsewhere outside the city. At their peak in the late 1960s and early 1970s, the four large estates accommodated around 200,000 people, almost exclusively in local authority housing. At over five miles from the city centre, the large post-war housing and urban renewal programmes created a new form and layer of spatial segregation within the city, superimposed on those patterns of residential divisions laid down in previous periods.

In the rush to build as many houses as possible in the shortest available time, little attention was given to the provision of 'civic amenities', a picture repeated in many British cities at the time and well documented in some examples of the 'community studies' literature in the 1950s and 1960s. From being the solution to Glasgow's housing problems in the immediate post-war period, by the late 1960s the peripheral estates were climbing the league table of deprived areas in the city. While in the early 1970s such areas were largely confined to older quarters of declining industrial activity and districts with private-rented housing along the Clyde and in the inner East End, by 1981 the four large peripheral estates, together with several inner suburban inter-war estates, had become significant locales of multiple deprivation. This was reflected in the large number of local authority housing estates identified as 'Areas of Priority Treatment' by Strathclyde Regional Council at this time. During the 1970s, then, the spatial distribution of urban deprivation in Glasgow had significantly changed, partly as a consequence of urban renewal and slum clearance programmes in the inner city, which led to dramatic falls in inner city populations (Pacione 1993). Glasgow's outer estates were built at a time of relative economic growth in the city. But by the late 1960s and

1970s, its economic base had dramatically declined, reflecting the long-term de-industrialisation of the city's economy. Lee highlights the ways in which the changing (and declining) economic fortunes of Britain's older industrial cities impact on outer estates; indeed his comments about Liverpool's overspill estates apply directly to Glasgow (Lee 1988, p.69).

During the 1980s, levels of unemployment, poverty and deprivation rose steadily in the outer estates, and the increasing attention which was focused on these areas by the media and policy-makers led the Scottish Office in 1988 to launch the 'New Life For Urban Scotland' programme, in four outer estates across Scotland (Scottish Office 1988). For Pacione, the results of the 1991 Census confirmed arguments that the 'urban crisis' was becoming particularly acute in such areas (Pacione 1993).

This brief historical backdrop shows the extent to which the peripheral estate 'problem' had been climbing the policy-making agenda since the late 1970s. In contrast with other parts of Britain, where the inner city remained the main focal point for state urban policy, in Scotland the peripheral estates dotted around the main Scottish cities had become the main targets for intervention (although to some extent outer estates in English cities were also beginning to figure in accounts of urban deprivation).

Glasgow's Urban Divide

In the main, the dual city/two city idea has been grasped by those eager to account for increasing levels of poverty at a time of economic renewal and substantial private sector investment in the city. It was Michael Keating in *The City That Refused To Die* (1988) who was among the first to popularise and apply the notion to a Glasgow context. Previously, Keating and Boyle (1986) had explored Glasgow's dual economy: a situation whereby city centre renewal and inward investment were in marked contrast to the underfunded peripheral estates. While the population of these estates was characterised by unemployment, low skill levels and a life of poverty, there had been little opposition to the growing social and spatial divide within the city. The 'problems of the periphery' would only be overcome by extending economic regeneration programmes to the peripheral areas according to Boyle (1990, p.129).

Keating (1988) argued that urban restructuring and renewal programmes, while improving Glasgow's image, had heightened social and geographical inequalities, increasing the isolation of the populations of the outer estates. Large public sector housing programmes in the post-war period had created a spatially divided city, wherein outlying estates would be largely cut off from inward investment in the city centre. As opposed to the entrepreneurial dynamism of the core, the peripheral estates could be seen as a 'welfare city', where the majority of the residents survived either on welfare benefits or on poor quality and low paid employment. But this 'dualism' would be further exacerbated by policies which saw these estates in isolation from the wider Glasgow and Strathclyde economies.

Pacione saw the outlying estates as typically 'cashless societies', characterised by high levels of welfare dependency (Pacione 1990, p.308). The conditions prevalent in this part of the city stood in marked contrast to those which characterised Glasgow's 'other city'.

While Keating, Boyle and Pacione sought to avoid a 'blame the victim' type of argument, and claimed that the 'problems' of the peripheral estates had to be seen in relation to the overall economy of Glasgow, their uncritical use of some of the concepts and terms characteristic of much of the underclass debate allows for a number of different interpretations of their arguments. Despite the call for regeneration programmes to be extended to include the peripheral estates, the language of 'two cities' allows the problems in the peripheral estates to be seen as residual, particularly by the policy-makers. This point will be taken up further in the conclusion.

The predominant themes which tended to emerge from the many newspaper reports were ones which focused on welfare 'dependency' and 'hopelessness' and the growing concentrations of single parent families. Numerous other articles provided human interest stories of the 'hell' of living in Glasgow's outer estates. Indeed the *Sunday Times*, when devoting space to Charles Murray's arguments about an emerging British underclass, pinpointed Easterhouse in particular as an example of a council estate 'consistent with reports from inner-city Washington and New York' (Murray 1989). One of the main ideas to emerge from these reports, and in a number of television programmes broadcast during 1990, was the growing isolation and marginalisation of the outer estate populations, cut off from processes of economic regeneration. Thus the peripheral estates were not only peripheral in geographical terms, but were also marginal in economic, social and political terms. The picture which dominated tended to stereotype the peripheral estates as uniformly rundown and deprived. The 'two Glasgows' – the 'old' (here depicted by the peripheral estates) and the 'new' (as represented by the Merchant City, Cultural Festivals and new shopping centres) – were starkly counterpoised. The peripheral estates were deprived, in contrast to the growing affluence of other areas of the city.

There is some evidence that the two city notion has begun to influence a number of public and private sector agencies which are operating in the city. In 1991 Glasgow City Council's Planning Department warned of the long-term consequences of ignoring the outer estates, which could undermine the regeneration of the entire city (Glasgow City Council 1991). This line of thinking has emerged most forcefully in the arguments made by the Glasgow Regeneration Alliance (GRA) (Mooney 1994). This Alliance, which comprises four public sector agencies, was launched with the promise of a £1.5 billion investment package for Glasgow's 'disadvantaged areas', which included the four peripheral estates. Continuing population decline had left Glasgow with an 'unbalanced social structure', increasingly marginalised and socially excluded in deprived areas. Of late, a more explicit description of the perceived position of these estates has gradually emerged, with the Glasgow Development Agency (GDA) apparently introducing the concept of 'exclusion' to the debate:

> But while Glasgow has every reason to pat itself on the back, Mr Gulliver [Chief Executive of GDA] warns there is still one major problem to be overcome – what he dubs the increasing impenetrability of 'excluded people'...'In these circumstances, the so-called excluded areas will find it particularly difficult as they may become even more detached from the conventional market,' he said. (Woods 1995)

For the GDA, Glasgow's long-term economic revitalisation was dependent on tapping the resources of such areas. Further, the threat to Glasgow's new image which such areas posed, particularly to the growing tourist sector, was also highlighted as a major cause for concern. The four large peripheral estates in particular offered considerable land development potential together with abundant supplies of labour. Despite claims that the GRA was committed to 'unlocking the full potential' of disadvantaged areas throughout Glasgow, it is not difficult to identify the attractiveness of the peripheral estates in terms of their land development potential. In other words, it was not the space occupied by the peripheral estates which was redundant, but sizeable chunks of their populations.

Population decline in the outer estates during the 1980s and early 1990s had led to proposals that at least one estate should be completely demolished, with the population being rehoused in the 20,000 empty council houses dotted across the rest of the city. While such proposals were not fully developed, the thinking that lay behind them illustrates the extent to which over the past 10–15 years the outer estates have come to be regarded as the key urban problem in Glasgow. Claims that they have become in some sense 'surplus' to requirements have not been hard to find, particularly in press coverage.

By the early 1990s, then, the idea that the peripheral estates had become 'outcast Glasgow' or Glasgow's 'second city' had been clearly established. More recently they have become the places to visit for stories of poverty, unemployment, deprivation and for illustrating the growing health divide in Britain's urban areas (for example, *Panorama*, 13 February 1995).

What emerges from this discussion is the language of much of the underclass debate. While references to the underclass in the Glasgow context have been few in number thus far, ideas of dependency, exclusion, marginalisation, hopelessness and despair have dominated the accounts of the emerging socio-spatial divide in the city. The portrayal of the peripheral estates in particular as uniformly depressed and welfare-dependent, as *the* locales of poverty in Glasgow, has been widely reported. Such views tend to regard these areas as residual problems. But how adequate are such claims and how far is the problem of poverty a problem of – or confined to – peripheral estates?

Social Polarisation and Social Exclusion in British Cities

In a recently published report commissioned by the Department of the Environment, Boddy and colleagues explored the growing incidence of poverty and associated disadvantage in inner urban areas (Department of the Environment 1995). Again, socio-spatial polarisation was highlighted as an issue of particular concern: 'One significant development in inner cities in recent years has been the increasing incidence of areas of deprivation existing in close proximity to neighbourhoods undergoing socio-demographic change in the form of gentrification and inner area redevelopment schemes' (Department of the Environment 1995, para. 4:61).

While the focus of this research was on inner urban areas in England and Wales, the growing incidence of poverty and deprivation in outer estates was also evident. The conclusion reached was that there was a growing gap between inner cities/outer estates and other areas in terms of spatially concentrated disadvantage. This growing awareness of the plight of peripheral estates was also a theme of another recent study on the spatial distribution of poverty and wealth (Green 1994). Once again, concerns regarding the increased marginalisation of the poor and disadvantaged in 'extreme poverty areas' leading to further social exclusion from 'mainstream' society were voiced (Green 1994, p.3). Further, the socio-spatial isolation of the poor tended to be at its most marked in large urban centres.

While much of the discussion of 'urban problems' in Britain has focused on inner cities, we would argue that issues of social exclusion and isolation are particularly significant in the context of peripheral estates. High incidences of poverty and multiple deprivation are reinforced and exacerbated by physical isolation, inadequate public transport, the relative lack of facilities and the absence of employment opportunities within the immediate area.

Similar issues have been raised by the European Commission in its Green Paper on Social Policy: 'social exclusion...by highlighting the flaws in the social fabric...suggests something more than social inequality, and, concomitantly, carries with it the risk of a dual or fragmented society' (Commission of the European Communities 1993, p.551).

While questioning the rather simplistic conclusion here, what is clear is that the consequences of poverty and isolation can be far-reaching and more significant than the figures alone might suggest. The key question concerns the adequacy of the dominant imagery and representations emerging about Glasgow's peripheral estates as socially excluded locales.

The Spatial Distribution of Poverty in Glasgow

Thousands of Glaswegians are sinking in a quicksand of deprivation. We can throw some of them a life-line but it will take national and international action to pull them free. (Glasgow City Council 1993, p.1)

The whole issue of poverty and deprivation in both Glasgow and Strathclyde has been in sharp focus over the past few years. In part this is due to the publication of a number of reports from both Glasgow City Council (1993) and Strathclyde Regional Council (1994a, b, 1995). But at a national level also, the deteriorating position of Glasgow in relation to the incidence of poverty has been highlighted. In terms of the intensity of poverty, as measured by the proportion of households with no earners and the proportion of households with no cars, Glasgow ranked first ahead of all other towns and cities in Britain (Green 1994). More recently there has been widespread media coverage devoted to claims that poverty in parts of Glasgow's peripheral estates is as bad as, if not worse, than in certain areas of the 'Third World' (Bell 1995).

In a multi-layered and multi-dimensional portfolio of strategies, Strathclyde Regional Council (1994a) and other social partners target their resources to priority communities in a hierarchy of initiative areas, defined according to a number of indicators of poverty. In delineating these areas, data are collated and analysed to produce statistics on 'areas of priority treatment' (APT), and are now being revised in response to the 1991 Census of Population. Although the data suggest that the extent of relative poverty and deprivation became more widespread between 1981 and 1991, in Glasgow and Renfrewshire multiple deprivation especially became even more focused on specific areas during the last decade (Strathclyde Regional Council 1994b), with all the peripheral estates included in the poorest areas. Nevertheless, the region possesses a dispersed and varied deprivation in the rest of Strathclyde, with many of the poorest living outside the worst areas of poverty.

In other words, poverty has become deeper and more widespread throughout Strathclyde, questioning the idea of a spatially concentrated, well defined and distinct group of the poor or underclass. And, if an underclass or dual city does exist, then unique concentrations of multiple deprivation would be expected and so the APT definitions hold promise in the pursuit and identification of an excluded people.

The 1980s witnessed a major restructuring in the Clydeside economy, with 44 per cent of manufacturing and 5 per cent of service jobs disappearing from the city over the decade (Strathclyde Regional Council 1994b). Despite this degree of dislocation, a significant change from the previous Census shows that the incidence of unemployment is now so widespread throughout the region and city that it is not a good discriminator of degrees of relative poverty between areas (Strathclyde Regional Council 1994b). Unemployment, therefore, is not highly correlated with the other key indicators of poverty, such as numbers of lone parents, elderly or disabled. As the poor earn their poverty, suffer from debilitating illnesses, struggle to raise a family single handedly or carry these burdens into old age, so they may be concentrated with similar people, but not exclusively or comprehensively with all such groups.

Equivalent analyses in previous Censuses have shown an overwhelming concentration of the very worst (1%) of enumeration districts in Glasgow, not only at the regional level but also for Scotland and Britain as a whole (Strathclyde Regional Council 1994b). Figures for 1981 and 1991 show that while poverty has become much more widespread, the city has continued to suffer from concentrations of relative multiple deprivation: almost half of all poverty in the region is suffered by the city of Glasgow, compared with its population share of under one-third. More detailed analysis further shows that the old industrial districts on the periphery of the conurbation have also deteriorated since 1981. Despite their massive industrial declines of the previous decade, Monklands and Motherwell demonstrate a high proportion of the population in poverty in 1991 but a low incidence of multiple deprivation. By way of contrast, the position of the areas of traditional deprivation in the more western districts, in Inverclyde and Renfrew, indicates that the deleterious effects of similar industrial restructuring have been evident, with increased commuting and suburbanisation alongside areas of multiple deprivation.

The focus on multiple deprivation means that the distribution of the population covered by the various social strategy schemes is skewed towards Glasgow, Renfrew and Inverclyde, each of these being over-represented compared with the share expected from a simple count of their residents. In total, 12 per cent (280,000) of the regional population live in the areas of severe deprivation designated as Priority 1 or 'Major Social Strategy Initiative Areas'; all but 48,000 living in Glasgow (Strathclyde Regional Council 1994b). All of the Glasgow APTs are included in the priority areas of the government quangos and public/private sector partnerships in Clydeside, Scottish Homes and the GRA. In none was unemployment below 27 per cent, lone parents headed between 35 and 52 per cent of households, while the lives of 13–21 per cent of the non-elderly population were limited by long-term illnesses. For the deprived communities of Paisley and Greenock/Port Glasgow (Inverclyde), similar levels of multiple deprivation were in evidence in 1991.

The Priority 2 or 'Smaller Social Strategy Urban Initiative Areas and Priority Rural Areas', tend to have lower populations and unemployment is again over 27 per cent, with lone parents usually being in charge of 30 per cent or more of households with children, with between 9 and 17 per cent of the population with long-term sickness. Few of these areas have instances of the very worst enumeration districts, however, where there are incidences of multiple deprivation they tend to fall in the Glasgow area. The Priority 3 areas are either 'Urban Programme Eligible Areas' or 'Other Deprived Rural Areas'. As the local authority document notes (Strathclyde Regional Council 1994b), however, some elements of deprivation in the latter are not addressed by the Census, for example, access to health care, employment, and so on. The Census thus confirms the city's position as the centre for poverty and deprivation in the region. On a range of indicators (unemployment, lone parents, overcrowding and vacancy rates), Glasgow appears as the worst district in Strathclyde, non-elderly illness being the exception. Glasgow has 50 per cent of enumeration districts in the worst 10 per cent in Scotland and 87 per cent of the worst 5 per cent in Strathclyde.

Comparing the city with its wider region suggests that the population characteristics are very similar, which implies that demographic factors are not the main causes of these relative concentrations. There are some notable differences, however. The proportions of lone parent households, large families, single adult households and elderly households are all higher in Glasgow. This suggests that couples tend to move out to the suburbs when they are newly married or otherwise ready to start a family – a standard pattern of mobility. Unemployment is worse, at 23.6 per cent compared with 16.3 per cent in the region for men, and 13.4 per cent against 9.5 per cent for women. A higher proportion of the economically active are on government training schemes, though this disguises the fact that more school leavers are unemployed in Glasgow and fewer on 'youth training', while the city suffers both higher numbers of adults unemployed and on schemes. The relatively low numbers of ethnic minorities in Strathclyde are concentrated in the city. While a higher proportion of the elderly have a limiting long-term illness, the differential is greater for younger age groups. A much higher proportion of households have no car, again a common large city phenomenon. Housing tenure is biased to the rented sector in Glasgow, above the regional average. Although the proportion is low, twice as many households lack basic amenities, and overcrowding is a more widespread problem.

The Census does not indicate comparative wage rates, mortality, and so on, but extending the analysis to other measures of standards of living, it can be shown that the metropolitan core has the worst ranked indicators across a number of factors. From other indicators it is apparent that age-specific death and morbidity rates are higher in Glasgow than elsewhere in the region, in the UK and, indeed, in Europe (Save The Children/Glasgow Caledonian University 1995, p.36). Wage and income data suggest a higher dependence on the benefit system and basic pensions, with a greater proportion of jobs in low paying sectors (Strathclyde Regional Council 1994b). The proportions of the relevant population receiving free school meals, income support, housing benefit and clothing grants are all highest in Glasgow. Mortality rates (all causes) are the third highest in Strathclyde.

Together, these data suggest that Glasgow has suffered and continues to suffer from the aftermath of decline and stagnation. Moreover, the large expansion in the new service sectors of the 1980s – banking, insurance and finance, personal services and public and private administration: all promoted as key elements of the 'post-industrial' city and as compensation for the haemorrhaging of skilled manufacturing employment – have overwhelmingly benefited commuters from outside the city. Nearly half of all jobs are now taken by residents of the dormitory suburbs, of satellite towns and of other regions within daily travelling distance. The widely accepted presence of 'trickle-down' processes of regeneration are difficult to discern in this evidence. Yet mobility out of the city and the widespread levels of multiple deprivation throughout Strathclyde suggest that Glasgow is not simply home to a new regional underclass, made redundant by the restructuring of the last quarter-century. To determine how concentrated the poverty is within Glasgow, it is necessary to look at the peripheral estates and renewal areas of the city.

Between 1981 and 1991, population loss was especially severe in the peripheral estates (30.4%) and the renewal areas in general (20.5%) compared with the rest of Glasgow (4%). There has therefore been a relative move from the peripheral estates into the wider city. This in itself undermines the notion that a permanently excluded underclass exists with limited mobility to the rest of the community, or that poverty is concentrated in certain areas alone. As to the social composition of the peripheral estates and renewal areas, the proportion of all households with children is highest in the former peripheral estates, and while the proportion of lone parents has increased across the city, the incidence is still greatest in these areas. There is a significant concentration of lone parents in poorer areas, therefore, with 70 per cent of all lone parents in the city living in renewal areas, half of whom are in the peripheral estates.

Another group subject to poverty and deprivation is the single elderly, yet these are under-represented in the poorest areas. This demonstrates that the deprived communities are themselves of different histories and structures. The old industrial communities of Govan and Shettleston, for instance, are deprived because of the redundancy of their populations' skills and networks in the 1970s, with induced and institutionalised immobility concentrating poverty locally. The new concentrations of single parents in some parts of some peripheral estates, for instance, are created no less by economic, housing and family interactions, but give rise to different areas of multiple deprivation.

Critically, therefore, the areas where the poor live cannot be explained simply in one dimension; by extension, there is not a class defined by different criteria from the rest of the working class; rather they are a heterogeneous sub-set of the population that is often concentrated in particular parts of the city, region and nation. Many of their number can be found beyond the 'areas for priority treatment', that is, the areas defined as having the worst problems of poverty and deprivation.

Conclusion

The conclusion which we draw from this examination of the spatial distribution of poverty in contemporary Glasgow/Strathclyde is thus not supportive of a simple dual city model. However, this is certainly not to deny that there is an uneven distribution of poverty or that poverty is concentrated in certain areas, particularly, as we have seen, in Glasgow itself. But there is little evidence that there is a distinctive underclass culture specific to such areas.

What is being contested is the usefulness of the dual city argument for our understanding of such spatial patterns and the processes which contribute to it. The language of the 'two city' perspective is one which is plagued by definitional and conceptual difficulties. Despite the continuing use of concepts such as polarisation, underclass, exclusion and marginalisation, the processes which are viewed as contributing to such developments tend to be obscured. In this respect the dual city perspective and its underlying arguments about growing socio-spatial polarisation are characterised by ambiguity and vagueness (Fainstein *et al.* 1992; Hamnett 1994; Marcuse 1989; Van Kempen 1994). Further, and importantly, the model tends to be a static one and offers little understanding of the shifting patterns of poverty in the city over time. Socio-spatial trends and divisions in the contemporary city are continually changing and are superimposed on previous patterns. Thus the pattern which appears dominant today is one which has been built up historically.

In discussions of the emerging 'tale of two cities' in Glasgow, the attention which the peripheral estates have received does not relate directly to the levels and proportions of poverty to be found there. In part this is a consequence of the reluctance to define adequately the areas or social groups concerned. Further, within peripheral estates there is a marked differentiation between the various component parts in terms of unemployment, poverty and deprivation. This is almost completely neglected in the dominant picture of these estates which has emerged in recent years which stereotypes them as locales of 'despair' or 'hopelessness'.

It is also evident from the analysis of the spatial distribution of poverty in Strathclyde that the situation *throughout* Glasgow is deteriorating relative to the rest of the region. Only in two other Strathclyde districts – Renfrew and Inverclyde – is there an increase in the concentration of poverty. This raises a major problem with the dual city concept – namely, that of scale (Van Kempen 1994). Middle-class suburban areas outside Glasgow, particularly Bearsden/Milngavie and Eastwood (Green 1994), have continued to prosper, largely at the expense of other parts of the region. Such a pattern may then justify the fears of policy-makers in the city that the continuing population exodus may be leaving Glasgow as a whole with an increasingly welfare-dependent population and an even more 'unbalanced' social structure. Despite the arguments that the peripheral estates of Glasgow are essential to the long-term economic future of the city, at present the dominant representation is one which sees such areas as a residual problem, a relic of the past. In this respect the dual city notion gives rise to a 'poor versus the rest' type of argument which, for Marcuse, serves to obscure the fundamental relations of power and profit in the modern city (Marcuse 1989, p.707).

The media have increasingly stigmatised Glasgow's outer estates as 'excluded communities'. A consequence of this has been to 'marginalise' the population of such localities further. The peripheral estates are dystopian: they have become symbolic of the 'dark side' of contemporary Glasgow: the 'city of despair' in contrast to the 'city of hope and splendour' (Van Kempen 1994). But such symbolic representations tell us little about the realities of an economically depressed city. From being the solution to post-war housing and planning problems, they are now represented as the major stumbling block in Glasgow's ongoing regeneration. Glasgow is a city in transition. But in transition to what?

The picture depicted here stands in opposition to the imagery associated with a successful post-industrial city. But while the evidence provided seriously questions much of the hype of the 'new' Glasgow, the imagery and representation of urban pathology which characterise many accounts of the city's major estates should also be directly challenged. Cities may have increasingly become 'places of sharp contrasts' (Beauregard 1993, p.259), but the dominant representations of such contrasts should always be subjected to critical and rigorous interrogation. The questions raised here are pertinent beyond the city of Glasgow itself, especially in the wider European urban context.

This chapter was originally written in 1995.

CHAPTER 11

The Policy Challenge

Paul Lawless

Introduction

The chapters in this book collectively embrace a wide range of perspectives on unemployment and its relationship to social exclusion. Some of the papers are primarily concerned with manifestations of, and explanations for, unemployment at the regional scale. Others focus on the interface between inequality and the labour market at the local or city-regional level. Some papers examine changes at the macro level, whilst others explore interrelationships between the operation of labour markets and their impact on specific sectors in society. Nevertheless, despite this catholic range of contributions, a number of overarching themes can be identified which characterise much of this material.

First, whatever the manifestations of unemployment, it is evident that, on the broad canvas, things are getting worse. There is little to suggest that existing policies have diminished inequalities within the labour market in any persistent and meaningful way. Indeed some of the evidence presented here strongly indicates that official figures may substantially underestimate the real problems of unemployment at national, regional and local scales. Clearly, in the UK context, the myriad revisions of unemployment statistics in the last 15 years or so have seriously undermined the credibility of official figures. But arguments presented in this book add a further dimension to this debate. Beatty and Fothergill's chapter, for instance, points to a widespread under-recording of the levels of unemployment in the British coalfields. Lawless and Smith, and Danson and Mooney indicate a similar situation at the local, intra-urban scale, where, for example, official unemployment figures for women bear little relationship to reality on the ground. This apparent under-recording of unemployment levels only serves to confirm the generally pessimistic message emerging from these papers.

Second, and very much a related point, there is a strong dynamic element to all of this. The relationship between the operation of the labour market and social exclusion is very much characterised by a sense of process. Market changes, and policy initiatives, can create and sustain real changes in labour market dynamics, sometimes over relatively short time spans. For instance, as Martin shows, the earnings distribution in the UK widened sharply between 1978 and 1992. In a similar vein, Green, Gregg and Wadsworth highlight the accentuating inequalities in relation to local unemployment rates after 1989. Moreover, Perrons points to an increase in income differentials between men and women across the EU in the 1980s and early 1990s. This dynamic feature inherent to the social exclusion/labour market nexus adds a further layer of complexity for those analysing its evolving nature or proposing policy innovation.

Third, one dimension through which many commentators wish to address relationships between social exclusion and the labour market, is that of space. It is interesting to reflect that virtually all of the chapters in this book employ space as one filter through which to explore social exclusion in the labour market. The scale employed varies: regional, local authority and neighbourhood levels are all used. And whilst authors are careful to avoid the fallacy of using space to explain change, some important observations with regard to the spatial patterns of labour market disadvantage nevertheless do emerge. Green, Gregg and Wadsworth's finding that, in the UK, unemployment inequality has tended to increase markedly within, rather than between, regions, is one especially apt example. In some respects, spatial inequalities can be seen not merely to reflect, but also to accentuate, inequalities in the labour market. Whilst wary of uncritically accepting notions of the 'dual city', Danson and Mooney's review of disadvantage in Glasgow clearly points to the existence of a number of interconnected processes collectively imposing multiple deprivation in some peripheral Glasgow estates. Lawless and Smith's micro-level assessment of the operation of the labour market in Sheffield and York similarly highlights the reality of estate stigmatisation and its concomitant impact on job opportunities for local residents. As many of the contributions in this book make clear, the operation of the labour market, and its implications for social exclusion, is mediated through space.

And fourth, one issue which emerges from many of these pieces is the interconnectedness of those processes and policies which constitute the 'labour market'. So often the evidence presented in these chapters has implications for other labour market trends or interventions. Danson and Mooney's review of disadvantage in Glasgow embraces issues of urban planning and housing policy. Harkness, Machin and Waldfogel's assessment of female employment and income contains important lessons in policy arenas such as low pay, child care and benefits for part-time employees. Williams and Windebank's examination of the paid informal sector raises policy considerations surrounding local demand for informal work and the ability of institutions to embrace and foster such activity. And Beatty and Fothergill's examination of hidden unemployment in UK coalfields raises, as a central policy issue, the inability of local regeneration programmes effectively to re-employ human, and other, resources within new areas of economic activity. One central theme to this book is the degree to which an understanding of trends within, and a consideration of policies relevant to, aspects of the job market, impinge on other dimensions to social exclusion.

Social Exclusion and the Labour Market

Issues of poverty, deprivation and disadvantage have figured prominently in British academic and political debate for more than 30 years. Abel Smith and Townsend (1965) and Townsend (1979), for example, mapped aspects of inequality in the 1960s and 1970s, showing conclusively that the welfare state introduced in the aftermath of the Second World War had not eradicated deprivation. The policy implications this raised were also subject to detailed neighbourhood-level examination by the Community Development Projects (NCDP 1977) and the Inner Area Studies (Department of the Environment 1977). In the post-1979 period, too, issues of poverty and deprivation have remained a central concern for academic and policy communities. The Rowntree research programme on income and wealth, which revealed a widening gap between rich and poor in Britain, has proved particularly significant in this context (Barclay 1995; Hills 1995).

But if issues of poverty and deprivation have figured prominently for more than 30 years, the concept of 'social exclusion' is of more recent vintage. It has emerged out of both transatlantic and, especially, European thinking. In the case of the former, Murray's perspectives on an 'underclass', apparently evident in both North America (Murray 1984) and Britain (Murray 1990), was to receive considerable public and political attention in the late 1980s and early 1990s. More reflective observers of the American scene identified a rather more complex interaction amongst welfare, employment and poverty than that emerging from Murray's analysis (Wilson 1987). In any event, issues of race and associated residential segregation in the US impose an additional tier of complexity still not evident in most disadvantaged areas in Britain (Massey and Denton 1994).

The European case is more pressing and crystallises out a number of policy interventions. The three Poverty programmes, the first of which began in the mid 1970s and the last of which ended in 1994, explored and evaluated mechanisms through which to combat social exclusion via direct intervention and cross-national evaluation through the aegis of a 'Social Exclusion' Observatory (Robbins *et al.* 1994; Room *et al.* 1992). But whereas the Poverty programmes may be perceived as relatively marginal to the main thrust of European Union activity, other manifestations of the growing significance of the social exclusion debate came from other mainstream interventions. Some of these were not surprising. For example the 'Flynn' White Paper on European social policy laid considerable emphasis on initiatives designed to moderate social exclusion (European Commission 1994). Indeed, following Maastricht the whole tenor of political debate within most of the member states, if not the United Kingdom, demonstrated a much stronger commitment towards eradicating social exclusion at the European level, even if the competencies to do so remained uncertain (Berghman 1995). This in turn reflected, at least in part, the thrust of much of the thinking inherent to the Delors White Paper on growth, competitiveness and employment (European Commission 1993). Some of the policies proposed in this White Paper, such as enhancing labour market flexibility, may well act to accentuate social exclusion for some vulnerable groups. But equally so, one of its central messages was the need for policies to address youth, and long-term, unemployment and labour market exclusion.

It is not therefore difficult to see why the issue of social exclusion has come to figure much more prominently in political policy and academic discourse within the UK. It builds on a well-established tradition of policy and deprivation studies; it reflects complementary thinking in the US; and it has been driven by a markedly more 'social' feel to policy interventions emanating from many member states of the EU.

Nevertheless, despite the growing interest in the notion of social exclusion, it remains a slippery concept. In political circles, and to some extent within the policy community too, there has often been little effort systematically to distinguish amongst 'social exclusion', 'poverty', 'deprivation', 'polarisation' and 'differentiation'. In an everyday sense this is entirely understandable. But the introduction of effective policy innovation requires more rigorous definition.

In the context of social exclusion, there are perhaps three definitional axes which merit consideration. Two of these appear generally uncontested. Social exclusion is widely perceived as a process, the end product of which is deprivation. There is hence a strongly dynamic element inherent to social exclusion. Most observers would also agree that social exclusion can manifest itself in various ways. The chapters of this book deal with the relationships between individuals, households and communities on the one hand, and the labour market on the other. But social exclusion is not limited to this nexus.

Other commentators have, for example, explored the dynamics of social exclusion within the housing market (Hamnett 1996; Lee 1994), citizenship (Lowndes 1995) and welfare (Alcock 1997).

However, a third definitional consideration raises rather more complex issues. As those centrally involved in the European Observatory on Policies to Combat Social Exclusion point out, there are at least two broad interpretations of social exclusion (Room 1995). There is a more conservative, and hierarchical, perspective. This perceives society as a, 'status hierarchy or as a set of collectivities, bound together by sets of mutual rights and obligations that are rooted in some broader moral order. Social exclusion is the process of becoming detached from this moral order...' (Room 1995, p.6). One potential implication of this interpretation is that the fundamental causes for social exclusion lie, at least in part, in the behaviour of those being excluded. An alternative interpretation would, however, perceive exclusion in relational terms. This approach accepts that there is a distributional context to social exclusion. Sufficiency of resources available to individuals and households is seen as a factor in creating and sustaining social exclusion. But crucially such deficiencies have to be framed within a relational context. In this perspective, social exclusion emerges out of the effects which institutions, agencies and individuals have on others. Social exclusion, therefore, needs to be seen within a wider interpretation of society which embraces not simply the excluded, but also the included.

The Policy Challenge: Some Guiding Principles

It is not possible, or indeed appropriate, to attempt to provide a comprehensive overview of that full diet of initiatives which might be designed to integrate the socially excluded within the labour market. Instead, in this section, some of the key dilemmas and debates are explored. Four issues are considered:

- the complexities of labour market intervention
- the local/national debate
- the people or places dilemma
- issues of linkage.

The complexities of labour market intervention

The papers collected together in this book, taken within the context of the labour market as a whole, point to a wide range of complexities, many of which will have implications for policy innovation. At one level it is important to stress the symbiotic relationships between analysis and prescription. Policy-makers may frequently be operating within a flawed, if conventional, analytical framework. Martin, for example, in Chapter 1, shows that the traditional approach towards long-term unemployment has been to focus attention on initiatives designed to encourage outflows into employment. But as he points out, evidence suggests that long-term unemployment may be as much a consequence of high unemployment as a cause. If this is the case, intervention might most sensibly be concentrated on intercepting inflows, an approach not traditionally invoked by the policy community.

A number of other contributors highlight issues of analysis and interpretation which have profound, usually unrecognised, implications for policymakers. Green and her colleagues point to the growing urban/rural dimension to unemployment patterns in the UK. Although we have witnessed a wide range of urban initiatives in recent decades, few have tackled the growing imbalance between job opportunities apparent within different parts of the city regions. Opportunities for reverse commuting have, for example, hardly been explored. Beatty and Fothergill re-confirm the substantial under-reporting of unemployment at the local level. Labour market intervention would appear far more pressing if accurate local unemployment statistics were available. In a similar vein, Williams and Windebank stress the close interrelationships between paid informal work and the welfare benefits system. Whatever the specific empirical base for each of these papers, one underlying theme to emerge from all of them is that labour market analysis is complex. Frequently it is too easily circumscribed into ostensibly self-evident truisms. Material contained in these chapters suggests that the analytical cement upon which interventions need to be secured is often inadequate or incomplete. Certainly one common experience for many researchers evaluating local and national programmes designed to moderate labour market inequalities is the degree to which interventions are rarely located within what might reasonably be perceived as a sound, and structured, analytical base.

The complexities of labour market intervention are not, however, limited solely to questions of analytical inadequacy. Any intervention in the labour market will need to be perceived within that constellation of criteria which play an increasing role in policy appraisal and evaluation (HM Treasury 1995). Issues of dead-weight and displacement will be likely to figure prominently. In reality, the former will be a factor likely to be taken into consideration in the evaluation of any policy initiative. Questions of displacement and leakage, whilst by no means confined to labour market interventions, are, however, especially relevant to them. Any subsidy designed to enhance job creation is liable to displace activity and jobs elsewhere. The reviews of enterprise zones, one of whose original objectives was job creation, show how acute this problem can be (Department of the Environment 1995a). Moreover, where attempts have been made specifically to target the benefits of intervention to those living in deprived areas, the limited evidence which is available points to a substantial leakage of benefits. For example, those gaining jobs through urban development grant support for an inner city brewery in Manchester, tended overwhelmingly to use enhanced household income to relocate to more affluent areas (Haughton, Peck and Stewart 1987). In short, intervention in the labour market is fraught with a range of operational complexities. Prescription needs to be rooted in a thorough and pertinent analytical framework. Existing secondary data will not usually reveal the full complexity of local, regional or national labour market dynamics. Moreover, interventions in the labour market are especially subject to the problems of displacement and leakage.

Local / national debates

Should policy innovation be articulated at the local or the national level? This is, of course, in part a false dualism. These options need not be mutually incompatible. A nested hierarchy of interventions might be created appropriate for intervention at international, national, regional and local levels. It can equally be argued that the administrative tier at which interventions are effected is less important than what those interventions might be. Nevertheless, despite these caveats, there are issues of debate pertinent to the scale at which intervention occurs.

At the European scale, the Commission is caught in a potential dilemma. Aspects of its interventions, notably in the Social Chapter emerging out of the 1993 Green Paper on social policy (European Commission 1994) and through the European Social Fund, are designed to moderate social exclusion via training, education, limiting hours of work, and so on. But there are other pressing political imperatives. In part these reflect the determination by the Commission and the 'core' member states to introduce a common currency, an initiative driven by eligibility criteria which are likely to impose markedly deflationary trends throughout Europe.

In addition, some member states, of which Britain is the most obvious example, continue to argue for a more 'flexible' labour market based on supply-side initiatives. The aetiology and consequences of this are discussed by Martin in the first chapter of this book, and by others, in both the American (Galbraith 1992) and the British (Jessop 1994) contexts. As these observers point out, the beneficial implications of these processes are far from clear. In the UK it is not easy to identify substantial, if, indeed, any, longer-term benefits for many in the labour market. Moreover, within the more narrow confines of social exclusion, policies designed to enhance labour market flexibility appear sharply to have accentuated job insecurity and part-time, poorly paid, employment. However, it remains apparent that, if political realities ever allow the European Union to be in a position to provide a more coherent attack on social exclusion, a number of important initiatives could be effected. Programmes which merit prioritisation include a more determined effort to eke 'social' benefits from the Structural Funds, early retirement programmes, encouragement of minimum wages, and job subsidies for the long-term unemployed.

The debate surrounding policy innovation at the national level must, of necessity, focus on questions of welfare. There is ample evidence to suggest that the operation of the social security system conspires to impose a poverty trap for many lower paid workers (Dilnot 1992). For those on the margins of the labour market, enhanced job income may be more than counter-balanced by reduction in welfare benefits. It is not possible here to examine the operation of the social security system in any detail. And, of course, innovations in other national policy arenas such as housing, education, transport and health, all have the capacity to impact on the articulation of social exclusion. But if there is one imperative for a socially reforming government to adopt to moderate social exclusion in the UK, it ought to focus on the dynamics of the poverty trap. This might involve, *inter alia*, introducing minimum wage levels, further relieving taxation on lower income groups and systematically integrating state welfare provision within the dynamics of the extant labour market. The root problem remains that a welfare system has been created which pays little, if any, cognisance to a rapidly changing labour market. And throughout the developed world, and especially within the UK, this interaction between jobs and welfare has, as other observers point out (Esping-Andersen 1993), proved to be a major factor in accentuating social exclusion.

Within the UK, the regional dimension to labour market policy remains relatively modest. It would be hard to argue that, even following the creation of Government Offices for the Regions, the eradication of social exclusion has emerged as a key policy objective in the regions. But two potential developments should be mentioned here. First, this may change. A long period of conservative hegemony has come to an end. There can be no easy assumption that the new Labour government will rapidly move towards regional government in England, or that, even if this were to occur, regional resources of any substantial nature would be made available through which to moderate social exclusion. But over a period of time, it is not inconceivable that elected regional assemblies might emerge which, bearing in mind their likely political composition, might well wish to prioritise social exclusion. And a second point here: comparative evidence does suggest, however, that innovative activity designed to moderate social exclusion can indeed be instigated at the regional or city-regional scale. The European Union has, for example, suggested that the integration of ERDF, spatial planning and community initiatives such as URBAN, is often most effectively developed at the regional scale (European Commission 1995b).

When, too, a detailed evaluation of the relative performance of different city-regions in Europe was attempted in the early 1990s, it became apparent that some cities, mainly by virtue of longer-term strategic partnerships, were proving much more effective than others in achieving economic growth and social cohesion (European Institute of Urban Affairs 1992).

However, many policies and programmes designed to moderate social exclusion will be formulated and implemented by councils, and other agencies, operating at the local level. There are several reasons why this should be so. Local authorities still remain key players in policy innovation. They might have endured a substantial diminution in powers and resources since the late 1970s, but nevertheless they are likely to prove to be the most creative, and pro-active, of local agencies when it comes to questions of social exclusion. This primacy is of particular relevance in the context of the Single Regeneration Budget (SRB). Because of cutbacks in mainstream expenditure, the SRB has rapidly become the major vehicle for socio-economic innovation at the local level. As an early review of the SRB made clear, it has its shortcomings. In particular there has been substantial over-bidding on available resources, and the competitive nature of the initiative inhibits longer-term, strategic, thinking (Centre for Urban and Regional Studies 1995). Nevertheless, the SRB has an important role to play in local strategies designed to moderate social exclusion. Its detailed articulation may, of course, alter as a result of political change at the centre, but the general principles underpinning the SRB are likely to continue, possibly in the guise of a Civic Grant. The SRB provides a locally articulated, integrative and catholic approach to social and economic regeneration.

The continuation of the SRB, or some similar initiative, is of particular relevance to the social exclusion debate. As the Bidding Guidance makes clear, the SRB is designed to address social as well as economic problems, to incorporate relevant agencies such as local authorities and TECs within regeneration strategies, and to liberate and to enhance voluntary sector and community-based resources (Government Offices for the Regions 1994). Within this policy environment, the SRB, or a subsequent equivalent, may well be especially relevant in assisting in the implementation of a wide range of local anti-poverty programmes. These have been subject to recent classification and evaluation (Alcock *et al.* 1995). It would be unrealistic to assume that these programmes, as currently effected, will make a substantial contribution to the eradication of social exclusion. Nevertheless, a range of programmes, such as debt counselling, the decentralisation of local services to areas of need, welfare rights and community economic development, have a key role to play at the local level. In an environment wherein financial pressures on local government are, at the very least, unlikely to moderate, urban regeneration funds are likely to play a crucial role in sustaining these modest, but useful, initiatives.

People or places?

Should social exclusion programmes concentrate on people or places? As with the issue of scale, these options are not mutually exclusive. But nevertheless, there has been a tension between on the one hand, introducing programmes designed to attack social exclusion at the level of the individual or household, and, on the other, area-based strategies. Both approaches have their merits.

There is a strong argument that nationally implemented welfare and income support measures targeted at deprived individuals and households, offer the best strategy through which to moderate social exclusion. For many of those in, or wishing to enter, the labour market, as is discussed above, the most appropriate innovations will include minimum wages, a more equitable relationship between income and benefits, and a recognition of the importance of unpaid work. And for those unlikely to be economically active, notably the young, single parents, the old and the disabled, state welfare represents the single most effective vehicle through which to enhance material standards and assist in social cohesion. The downside of an approach based on individuals and households is, obviously, that of cost. Even if some benefits were subject to income tax – and in some instances, notably child benefit, there is a strong case that they should – any government is likely to pause before effecting policies to welfare and income support programmes which would have the effect of increasing overall public expenditure.

Partly for that reason, governments have consistently sought to confine policy innovation within defined areas. This has, for instance, been a defining feature of both urban and regional policy. The disadvantages of the area approach have, however, been evident for many years: spatial targeting eliminates assistance for those in areas not 'selected' for support; many of those in targeted areas do not merit additional assistance; and the fundamental problems facing those in 'selected areas', such as unemployment, low income, poverty and poor housing, are unlikely to be resolved through locally based initiatives alone.

Yet there are factors which do point to the appropriateness of area-based interventions. Recent work at both the local level (Department of the Environment 1995b) and the local authority scale (Department of the Environment 1996), has indicated the intensity of multiple deprivation apparent at both the neighbourhood scale and within some local authorities as a whole. These trends are confirmed in this book by Green, and Danson and Mooney. If spatial segregation and polarisation are indeed accentuating, this suggests that area-based interventions may be entirely appropriate. It is probably true, too, that some manifestations of social exclusion may best be attacked through locally based activity. Housing is one example, of which more below. But there are others. Community economic development is especially well suited to neighbourhood-based activity. Job creation in fields such as environmental improvements, community care and housing repair, is well suited to localised interventions. There are also possibilities around that somewhat intangible notion of community cohesion. One neglected aspect of the social exclusion debate surrounds the degree to which more disadvantaged households are distanced from mainstream community networks and political channels. Localised interventions around programmes such as estate regeneration can act as a catalyst in assimilating a range of individuals and households within governmental and community institutions. It is not easy to achieve, but it can be done (Cole and Smith 1996).

Issues of Linkage

One of the major challenges facing policy-makers, at national and local levels, is to ensure that initiatives designed to enhance competitiveness and efficiency are able also to sustain goals of equity and inclusion. This has been a perennial dilemma in relation to urban policy for many years. The key innovations of the 1980s, enterprise zones and urban development corporations, laid a heavy emphasis on physical, and to some extent economic, development. The idea that distributional benefits would somehow 'trickle down' to residents in more disadvantaged areas has been widely seen as a bland and over-simplistic assumption. Evidence drawn from urban policy as a whole (Deakin and Edwards 1993), and from specific inner city initiatives (Haughton 1990), suggests that most urban policies bring very limited benefits to the more disadvantaged. Detailed macro-level research funded by the Department of the Environment in the early 1990s further confirmed that substantial inner city investment undertaken in the 1980s and early

1990s, had not improved material circumstances for people in the most deprived of English inner city areas (Department of the Environment 1994).

To its credit the government recognised this. In both of the major urban innovations instigated in the early 1990s, City Challenge and the SRB, efforts have been made, explicitly, to link social objectives to goals of economic efficiency. In the case of SRB, for example, one of the key objectives is to, 'enhance the employment prospects, education and skills of local people, particularly the young and those at a disadvantage' (Government Offices for the Regions 1994, p.5).

However, despite these developments, it would be difficult to argue that urban policy, or indeed other forms of government intervention, have proved especially adept in sustaining social or distributional objectives. Certainly there has been nothing like the same intensity of debate, with regard to linkage, in the UK as has occurred in the US. There, some urban administrations have sought directly to link planning permissions to, say, development levies deposited in community funds. In this instrumentalistic manner, some gains will therefore automatically occur for less disadvantaged residents via, for example, new investment in low cost accommodation, community economic development, local facilities, and so on.

Although notions of linkage within the UK have not been expounded as fully as has been evident in some American cities, there are, nevertheless, genuine opportunities to utilise investment in ways which will bring more in the way of benefits to the disadvantaged and excluded. Two examples might usefully be quoted here. First, the potential linkages between new housing investment and wider community gains are only just being realised (McGregor and McConnachie 1995). Housing expenditure in more deprived localities can create jobs for locals, enhance community skills, assist in the formation of new firms, and provide the disadvantaged with more in the way of managerial, technical and personal skills, and so on. Similar opportunities can be garnered from expenditure in health, education and community care. Policy-makers need to explore more thoroughly the notion of linkage. Many forms of public and private investment have the capacity to achieve a range of socio-economic goals.

Second, the EU has been especially innovative in exploring potential links between its programmes and social cohesion. One example of this is recently completed work examining the potential relationships between Structural Funds and social and economic cohesion within the UK (European Commission 1996b). This study outlines the mechanisms through which coherent and integrated local strategies can be devised which target ERDF and other resources at more disadvantaged areas. Building on exploratory work in Merseyside, the report concludes that community economic development can create and sustain tailored pathways for individuals and households to enable them to (re)engage with the mainstream. The ideas contained within this study may prove difficult to implement fully. But collectively the conclusions and recommendations provide one of the clearest justifications for, and expositions of, linkage yet to appear in Britain.

Conclusion: The Politics of Exclusion

The papers developed in this book present a generally gloomy review of social exclusion in the labour market. However, as is briefly developed in this chapter, there are real opportunities for change. It is not beyond the ability of the EU, combining with national and local governments, to introduce a diet of policies and projects which would help to moderate the more acute manifestations of social exclusion. However, perhaps ultimately the problem is not one of policies, but politics.

For nearly 20 years, in the Anglo-American world, neo-liberal, market-orientated, anti-collectivist thinking has dominated government. In the UK this political legacy has been sustained by a peculiar electoral system which, for example, allowed Mrs Thatcher to gain three electoral triumphs with about 43 per cent of the popular vote. Most people in the country, and even a substantial proportion of Conservatives, saw little of appeal in this message. But via electoral success, and buttressed by a compliant media, radical Conservative governments were able to impose a series of ideological assumptions on the national psyche: unions were bad; nationalised industries were over-manned and inefficient; the labour market needed 'shaking out' and made more flexible; wages had to be competitive; and so on. Whilst there might have been an element of truth in many of these slogans, too often the prevailing political debate was rooted in inaccuracies and misconceptions. Moreover, as several commentators point out in this book and others point out elsewhere (Morgan 1996), after almost two decades of Conservative government, the British economy is characterised by low wages, diminishing long-term investment, high unemployment and job insecurity.

Nevertheless, what progressive thinkers have to accept is that Mrs Thatcher, her colleagues and rightist observers generally, captured the high ground of political debate in the 1980s and into the 1990s. Tapping into strongly held misgivings concerning the power of the unions, Britain's role in Europe and the inefficiencies of nationalised industries, she offered a simple, and ostensibly 'objective', alternative based on opportunism, individualism and privatism. But this vision failed. The mid 1990s now offer new political opportunities. President Clinton has managed to prevent a further shift to the right in America. In Europe, the Union continues to locate questions of social exclusion at the centre of its deliberations. In the UK, after 18 years, the Conservatives have been ejected from office.

However, electoral success for non-rightist parties can no longer be seen as a harbinger of reform. For the Labour Party in the UK, for example, no hints of additional social welfare expenditure are allowed. As long as public sentiment, and hence electoral success, is seen to depend on low taxation, minimalist government and the continued protection of middle-class subsidies, any coherent attack on exclusion is unlikely to occur. In this context reformist thinkers must seize the possibilities emerging from a changing political environment. One of their central objectives must be to reintroduce questions of social stratification to the political agenda. At one level this will mean focusing on the implications and consequences of social exclusion. It will involve tabulating the social and economic costs of unemployment and other manifestations of disadvantage, for society as a whole. But it will also be about concentrating debate on the processes of inclusion. The mechanics of resource allocation in health, education, housing and other markets, tend consistently to benefit more affluent sectors in society. Exclusion is not the outcome of rational people electing to live off a generous welfare system. Rather, it reflects persistent and inequitable outcomes to processes which tend frequently further to marginalise the most disadvantaged. Progressive thinkers need to locate questions of equity, inclusion and exclusion at the centre of civil debate. It is a tall, but not impossible, task.

Bibliography

Abel Smith, B. and Townsend, P. (1965) *The Poor and the Poorest*. London: Bell and Hyman.

Adams, J.D. (1985) 'Permanent differences in unemployment and permanent wage differentials.' *Quarterly Journal of Economics 100*, 29–56.

Alcock, P. (1997) *Understanding Poverty*. 2nd Edition. Basingstoke: Macmillan.

Alcock, P., Craig, G., Dalgleish, K. and Pearson, S. (1995) *Combating Local Poverty; The Management of Anti-Poverty Strategies by Local Government*. Luton: Local Government Management Board.

Allen, J. and Henry, N. (1995) 'Growth at the margins: contract labour in a core region.' In C. Hadjimichalis and D. Sadler (eds) *Europe at the Margins: New Mosaics of Inequality*. London: Wiley.

Alogoskoufis, G., Bean, C., Bertola, G., Cohen, D., Dolado, J. and Saint-Paul, G. (1995) *Unemployment: Choices for Europe*. London: Centre for Economic Policy Research.

Anglin, R. and Holcomb, B. (1992) 'Poverty in urban America: policy options.' *Journal of Urban Affairs 14*, 3/4, 447–468.

Applebaum, E. (1990) 'Unbalanced growth and the US employment expansion.' *Structural Change and Economic Dynamics 1*, 1, 91–101.

Audas, R.P. and MacKay, R.R. (1996) 'A tale of two recessions.' Research Paper 96/21. Bangor: Institute of Economic Research, School of Accounting, Banking and Economics, University of Wales.

Aufhauser, E. (1995) 'Mapping changing patriarchal relations at the regional level: a cohort perspective on gendered life course restructuring.' Paper presented to the European Science Foundation Network on Gender Inequality and the European Regions, Bremen, July.

Auger, D.A. (1993) 'Urban realities, US national policy and the Clinton administration.' *Regional Studies 27*, 8, 807–816.

Baddeley, M., Martin, R.L. and Tyler, P. (1996) 'European regional unemployment: convergence or persistence?' Discussion Paper. Cambridge: Department of Land Economy, University of Cambridge.

Bagguley, P. and Mann, K. (1992) 'Idle thieving bastards? Scholarly representations of the underclass.' *Work, Employment and Society 6*, 113–126.

Barclay, P. (1995) *Inquiry into Income and Wealth*. Volume 1. York: Joseph Rowntree Foundation.

Barro, R. and Sala-I-Martin, X. (1991) 'Convergence across states and regions.' *Brookings Papers on Economic Activity 1*, 107–182.

Barthe, M.A. (1988) *L'economie cachee.* Paris: Syros Alternatives.

Barthelemy, P. (1990) 'Le travail au noir en Belgique et au Luxembourg.' In *Underground Economy and Irregular Forms of Employment.* Final Synthesis Report. Brussels: Office for Official Publications of the European Communities.

Bathelemy, P. (1991) 'La croissance de l'economie southerraine dans les pays occidentaux: un essai d'interpretation.' In J.-L. Lespes (ed) *Les Pratiques Juriediques, Economiques et Sociales Informelles.* Paris: PUF.

Beatty, C. and Fothergill, S. (1994) 'Registered and hidden unemployment in areas of chronic industrial decline: the case of the UK coalfields.' In S. Hardy, G. Lloyd and I. Cundell (eds) *Tackling Unemployment and Social Exclusion: Problems for Regions, Solutions for People.* London: Regional Studies Association.

Beatty, C. and Fothergill, S. (1996) 'Labour market adjustment in areas of chronic industrial decline: the case of the UK coalfields.' *Regional Studies 30,* 7, 627–640.

Beauregard, R.A. (1993) *Voices of Decline: The Post-War Fate of US Cities.* Cambridge, Massachusetts: Blackwell.

Begg, I., Moore, B.C. and Rhodes, J. (1986) 'Economic and social change in urban Britain and the inner cities.' In V. Hausner (ed) *Critical Issues in Urban Economic Development.* Vol. 1, pp.10–44. Oxford: Clarendon Press.

Bell, I. (1995) '"Third World" label drives Glaswegians to despair.' *The Observer,* 11 March.

Benton, L. (1990) *Invisible Factories: The Informal Economy and Industrial Development in Spain.* New York: State University of New York Press.

Berghman, J. (1995) 'Social exclusion in Europe: policy context and analytical framework.' In G. Room (ed) *Beyond the Threshold; The Measurement and Analysis of Social Exclusion.* Bristol: The Policy Press.

Berry, B.J.L. (1985) 'Islands of renewal in seas of decay.' In P. Peterson (ed) *New Urban Reality.* Washington, DC: The Brookings Institute.

Bertola, G. and Ichino, A. (1996) *Wage Inequality and Unemployment: US vs Europe.* London: Discussion Paper No. 1186, Centre for Economic Policy Research.

Bettio, F. and Villa, P. (1996) 'Changing pay differentials and the position of women in the Italian economy.' European perspectives on changing labour markets and equal opportunities. ESRC Seminar Economics of equal opportunities. London School of Economics, May.

Blanchard, O.J. and Diamond, P. (1989) 'Ranking, unemployment duration and wages.' *Review of Economic Studies 61,* 417–434.

Blanchard, O. and Katz, L. (1992) 'Regional evolutions.' *Brookings Papers on Economic Activity 1,* 1–75.

Blanchard, O.J. and Summers, L.H. (1986) *Hysteresis and the European Unemployment Problem.* NEBR Macroeconomics Annual, Cambridge, Massachusetts: MIT Press.

Blanchflower, D.G. and Oswald, A.J. (1995) *The Wage Curve.* Cambridge, Massachusetts: MIT Press.

Boyle, R. (1990) 'Regeneration in Glasgow: stability, collaboration, and inequity.' In D. Judd and M. Parkinson (eds) *Leadership and Urban Regeneration*. Newbury Park, California: Sage.

Brannen, J. and Moss, P. (1991) *Managing Mothers: Dual Earner Households After Maternity Leave*. London: Unwin Hyman.

Braverman, H. (1974) *Labour and Monopoly Capital, The Degradation of Work in the Twentieth Century*. London: Monthly Review Press.

Bruegel, I. and Perrons, D. (1995) 'Where do the costs of unequal treatment fall? An analysis of the incidence of the costs of unequal pay and sex discrimination in the UK.' *Gender, Work and Organization 2*, 3, 113–124.

Bruegel, I. and Perrons, D. (1996) 'Deregulation and women's employment: the diverse experiences of women in Britain.' Gender Institute Discussion Paper No. 2. London School of Economics.

Bryson, A. and McKay, S. (1994) *Is It Worth Working?* London: PSI.

Burgess, S. (1994) *Where did Europe Fail? A Disaggregate Comparison of Net Job Generation in the USA and Europe*. London: Discussion Paper 192, Centre for Economic Performance, London School of Economics.

Cambridge Economic Policy Group (1980) 'Urban and regional policy with provisional regional accounts for 1966–78.' *Cambridge Economic Policy Review 6*.

Cambridge Economic Policy Group (1982) 'Employment problems in the cities and regions of the UK: prospects for the 1980s.' *Cambridge Economic Policy Review 8*.

Campbell, M. and Duffy, K. (1992) *Local Labour Markets: Problems and Policies*. London: Longman.

Castells, M. (1989) *The Informational City*. Cambridge: Blackwell.

Castells, M. (1994) 'European cities, the informational society, and the global economy.' *New Left Review 204*, March–April, 18–32.

Centre for Regional Economic and Social Research (1993) *Bell Farm Skills Survey*. Sheffield: Centre for Regional Economic and Social Research and Survey and Statistical Research Centre.

Centre for Urban and Regional Studies (1995) *The Single Regeneration Budget: The Stocktake*. Birmingham: CURS, University of Birmingham.

Champion, A.G., Green, A.E., Owen, D.W., Ellin, D.J. and Coombes, M.G. (1987) *Changing Places: Britain's Demographic, Economic and Social Complexion*. London: Edward Arnold.

Cheshire, P. (1990) 'Explaining the recent performance of the European Community's major urban regions.' *Urban Studies 27*, 3, 311–333.

Cheshire, P.C. and Hay, D.G. (1989) *Urban Problems in Western Europe*. London: Unwin Hyman.

Chick, V. (1983) *Macroeconomics after Keynes, Reconsideration of the General Theory*. Oxford: Philip Allan.

Cisneros, H.G. (ed) (1993) *Interwoven Destinies: Cities and the Nation*. New York: W.W. Norton.

Cockburn, C. (1991) *In the Way of Women – Men's Resistance to Sex Equality in Organisations.* London: Macmillan.

Coffield, F., Borill, C. and Marshall, S. (1983) 'How young people try to survive being unemployed.' *New Society,* 2 June, 332–334.

Cole, I. and Smith, Y. (1993) *Bell Farm in the Midst of Change.* Sheffield: Centre for Regional Economic and Social Research, Sheffield Hallam University.

Cole, I. and Smith, Y. (1996) *From Estate Action to Estate Agreement: Regeneration and Change on the Bell Farm Estate, York.* Bristol: Policy Press.

Commission of the European Communities (1991) *Employment in Europe.* Luxembourg: Office for Official Publications of the European Communities.

Commission of the European Communities (1993) *European Social Policy: Options for the Union.* Brussels: Com (93).

Commission of the European Communities (1993a) *Medium-Term Action Programme to Combat Exclusion and Promote Solidarity: A New Programme to Support and Stimulate Innovation (1994–1999) and Report on the Implementation of the Community Programme for the Social and Economic Integration of the Least-Privileged Groups (1989–1994).* Brussels: COM (93) 435.

Commission of the European Communities (1993b) *Green Paper: European Social Policy: Options for the Union.* Brussels: COM (93) 551.

Commission of the European Communities (CEC) (1993c) *Growth, Competitiveness and Unemployment.* Brussels: CEC.

Commission of the European Communities (1994) *White Paper: Growth, Competitiveness, Employment: The Challenges and Ways Forward into the 21st Century.* Luxembourg: European Commission.

Community Development Foundation/OECD (1993) *Trickle Down or Bubble Up; The Challenge of Urban Regeneration.* Report of an International Conference. London: CDF.

Conrad, J. (1899, 1983) *Heart of Darkness.* London: Penguin Classics.

Cook, D. (1989) *Rich Law, Poor Law: Different Responses to Tax and Supplementary Benefit Fraud.* Milton Keynes: Open University Press.

Cornuel, D. and Duriez, B. (1985) 'Local exchange and state intervention.' In N. Redclift and E. Mingione (eds) *Beyond Employment.* Oxford: Basil Blackwell.

Cornwall, J. (1990) *The Theory of Economic Breakdown.* Oxford: Basil Blackwell.

Cortesi, G. and Marengo, M. (1992) 'Women in the Italian workplace: evolution of a role.' International Geographical Union Study Group on Gender and Geography. Working Paper 17.

Crompton, R. (1994) 'Occupational trends and women's employment patterns.' In R. Lindley (ed) *Labour Market Structures and Prospects for Women.* Manchester: EOC.

Cross, R. (ed) (1988) *Unemployment, Hysteresis and the Natural Rate Hypothesis.* Oxford: Basil Blackwell.

Dahrendorf, R. (1987) 'The erosion of citizenship and its consequences for us all.' *New Statesman* 12 June, 12–15.

Dallago, R. (1991) *The Irregular Economy: The 'Underground' and the 'Black' Labour Market.* Aldershot: Dartmouth.

Damer, S. (1990) *Glasgow: Going for a Song.* London: Lawrence and Wishart.

Damer, S. (1992) *Last Exit to Blackhill: The Stigmatisation of a Glasgow Housing Scheme.* Glasgow: Centre for Housing Research, University of Glasgow.

Dangschat, J.S. (1994) 'Concentrations of poverty in the landscapes of 'Boomtown' Hamburg: the creation of a new urban underclass?' *Urban Studies 31*, 7, 1133–1147.

Danson, M.W. (1982) 'The industrial structure and labour market segmentation: urban and regional implications.' *Regional Studies 16*, 4, 255–265.

Danson, M.W. (1991) 'The Scottish economy: the development of underdevelopment?' *Planning Outlook 34*, 2, 89–95.

Darwin, C. (1890) *The Descent of Man, and Selection in Relation to Sex.* London: John Murray.

Dawes, L. (1993) *Long-Term Unemployment and Labour Market Flexibility.* Leicester: Centre for Labour Market Studies, University of Leicester.

Deakin, N. and Edwards, J. (1993) *The Enterprise Culture and the Inner City.* London: Routledge.

Decressin, J. and Fatas, A. (1994) Regional Labour Market Dynamics in Europe. Discussion Paper No 1085. Centre for Economic Performance, London School of Economics.

Del Boca, D. and Forte, F. (1982) 'Recent empirical surveys and theoretical interpretations of the parallel economy.' In V. Tanzi (ed) *The Underground Economy in the United States and Abroad.* Lexington: Lexington Books.

Department of the Environment (1977) *Final Report to the Liverpool Inner Area Study, Change or Decay.* London: HMSO.

Department of the Environment (1994) *Assessing the Impact of Urban Policy.* London: HMSO.

Department of Employment (1995) *How Exactly is Unemployment Measured?* London: Department of Employment.

Department of the Environment (1995a) *Second Interim Evaluation of Enterprise Zones.* London: HMSO.

Department of the Environment (1995b) *Socio-Demographic Change and the Inner City.* London: HMSO.

Department of the Environment (1996) *Urban Trends in England, Latest Evidence from the 1991 Census.* London: HMSO.

Dilnot, A. (1992) 'Social security and labour market policy.' In E. McLaughlin (ed) *Understanding Unemployment: New Perspectives on Active Labour Market Policies.* London: Routledge.

Doeringer, P.B. and Piore, M.J. (1985) *Internal Labour Markets and Manpower Analysis.* New York: Sharpe.

Donnison, D. and Middleton, A. (eds) (1987) *Regenerating the Inner City: Glasgow's Experience.* London: Routledge and Kegan Paul.

Donzel, A. (1993) 'Suburban development and policy making in France: the case of Marseilles.' In S. Mangen and L. Hantrais (eds) *Polarisation and Urban Space.* London: Cross-National Research Papers.

Dreze, J.H. and Bean, C.R. (eds) (1990) *Europe's Unemployment Problem.* Cambridge, Massachusetts: MIT Press.

Duffy, K. (1994) *A Local Partnership Approach to Social Policy: The Experience of Poverty 3.* Leicester: De Montfort University.

Duncan, S. (1991) 'The geography of gender division of labour in Britain.' *Transactions of the Institute of British Geographers New Series 16*, 4, 420–439.

Duncan, S. (1996) 'The diverse worlds of European patriarchy.' In M.D. García-Ramon and J. Monk (eds) *Women of the European Union.* London: Routledge.

Dunford, M. and Fielding, A. (1994) 'Greater London, the South East region and the wider Britain: metropolitan polarisation, uneven development and interregional migration.' Brighton, University of Sussex, mimeograph.

Dunford, M. and Perrons, D. (1994) 'Regional inequality, regimes of accumulation and unequal development in contemporary Europe.' *Transactions of the Institute of British Geographers New Series 19*, 2, 163–182.

Dunkerley, M. (1996) *The Jobless Economy?* Cambridge: Polity Press.

Eck, R. Van, and Kazemier, B. (1985) *Swarte Inkonsten uit Arebeid: Resultaten van in 1983 Gehouden Experimentele Enquetes (Black Income Out of Labour: Results from Experimental Surveys Held in 1983).* Den Haag: CBS-Statistische Katernen nr 3, Central Bureau of Statistics.

Economic Report to the President (1991) Washington: US Government Printing Office.

Economic Report to the President (1992) Washington: US Government Printing Office.

Economist Intelligence Unit (1982) *Coping with Unemployment: The Effects on the Unemployed Themselves.* London: Economist Intelligence Unit.

Edwards, J. and Batley, R. (1978) *The Politics of Positive Discrimination.* Andover: Tavistock Publications.

Eichengreen, B. (1990) 'One money for Europe? Lessons from the US currency union.' *Economic Policy 10*, 117–187.

Eichengreen, B. (1993) 'Labour markets and European monetary integration.' In P. Masson and M.P. Taylor (eds) *Policy Issues in the Operation of Currency Unions.* Cambridge: Cambridge University Press.

Eichengreen, B. (1995) 'European monetary unification and regional unemployment.' In L. Ulman, B. Eichengreen and W.T. Dickens (eds) *Labour in an Integrated Europe.* Washington: The Brookings Institute.

Engberson, G., Schuyt, K., Timmer, J. and Van Waarden, F. (1993) *Cultures of Unemployment: A Comparative Look at Long-Term Unemployment and Urban Poverty.* Oxford: Westview.

Esping-Andersen, G. (1990) *The Three Worlds of Welfare Capitalism.* Cambridge: Polity Press.

Esping-Andersen, G. (1993) *Changing Classes; Stratification and Mobility in Post-Industrial Societies.* London: Sage.

European Commission (1993) *Growth, Competitiveness and Employment – the Challenges and Ways Forward into the 21st Century.* Bulletin of the European Communities, Supplement 6/93, Brussels.

European Commission (1994) *European Social Policy – the Way Forward for the Union.* Brussels: COM (94) 333.

European Commission (1995a) *Employment in Europe.* Luxembourg: European Commission.

European Commission (1995b) *Guide to Innovative Actions for Regional Development.* Brussels: European Commission.

European Commission (1996a) *First Report on Economic and Social Cohesion.* Luxembourg: European Commission.

European Commission (1996b) *Social and Economic Inclusion through Regional Development.* Brussels: European Commission.

European Institute of Urban Affairs (1992) *Urbanisation and the Functions of Cities in the European Communities.* DGXVI. Liverpool: Liverpool European Institute of Urban Affairs, John Moores University.

Eurostat (1994) *REGIO: Regional Data Bank.* Luxembourg: Eurostat.

Evans, P. and McCormick, B. (1994) 'The new pattern of regional unemployment: causes and policy significance.' *Economic Journal* May, 633–647.

Fainstein, S.S., Gordon, I. and Harloe, M. (eds) (1992) *Divided Cities.* Cambridge: Blackwell.

Flanagan, R.J. (1987) 'Labour market behaviour and European economic growth.' In R. Lawrence and C. Schultz (eds) *Barriers to European Growth: A Transatlantic View.* Washington, DC: Brookings Institute.

Flanagan, R.J. (1993) 'European wage equalisation since the treaty of Rome.' In L. Ulman, B. Eichengreen and W.T. Dickens (eds) *Labor and an Integrated Europe.* Washington, DC: Brookings Institute.

Foudi, R., Stankiewicz, F. and Vanecloo, N. (1982) 'Chomeurs et economie informelle.' *Cahiers de l'observation du changement social et culturel,* 17, ed. du CNRS, Paris.

Freeman, R. (ed) (1994) *Working Under Different Rules.* New York: Russell Sage.

Freeman, R. (1995) *Doing it Right? The US Labour Market Response to the 1980s–1990s.* Discussion Paper 231, Centre for Economic Performance. London: London School of Economics.

Freeman, R. and Katz, L.F. (1994) 'Rising wage inequality: the United States versus other advanced countries.' In R. Freeman (ed) *Working Under Different Rules.* New York: Russell Sage.

Freud, S. (1930) *Civilisation and its Discontents.* Vol. 21 of Collected Works. London: Hogarth Press.

Gaffikin, F. and Morrisey, M. (1994) 'In pursuit of the holy grail: combating local poverty in an unequal society.' *Local Economy 9*, 100–16.

Galbraith, J.K. (1992) *The Culture of Contentment*. London: Sinclair-Stevenson.

Gallie, D. (1985) 'Directions for the future.' In B. Roberts, R. Finnegan and D. Gallie (eds) *New Approaches to Economic Life: Economic Restructuring, Unemployment and Social Divisions of Labour*. Oxford: Oxford University Press.

Gans, H. (1990) 'Deconstructing the underclass: the term's dangers as a planning concept.' *APA Journal* Summer, 271–277.

Geddes, M. (1994) 'Public services and local economic regeneration in a post-Fordist economy.' In R. Burrows and B. Loader (eds) *Towards a Post-Fordist Welfare State?* London: Routledge.

Geuns, R. Van., Mevissen, J. and Renooy, P. (1987) 'The spatial and sectoral diversity of the informal economy.' *Tijdschrift vor eco. en soc. geografie 78*, 5, 389–398.

Gilbert, N., Burrows, R. and Pollert, A. (eds) (1992) *Fordism and Flexibility: Divisions and Change*. London: Macmillan.

Glasgow City Council (1991) *City Planning Aims For The Next Decade*. Glasgow: GCC Planning Department.

Glasgow City Council (1993) *Glasgow Poverty Profile*. Glasgow: GCC Planning Department.

Glatzer, W. and Berger, R. (1988) 'Household composition, social networks and household production in Germany.' In R.E. Pahl (ed) *On Work: Historical, Comparative and Theoretical Approaches*. Oxford: Basil Blackwell.

Glendinning, C. and Millar, J. (1991) 'Poverty: the forgotten Englishwoman reconstructing research and policy on poverty.' In M. Maclean and D. Groves (eds) *Women's Issues in Social Policy*. London: Routledge.

Glucksmann, M. (1994) 'The work of knowledge and the knowledge of womens work.' In M. Maynard and J. Purvis (eds) *Researching Women's Lives from a Feminist Perspective*. London: Taylor and Francis.

Glyn, A. (1995) 'The assessment: unemployment and inequality.' *Oxford Review of Economic Policy 11*, 1, 1–25.

Glyn, A. and Miliband, D. (eds) (1994) *Paying for Inequality: The Economic Cost of Social Injustice*. London: IPPR/Rivers Oram Press.

Gonas, L. (1995) 'Labour market regimes and gender labour relations.' Paper presented to the European Science Foundation Network on Gender Inequality and the European Regions, Bremen, July.

Gordon, I. (1980) 'Regional unemployment differentials: migration not registration.' *Scottish Journal of Political Economy 27*, 97–102.

Gosling, A., Machin, S. and Meghir, C. (1994) 'What happened to the wages of men since the mid-1960s.' *Fiscal Studies 14*, 63–87.

Government Offices for the Regions (1994) *Bidding Guidance, A Guide to Funding from the Single Regeneration Budget*. London: HMSO.

Green, A.E. (1994) *The Geography of Poverty and Wealth.* Coventry: University of Warwick Institute for Employment Research.

Green, A.E. (1995) 'Discrimination and exclusion: comparative experiences.' Closing plenary discussion, Regional Futures Conference, Regional Studies Conference, Gothenberg, May.

Green, A.E., Owen, D. and Winnett, C. (1994) 'The changing geography of recession: analyses of local unemployment times series.' *Transactions of the Institute of British Geographers 19*, 142–162.

Green, A.E. (1995a) 'A comparison of alternative measures of unemployment.' *Environment and Planning A 27*, 535–556.

Green, A.E. (1995b) 'The changing structure, distribution and spatial segregation of the unemployed and economically inactive in Great Britain.' *Geoforum 26*, 373–394.

Green, A.E. and Owen, D.W. (1991) 'Local labour supply and demand interactions in Britain during the 1980s.' *Regional Studies 25*, 4, 295–314.

Green, A.E. and Owen, D.W. (1995) 'A labour market definition of disadvantage: towards an enhanced local classification.' Report to the Department for Education and Employment.

Green, A.E. and Owen, D.W. (1996) 'A labour market definition of disadvantage: towards an enhanced local classification.' *Department for Education and Employment Research Series 11.* London: HMSO.

Greene, R. (1991) 'Poverty concentration measures and the urban underclass.' *Economic Geography 67*, 240–252.

Gregg, P. (1994) 'Out for the count: a social scientist's analysis of unemployment statistics in the UK.' *Journal of the Royal Statistical Society A 157*, 253–270.

Gregg, P. and Machin, S. (1994) 'Is the UK rise in inequality different?' In R. Barrell (ed) *The UK Labour Market.* Cambridge: Cambridge University Press.

Gregg, P. and Wadsworth, J. (1994) 'Women, households and access to employment: who gets it and why?' Paper presented to the EOC Economics of Equal Opportunities Seminar, Wilmslow, October.

Gregg, P. and Wadsworth, J. (1995) 'A short history of labour turnover, job tenure, and job security, 1975–93.' *Oxford Review of Economic Policy 11*, 73–90.

Gregg, P. and Wadsworth, J. (1996) 'More work in fewer households. In J. Hills (ed) *The New Inequality.* Cambridge: Cambridge University Press.

Gregson, N. and Lowe, M. (1994) *Servicing the Middle Classes: Class, Gender and Waged Domestic Labour in Contemporary Britain.* London: Routledge.

Gregory, J. and O'Reilly (1995) 'Checking out and cashing up: the prospects and paradox of regulating part-time work in Europe.' In R. Crompton, D. Gallie and K. Purcell (eds) *Changing Forms of Employment: Organisation, Skills and Gender.* London: Routledge.

Griffin, G., Wood, S. and Knight, J. (1992) *The Bristol Labour Market*. Employment Department Research Paper 82. Leicester: Centre for Labour Market Studies, University of Leicester.

Gutmann, P.M. (1978) 'Are the unemployed, unemployed?' *Financial Analysts Journal* 35, Sept–Oct, 26–27.

Guy, N. (1994) *Dole not Coal: Redundant Miners Survey*. Barnsley: Coalfield Communities Campaign.

Hadjimichalis, C. and Vaiou, D. (1989) 'Whose flexibility? The politics of informalisation in Southern Europe.' Paper presented in April to the IAAD/SCG Study Groups of the IBG Conference on Industrial Restructuring and Social Change: The Dawning of a New Era of Flexible Accumulation?, Durham.

Hall, P. (ed) (1989) *The Political Power of Economic Ideas: Keynesianism Across Countries*. Princeton: Princeton University Press.

Hamnett, C. (1994) 'Social polarisation in global cities: theory and evidence.' *Urban Studies 31*, 3, 401–424.

Hamnett, C. (1996) 'Social polarisation, economic restructuring and welfare state regimes.' *Urban Studies 33*, 1407–1430.

Hanson, S. and Pratt, G. (1992) 'Dynamic interdependencies: a geographical investigation of local labour markets.' *Economic Geography 68*, 4, 373–405.

Harkness, S. (1996) 'The gender earnings gaps: evidence from the UK.' *Fiscal Studies 17*, 2, 1–36.

Harkness, S., Machin, S. and Waldfogel, J. (1995) 'Evaluating the pin money hypothesis: the relationship between women's labour market activity, family income and poverty in Britain.' WSP Discussion Paper 103, STICERD.

Harloe, M., Pickvance, C. and Urry, J. (1990) *Place, Policy and Politics: Do Localities Matter?* Andover: Tavistock Publications.

Harvey, D. (1989) *The Condition of Post-Modernity*. Oxford: Basil Blackwell.

Hasluck, C. (1994a) *People and Skills in North East Wales*. Coventry: IER, University of Warwick.

Hasluck, C. (1994b) *People and Skills in Southern Derbyshire*. Coventry: IER, University of Warwick.

Hasluck, C., Siora, G. and Green, A.E. (1995) *People and Skills in Central London*. Coventry: IER, University of Warwick.

Haughton, G. (1990) 'Targeting jobs to local people: the British urban policy experience.' *Urban Studies 27*, 185–198.

Haughton, G., Peck, J. and Stewart, A. (1987) 'Local jobs and local houses for local workers; a critical analysis of spatial employment targeting.' *Local Economy 2*, 201–207.

Heath, A. (1992) 'The attitudes of the underclass.' In D. Smith (ed) *Understanding the Underclass*. London: Policy Studies.

Hellberger, C. and Schwarze, J. (1987) 'Nebenerwerbstatigkeit: ein indikator fur arbeitsmarkt-flexibilitat oder schattenwirtschaft.' *Wirschaftsdienst 2*, 83–90.

Hills, J. (1995) *Inquiry into Income and Wealth, Volume 2, A Summary of the Evidence.* York: Joseph Rowntree Foundation.

HM Treasury (1995) *A Framework for the Evaluation of Regeneration Projects and Programmes.* London: HM Treasury.

Houseman, S.N. and Abraham, K.G. (1990) 'Regional labour market responses to demand shocks: a comparison of the United States and West Germany.' Paper presented at the Conference of the Association for Public Policy and Management, San Francisco (October).

Howe, L.E.A. (1988) 'Unemployment, doing the double and local labour markets in Belfast.' In C. Cartin and T. Wilson (eds) *Ireland from Below: Social Change and Local Communities in Modern Ireland.* Dublin: Gill and Macmillan.

Hughes, M.A. (1989) 'Mis-speaking truth to power: a geographical perspective on the "underclass" fallacy'. *Economic Geography 65,* 189–207.

Hula, R.C. (1990) 'The two Baltimores.' In D. Judd and M. Parkinson (eds) *Leadership and Urban Regeneration.* Newbury Park, California: Sage.

Humphries, J. and Rubery, J. (1992) 'The legacy for women's employment: integration, differentiation and polarisation.' In J. Michie (ed) *The Economic Legacy 1972–1992.* London: Academic Press.

Hutton, W. (1995) *The State We're In.* London: Jonathan Cape.

International Labour Office (ILO) (1995) *World Employment Report.* Geneva: ILO.

Jackman, R. (1995) *Unemployment and Wage Inequality in OECD Countries.* Discussion Paper 235. Centre for Economic Performance. London: London School of Economics.

Jackman, R. and Savouri, S. (1991) *Regional Wage Determination in Great Britain.* Discussion Paper No.47. London: Centre for Economic Performance.

Jahoda, M. (1982) *Employment and Unemployment: A Social-Psychological Analysis.* Cambridge: Cambridge University Press.

Jessop, B. (1994) 'The transition to post-Fordism and the Schumpeterian workforce state.' In R. Burrows and B. Loader (eds) *Towards a Post-Welfare State?* London: Routledge.

Jones, D. (1992) 'Unemployment resistance and labour mobility in the UK: a spatial perspective.' In C.H.A. Verhaar and L.G. Jansma (eds) *On the Mysteries of Unemployment.* Amsterdam: Kluwer.

Jones, D. and Martin, R.L. (1986) 'Voluntary and involuntary turnover in the labour force.' *Scottish Journal of Political Economy 33,* 124–144.

Joshi, H. and Davies, H. (1993) 'Mother's human capital and childcare in Britain.' *National Institute Economic Review.* November, 50–63.

Kalecki, M. (1943, 1972) 'Political aspects of full employment.' In E.K. Hunt and J.G. Scwartz (eds) *A Critique of Economic Theory.* Middlesex: Penguin Modern Economic Readings.

Kasarda, J.D. (1990) 'Structural factors affecting the location and timing of urban underclass growth.' *Urban Geography 11,* 3, 234–264.

Kasarda, J.D. (1993) 'Inner city concentrated poverty and neighbourhood distress: 1970–1990.' *Housing Policy Debate 4*, 253–285.

Katz, M.B. (1989) *The Undeserving Poor.* New York: Pantheon Books.

Keating, M. (1988) *The City That Refused To Die.* Aberdeen: Aberdeen University Press.

Keating, M. (1989) 'The disintegration of urban policy: Glasgow and the New Britain.' *Urban Affairs Quarterly 24*, June, 513–536.

Keating, M. and Boyle, R. (1986) *Remaking Urban Scotland.* Edinburgh: Edinburgh University Press.

Keeble, D., Owens, P. and Thompson, C. (1982) 'Regional accessibility and economic potential in the European Community.' *Regional Studies 16*, 6, 419–432.

Kesteloot, C. and Meert, H. (1994) 'Les fonctions socio-economiques de l'economie informelle et son implantation spatiale dans les villes belges.' Paper presented to International Conference on Cities, Enterprises and Society at the Eve of the XXIst Century, Lille.

Keynes, J.M. (1933, 1972) *Essays in Persuasion.* Collected Writings Vol. 9. London: Macmillan.

Keynes, J.M. (1936, 1973) *The General Theory of Employment, Interest and Money.* Collected Writings Vol. 7. London: Macmillan.

Keynes, J.M. (1937, 1973) *The General Theory and After. Part 2: Defence and Development.* Vol 14. London: Macmillan.

Keynes, J.M. (1943, 1980) *Shaping the Post-War World: Employment and Commodities.* Collected Writings Vol. 27. London: Macmillan.

Keynes, J.M. (1944, 1980) *Activities 1941–46 in Shaping the Post-War World.* Bretton Woods Collected Writings Vol. 26. London: Macmillan.

Keynes, J.M. (1945, 1980) *Shaping the Post-War World: Employment and Commodities.* Collected Writings Vol. 27. London: Macmillan.

Klerk, L. de and Vijgen, J. (1985) 'Cities in post-industrial perspective: new economies, new lifestyles – new chances?' *Grote steden: verval of innovatie*, Reader ASVS, Lustrum Congress.

Kornai, J. (1971) *Anti-Equilibrium.* Oxford: North Holland.

Krugman, P. (1990) *The Age of Diminished Expectations.* Cambridge, Massachusetts: MIT Press.

Krugman, P. (1994a) *Inequality and the Political Economy of Eurosclerosis.* Discussion Paper 867. London: Centre for Economic Policy Research.

Krugman, P. (1994b) Europe Jobless, America Penniless. *Foreign Policy*, Fall.

Land, H. (1978) 'Who cares for the family?' *Journal of Social Policy 7*, 3, 257–284.

Lane, C. (1993) 'Gender and the labour market in Europe: Britain, Germany and France compared.' *Sociological Review 41*, 2, 274–301.

Lawless, P., Smith, Y. and Short, J. (1993) *Thorpe/Kelvin Skills Survey.* Sheffield: Centre for Regional Economic and Social Research, Sheffield Hallam University.

Lawlor, J. (1990) 'Monthly unemployment statistics: maintaining a consistent series.' *Employment Gazette*, December.

Layard, R. (1989) *European Unemployment: Cause and Cure.* Discussion Paper No 368. London: Centre for Economic Performance.

Layard, R. and Bean, C.R. (1990) 'Why does unemployment persist?' In S. Honkapohja (ed) *The State of Macroeconomics.* Oxford: Basil Blackwell.

Layard, R. and Nickell, S. (1985) 'The causes of British unemployment.' *National Economic Review 111,* 62–85.

Layard, R., Nickell, S. and Jackman, R. (1991) *Unemployment: Macroeconomic Performance and the Labour Market.* Oxford: Oxford University Press.

Lee, G. (1987) 'Implications of the social construction of stigma: the principle, policy and practice of equal opportunity.' In G. Lee and R. Loveridge (eds) *The Manufacture of Disadvantage.* Milton Keynes: Open University Press.

Lee, P. (1994) 'Housing and spatial deprivation: Relocating the underclass and the new urban poor.' *Urban Studies 31,* 7, 1191–1209.

Lee, R. (1988) 'Urban transformation: from problems in to problems of the city.' In D.T. Herbert and D.M. Smith (eds) *Social Problems and the City: New Perspectives.* Oxford: Oxford University Press.

Legrain, C. (1982) 'L'economie informelle a Grand Failly.' *Cahiers de l'OCS,* no.7. Paris: CNRS.

Leibfried, S. and Ostner, I. (1991) 'The participation of West German welfare capitalism: the case of women's social security.' In M. Adler and A. Sinfield (eds) *The Sociology of Social Security.* Edinburgh: Edinburgh University Press.

Leonard, M. (1994) *Informal Economic Activity in Belfast.* Adlershot: Avebury.

Leontidou, L. (1993) 'Informal strategies of unemployment relief in Greek cities: the relevance of family, locality and housing.' *European Planning Studies 1,* 1, 43–68.

Lever, W. (1993) 'Competition within the European urban system.' *Urban Studies 30,* 6, 935–948.

Lever, W. and Moore, C. (eds) (1986) *The City in Transition: Policies and Agencies for the Regeneration of Clydeside.* London: Oxford University Press.

Lewis, J. (1992) 'Gender and the development of welfare regimes.' *Journal of European Social Policy 2,* 3, 159–173.

Lindley, R. (ed) (1992) *Women's Employment: Britain in the Single European Market.* London: HMSO.

Littman, M.S. (1991) 'Poverty areas and the 'underclass': untangling the web.' *Monthly Labor Review,* March, 19–32.

Lobo, F.M. (1990) 'Irregular work in Spain.' In *Underground Economy and Irregular Forms of Employment.* Final Synthesis Report. Brussels: Office for Official Publications of the European Communities.

Loveridge, R. (1987) 'Stigma: the manufacture of disadvantage.' In G. Lee and R. Loveridge (eds) *The Manufacture of Disadvantage.* Milton Keynes: Open University.

Lowndes, V. (1995) 'Citizenship and urban politics.' In D. Judge, G. Stoker and H. Wolman (eds) *Theories of Urban Politics.* London: Sage.

MacDonald, M. (1995) 'The empirical challenge of feminist economics.' In E. Kuiper and J. Sap (eds) *Out of the Margin: Feminist Perspectives on Economic Theory*. London: Routledge.

MacGregor, S. (1994) 'The semantics and politics of urban poverty.' In S. Mangen and L. Hantrais (eds) *Polarisation and Urban Space*. Loughborough: Cross-National Research Papers.

Machin, S. (1995) *Changes in the Relative Demand for Skills in the UK Labour Market*. Discussion Paper 221. London: Centre for Economic Performance, London School of Economics.

Machin, S. (1996) 'Wage inequality in the UK.' *Oxford Review of Economic Papers 12*, 47–64.

MacKay, R.R. (1993) 'Local labour markets, regional development and human capital.' *Regional Studies 27*, 8, 783–795.

MacKay, R.R. (1994) 'Automatic stabilisers, European union and national unity.' *Cambridge Journal of Economics 18*, 6, 571–585.

MacKay, R.R. (1995) 'Non-market forces, the nation state and the European union.' *Papers in Regional Science 74*, 3, 209–231.

MacKay, R.R. and Jones, D.R. (1989) *Labour Markets in Distress: The Denial of Choice*. Aldershot: Gower.

Maddison, A. (1991) *Dynamic Forces in Capitalist Development: A Long-Run Comparative View*. Oxford: Oxford University Press.

Malone, A. (1994) 'A beggar's banquet.' *Sunday Times*, 20 February, p.1.14.

Marcuse, P. (1989) '"Dual city": a muddy metaphor for a quartered city.' *International Journal of Urban and Regional Research 13*, 4, 697–708.

Marris, D. and Rein, M. (1974) *Dilemmas of Social Reform, Poverty and Community Action in the US*. 2nd edition. Harmondsworth: Pelican.

Marston, S.T. (1985) 'Two views of the geographical distribution of unemployment.' *Quarterly Journal of Economics 110*, 57–79.

Martin, C. and Roberts, J. (1984) *Women and Employment, A Lifetime Perspective*. London: HMSO.

Martin, R.L. (ed) (1981) *Regional Wage Inflation and Unemployment*. London: Pion.

Martin, R.L. (1984) 'Redundancies, labour turnover and employment contraction in the recession.' *Regional Studies 18*, 445–458.

Martin, R.L. (1986) 'Getting the labour market into geographical perspective.' *Environment and Planning A*, 18, 569–572.

Martin, R.L. (1993) 'Remapping British regional policy: the end of the North–South divide?' *Regional Studies 27*, 797–806.

Martin, R.L. (1995) 'Income and poverty inequlaities across regional Britain: the North-South divide lingers on.' In C. Philo (ed) *Off the Map: The Social Geography of Poverty in the UK*. London: CPAG.

Martin, R.L. (1997) 'Regional unemployment disparities and their dynamics.' *Regional Studies 31*, 3, 237–252.

Martin, R.L. and Sunley, P. (1997) Regional Unemployment Flows and the Geography of Unemployment. Paper submitted to *Environment and Planning, A*.

Martin, R.L., Sunley, P. and Wills, J. (1996) *Union Retreat and the Regions: The Shrinking Landscape of Organised Labour*. London: Jessica Kingsley Publishers.

Martin, S. and Roberts, J. (1984) *Women and Employment: A Lifetime Perspective*. Social Survey Report SS1143. London: HMSO.

Marx, K. (1975) *Early Writings*. R. Livingston and G. Benton (trans). Harmondsworth: Penguin and New Left Review.

Massey, D.S. and Denton, N.A. (1988) 'The dimensions of residential segregation.' *Social Forces 67*, 281–315.

Massey, D.S. and Denton, N.A. (1994) *American Apartheid, Segregation and the Making of the Underclass*. London: Harvard University Press.

Matthews, K. (1983) 'National income and the black economy.' *Journal of Economic Affairs 3*, 261–267.

Mayer, M. (1992) 'The shifting local political system in European cities.' In M. Dunford and G. Kafkalas (eds) *Cities and Regions in the New Europe*. London: Belhaven.

Maynard, M. (1994) 'Methods, practice and epistemology: the debate about feminism and research.' In M. Maynard and J. Purvis (eds) *Researching Women's Lives from a Feminist Perspective*. London: Taylor and Francis.

McDowell, L. (1991) 'Life without father and Ford: the new gender order of post-Fordism.' *Transactions of the Institute of British Geographers 16*, 4, 400–419.

McDowell, L. and Court, G. (1994) 'Gender divisions of labour in the post-Fordist economy: the maintenance of occupational sex segregation in the financial services sector.' *Environment and Planning A 26*, 9, 1397–1418.

McDowell, L. and Massey, D. (1984) 'A woman's place.' In D. Massey and J. Allen (eds) *Geography Matters*. Cambridge: Cambridge University Press.

McGregor, A. and McConnachie, M. (1995) 'Social exclusion, urban regeneration and economic reintegration.' *Urban Studies 32*, 1587–1600.

Metcalf, H. and Leighton, P. (1989) The Under-Utilisation of Women in the Labour Market. Institute of Manpower Services, Report 172. Brighton: University of Sussex.

Meulders, D., Plasman, R. and Vander Stricht, V. (1993) *Position of Women on the Labour Market in the European Community*. Aldershot: Dartmouth.

Michie, J. and Grieve Smith, J. (eds) (1994) *Unemployment in Europe*. London: Academic Press.

Miguelez, F. and Recio, A. (1986) 'Catalunya: la economia ignota.' In *Economia Sumergida en Espana*. Valencia: Institut Alfons el Magnanim.

Miller, R. (1988) *The End of Unemployment*. Hartfield: Atlas Economic Research Foundation.

Mingione, E. (1991) *Fragmented Societies: A Sociology of Economic Life Beyond the Market Paradigm*. Oxford: Basil Blackwell.

Mingione, E. (1993) 'The new urban poverty and the underclass: introduction.' *International Journal of Urban and Regional Research 17.*

Mingione, E. and Morlicchio, E. (1993) 'New forms of urban poverty in Italy: risk path models in the North and South.' *International Journal of Urban and Regional Research 17,* 3, 413–427.

Mogensen, G.V. (1985) Sort arbejde i Danmark. Copenhagen: Institut for Nationalokonomi.

Mollenkopf, J.H. and Castells, M. (eds) (1991) *Dual City: Restructuring New York.* New York: Russell Sage Foundation.

Mooney, G. (1994) 'The Glasgow regeneration alliance: the way forward for peripheral estates?' *Regions 192,* August.

Morgan, J. (1996) 'Labour market recoveries in the UK and other OECD countries.' *Labour Market Trends 104,* 529–539.

Morrill, R.L. (1991) 'On the measure of geographic segregation.' *Geography Research Forum 11,* 25–36.

Morris, L. (1987) 'Local polarisation: a case study of Hartlepool.' *International Journal of Urban and Regional Research 11,* 3, 331–349.

Morris, L. (1990) *The Workings of the Household: A US UK Comparison.* Cambridge: Polity Press.

Morris, L. (1993) 'Is there a British underclass?' *International Journal of Urban and Regional Research 17,* 3, 404–412.

Morris, L. (1994a) *Dangerous Classes.* London: Routledge.

Morris, L. (1994b) 'Informal aspects of social divisions.' *International Journal of Urban and Regional Research 18,* 112–126.

Murray, C. (1984) *Losing Ground: American Social Policy 1950–1980.* New York: Basic Books.

Murray, C. (1989) 'Underclass.' *The Sunday Times Magazine,* 26 November, p.30.

Murray, C. (1990) *The Emerging British Underclass.* London: Institute of Economic Affairs.

Murray, C. (1994) *Underclass: The Crisis Deepens.* London: Institute of Economic Affairs.

National Community Development Projects (1977) *Gilding the Ghetto, The State and Poverty Experiments.* London: CDP Inter Project Editorial Team.

Neathey, F. and Hurstfield, J. (1995) *Flexibility in Practice: Women's Employment and Pay in Retail and Finance.* EOC/IRS Discussions Series no 16.

Neumann, G. and Topel, R. (1991) 'Employment risk, diversification and unemployment.' *Quarterly Journal of Economics 56,* 4, 1341–1366.

Nicaise. I., Bollens, J., Dawes, L., Laghaei, S., Thaulow, I., Verdie, M. and Wagner, A. (1994) *Pitfalls and Dilemmas in Labour Market Programmes for Disadvantaged Groups – and How to Avoid Them.* Leuven: HIVA, KU Leuven.

Noble, M. and Turner, R. (1985) 'The moral implications of unemployment and the hidden economy in a Scottish Village.' ESRC End of Award Report, Award no. G00232114.

OECD (1989) Regional unemployment in OECD countries. *Employment Outlook* (July). Paris: OECD.

OECD (1994a) *The OECD Jobs Study: Facts, Analyses, Strategies.* Paris: Organisation for Economic Co-operation and Development.

OECD (1994b) *The OECD Jobs Study, Part I: Labour Market Trends and Underlying Forces of Change.* Paris: Organisation Economic Co-operation and Development.

OECD (1994c) *The OECD Jobs Study, Part II: The Adjustment Potential of the Labour Market.* Paris: Organisation Economic Co-operation and Development.

Olson, M. (1965) *The Logic of Collective Action.* Cambridge, Massachusetts: Harvard University Press.

Oppenheim, C. (1993) *Poverty: The Facts.* London: Poverty Publications.

Oswald, A.J. (1994) *Four Pieces of the Unemployment Puzzle.* Discussion Paper. London: London School of Economics. Centre for Economic Performance.

Owen, D.W. (1993) *Ethnic Minorities in Great Britain: Economic Characteristics.* Census Statistical Paper 3. Coventry: NEMDA, Centre for Research in Ethnic Relations, University of Warwick.

Owen, D.W. (1994) 'Spatial variations in ethnic minority group populations in Great Britain.' *Population Trends 78,* 23–33.

Owen, D.W. and Green, A.E. (1989) 'Labour market accounts for travel-to-work areas 1981–84.' *Regional Studies 23,* 1, 27–42.

Pacione, M. (1986) 'The changing pattern of deprivation in Glasgow.' *Scottish Geographical Magazine 102,* 97–109.

Pacione, M. (1990) 'A tale of two cities: the migration of the urban crisis in Glasgow.' *Cities 7,* 4, 304–314.

Pacione, M. (1993) 'The geography of the urban crisis: some evidence from Glasgow.' *Scottish Geographical Magazine 109,* 87–95.

Pahl, R.E. (1984) *Divisions of Labour.* Oxford: Basil Blackwell.

Pahl. R.E. (1985) 'The politics of work.' *The Political Quarterly 56,* 4, 331–345.

Pahl, R.E. (1990) 'The black economy in the United Kingdom.' In *Underground Economy and Irregular Forms of Employment.* Final Synthesis Report. Brussels: Office for Official Publications of the European Communities.

Payne, G. (1977) 'Occupational transition in advanced industrial societies.' *Sociological Review 25,* 387–427.

Peck, J. (1992) 'Labour and agglomeration: control and flexibility in local labour markets.' *Economic Geography 68,* 4, 325–347.

Peck, J. (1994) 'Regulating labour: the social regulation and reproduction of local labour Markets.' In A. Amin and N. Thrift (eds) *Globalization, Institutions, and Regional Development in Europe.* Oxford: Oxford University Press.

Peck, J. (1996) *Work-Place: The Social Regulation of Labour.* New York: Guilford Press.

Pekkarinen, J., Pohjola, M. and Rowthorn, B. (1992) *Social Corporatism: A Superior Economic System?* Oxford: Clarendon Press.

Perrons, D. (1992) 'Regions and the single market.' In M. Dunford and G. Kafkalas (eds) *Cities and Regions in the New Europe*. London: Belhaven.

Perrons, D. (1995a) 'Economic strategies, welfare regimes and gender equality in European employment.' *European Urban and Regional Studies 2*, 2, 99–120.

Perrons, D. (1995b) 'Gender inequalities in regional development.' *Regional Studies 29*, 5, 465–476.

Pestieau, P. (1984) 'Belgium's irregular economy.' Paper Collogue IV, Economie Parallele, ULB, Brussels.

Pfau-Effinger, B. (1994) 'The gender contract and part-time paid work by women – Finland and Germany compared.' *Environment and Planning A 26*, 9, 1355–1376.

Pfau-Effinger, B. (1995) 'Social change in the gendered division of labour in cross-national perspective.' Second European conference of sociology, working group, Gender Relations and the labour market in Europe, Budapest, September.

Phelps Brown, M.J. (1990) 'The control of cost push.' *Political Quarterly 61*, 1, 8–22.

Phelps, E. (1980) 'The statistical theory of racism and sexism.' In A. Amsden (ed) *The Economics of Women and Work*. Harmondsworth: Penguin Books.

Phillips, K. (1990) *The Politics of Rich and Poor: Wealth and the American Electorate in the Reagan Aftermath*. New York: Random House.

Pinch, S. (1993) 'Social polarisation: a comparison of the evidence from Britain and the United States.' *Environment and Planning A 25*, 6, 779–795.

Pinch, S. and Storey, A. (1991) 'Social polarisation in a buoyant labour market: the Southampton case – a response to Pahl, Dale and Bamford.' *International Journal of Urban and Regional Research 15*, 3, 453–460.

Piore, M.J. (1987) 'Historical perspectives and the interpretation of unemployment.' *Journal of Economic Literature 25*, 4, 1834–1850.

Pissarides, C. and Wadsworth, J. (1989) 'Unemployment and the inter-regional mobility of labour.' *Economic Journal* September, 739–755.

Platenga, J. (1994) 'Part-time work and equal opportunities: the case of the Netherlands.' Paper presented to the EOC Economics of Equal Opportunities Seminar, Wilmslow, October.

Pollert, A. (ed) (1991) *Farewell to Flexibility*. Oxford: Basil Blackwell.

Portes, A. and Castells, M. (1989) 'World underneath: the origin, dynamics and effects of the informal economy.' In A. Portes, M. Castells and L. Benton (eds) *The Informal Economy: Studies in Advanced and Less Developed Countries*. Baltimore: Johns Hopkins University.

Portes, A., Castells, M. and Benton, L. (1989) (eds) *The Informal Economy: Studies in Advanced and Less Developed Countries*. Baltimore: Johns Hopkins University Press.

Pratt, G. and Hanson, S. (1991) 'On the links between home and work: family household strategies in a buoyant labour market.' *International Journal of Urban and Regional Research 115*, 1, 55–74.

Priestley, J.B. (1934, 1994) *English Journey*. London: Mandarin.

Quah, D. (1994) *Convergence Empirics Across Economies with (some) Capital Mobility.* Department of Economics Working Paper. London: London School of Economics.

Reissert, B. (1994) 'Unemployment compensation and the labour market: a European perspective.' In S. Mangen and L. Hantrais (eds) *Unemployment, the Informal Economy and Entitlement to Benefits.* Loughborough: Cross-National Research Papers, European Research Centre, Loughborough University.

Renooy, P. (1990) *The Informal Economy: Meaning, Measurement and Social Significance.* Amsterdam: Netherlands Geographical Studies no.115.

Robbins, D. *et al.* (1994) *National Policies to Combat Social European Commission Exclusion. Third Annual Report of the EC Observatory on Policies to Combat Social Exclusion.* Brussels: European Commission.

Robson, B. (1989) 'Social and economic futures for the large city.' In D.T. Herbert and D.M. Smith (eds) *Social Problems and the City: New Perspectives.* Oxford: Oxford University Press.

Robson, B., Bradford, M. and Tye, R. (1995) 'A matrix of deprivation in English authorities.' In Department of the Environment (ed) *1991 Deprivation Index: A Review of Approaches and a Matrix of Results.* London: HMSO.

Rodgers, G. and Rodgers, J. (1989) *Precarious Jobs in Labour Market Regulation: The Growth of Atypical Employment in Western Europe.* Geneva: International Labour Organisation.

Rodriguez-Pose, A. (1994) 'Socioeconomic restructuring and regional change: rethinking growth in the European Community.' *Economic Geography 70,* 4, 325–343.

Room, G. (ed) (1990) *New Poverty in the European Community.* London: Macmillan.

Room, G. *et al.* (1992) *National Policies to Combat Social Exclusion. Second Annual Report of the EC Observatory on Policies to Combat Social Exclusion.* Brussels: European Commission.

Room, G. (1995) 'Poverty and social exclusion: a new European agenda for policy and research.' In G. Room (ed) *Beyond the Threshold: The Measurement and Analysis of Social Exclusion.* Bristol: Policy Press.

Rosanvallon, P. (1980) 'Le developpement de l'economie souterraine et l'avenir des societes industrielles.' *Le debat,* no. 2.

Rowntree Foundation (1995) *Inquiry into Income and Wealth.* York: Rowntree Foundation.

Rowthorn, R.E. and Glyn, A. (1990) 'The diversity of unemployment experience since 1973.' *Structural Change and Economic Dynamics 1,* 1, 57–89.

Royal Statistical Society (1995) *Report of the Working Party on the Measurement of Unemployment in the UK.* London: Royal Statistical Society.

Rubery, J. (1989) 'Labour market flexibility in Britain.' In F. Green (ed) *The Restructuring of the UK Economy.* Hemel Hempstead: Harvester Wheatsheaf.

Rubery, J. (1992a) *Industrial Change, Retraining and Redeployment.* Employment Committee Report, Appendix 7. HCP 71, London: HMSO.

Rubery, J. (1992b) 'Pay gender and the social dimension to Europe.' *British Journal of Industrial Relations 30*, 4, 605–21.

Rubery, J. (1996) 'Mainstreaming gender in labour market policy debates.' In L. Hantrais and S. Mangen (eds) *Cross-National Research Methods in the Social Sciences.* London: Pinter.

Rubery, J. and Fagan, C. (1993) *Bulletin on Women and Employment in the EU.* No.2. Brussels: CEC.

Sackmann, R. and Haüssermann, H. (1994) 'Do regions matter? Regional differences in female labour-market participation in Germany.' *Environment and Planning 26*, 9, 1377–1418.

Sainsbury, D. (ed) (1994) *Gendering Welfare States.* London: Sage.

Sassen, S. (1991) *The Global City.* Princeton: Princeton University Press.

Sassen-Koob, S. (1984) 'The new labor demand in global cities.' In M.P. Smith (ed) *Cities in Transformation.* Beverley Hills: Sage.

Sassen-Koob, S. (1989) 'New York City's informal economy.' In A. Portes, M. Castells and L. Benton (eds) *The Informal Economy: Studies in Advanced and Less Developed Countries.* Baltimore: Johns Hopkins University Press.

Sassen, S. (1991) *The Global City: New York, London, Tokyo.* Princeton: Princeton University Press.

Save The Children/Glasgow Caledonian University (1995) *Child and Family Poverty in Scotland.* Glasgow: Save The Children.

Savitch, H.V. (1988) *Post Industrial Cities.* Princeton: Princeton University Press.

Sawyer, M. (1992) 'Unemployment and the dismal science.' Inaugural lecture, University of Leeds, mimeo.

Schmitt, J. (1995) 'The changing structure of male earnings in Britain, 1974–88.' In R. Freeman and L. Katz (eds) *Changes and Differences in Wage Structures.* Chicago: University of Chicago Press.

Schmitt, J. and Wadsworth, J. (1994a) *Why are 2 Million Men Inactive? The Decline in Male Labour Force Participation Rates in Britain.* Working Paper No. 338. London: Centre for Economic Performance.

Schmitt, J. and Wadsworth, J. (1994b) 'The rise in economic inactivity.' In A. Glyn and D. Miliband (eds) *Paying for Inequality: The Economic Cost of Social Injustice.* London: IPPR/Rivers Oram Press.

Schumpeter, J.A. (1943) *Capitalism, Socialism and Democracy.* London: Unwin University Books.

Scottish Office (1988) *New Life For Urban Scotland.* Edinburgh: Scottish Office.

Shackle, G.L.S. (1972) *Epistemics and Economics: A Critique of Economic Doctrines.* Cambridge: Cambridge University Press.

Sharpe, W. and Wallock, L. (1989) 'Tales of two cities: gentrification and displacement in contemporary New York.' In M.B. Campbell and M. Rollins (eds) *Begetting Images.* New York: Peter Lang.

Sheffield City Council (1993a) *Sheffield Economic Bulletin: Issue No. 4.* Sheffield: Department of Employment and Economic Development, Sheffield City Council.

Sheffield City Council (1993b) *Poverty and the Poor in Sheffield, 1993: Review of the Areas of Poverty.* Sheffield: Directorate of Planning and Economic Development, Sheffield City Council.

Silver, H. (1993) 'National conceptions of the new urban poverty: social structural change in Britain, France and the United States.' *International Journal of Urban and Regional Research 17*, 3, 336–353.

Simkin, C. and Hillage, J. (1992) *Family-Friendly Working: New Hope or Old Hype?* IMS Report 224. Brighton: IMS.

Sly, F. (1994) 'A comparison of the results from the 1991 Labour Force Survey and Census of Population.' *Employment Gazette 102*, 87–96.

Smith, A. (1776, 1904) *An Inquiry into the Nature and Causes of the Wealth of Nations.* E. Cannon (ed). London: Methuen.

Smith, J. (1979) 'The distribution of family earnings.' *Journal of Political Economy 87*, Supplement, S163–S193.

Smith, S. (1986) *Britain's Shadow Economy.* Oxford: Clarendon.

Sorrentino, C. (1993) 'International comparisons of unemployment indicators.' *Monthly Labor Review* March, 3–24.

Stafford, B. (1990) *Development of the York Economy to 2000: A Revised Projection.* York: Department of Economics and Related Studies, University of York.

Stedman-Jones, G. (1971) *Outcast London.* London: Penguin Books.

Strathclyde Regional Council (1993) *Poverty in Strathclyde: Key Facts.* Glasgow: Strathclyde Regional Council.

Strathclyde Regional Council (1994a) *The Social Strategy for the Nineties.* Glasgow: Strathclyde Regional Council.

Strathclyde Regional Council (1994b) *The Social Strategy for the Nineties: Priority Areas.* Glasgow: Strathclyde Regional Council.

Strathclyde Regional Council (1995) *Strathclyde Social Trends, No 4.* Glasgow: Strathclyde Regional Council.

Stratigaki, M. and Vaiou, D. (1994) 'Women's work and informal activities in Southern Europe.' *Environment and Planning A 26*, 8, 1221–1234.

Symes, V. (1995) *Unemployment in Europe: Problems and Policies.* London: Routledge.

Tarantelli, E. (1986) 'The regulation of inflation and unemployment.' *Industrial Relations 25*, 1, 1–15.

Taylor, D. (1989) *Creative Counting.* London: Unemployment Unit.

Terhorst, P. and Van de Ven, J. (1985) 'Zwarte persoonlijke dienstverlening en het stedelijk milieu' (*Black Personal Services and the Urban Environment*). Amsterdam: Social Geografisch Instituut.

Tievant, S. (1982) 'Vivre autrement: echanges et sociabilite en ville nouvell.' *Cahiers de l'OCS*, vol 6. Paris: CNRS.

Tomaney, J. (1994) 'Regional and industrial aspects of unemployment in Europe.' In J. Michie and J. Grieve Smith (eds) *Unemployment in Europe*. London: Academic Press.

Topel, R. (1986) 'Local labour markets.' *Journal of Political Economy 94*, 3, S111–S143.

Townroe, P. and Dabinett, G. (1993) 'Compounding confusion over coal: a reaction to the White Paper.' *Regional Studies 27*, 8, 827–834.

Townsend, P. (1979) *Poverty in the United Kingdom*. Harmondsworth: Penguin.

Ungerson, C. (1996) 'Qualitative methods.' In L. Hantrais and S. Mangen (eds) *Cross-National Research Methods in the Social Sciences*. London: Pinter.

Van Kempen, E.T. (1994) 'The dual city and the poor: social polarisation, social segregation and life chances.' *Urban Studies 31*, 7, 995–1015.

Veblen, T. (1978) 'The natural right of investment.' In C.B. Macpherson (ed) *Property, Mainstream and Critical Positions*. Oxford: Basil Blackwell.

Verhaar, C.H.A., de Klaver, P.M., de Goede, M.P.M., Van Ophem, J.A.C. and de Vires, A. (eds) (1996) *On the Challenges of Unemployment in a Regional Europe*. Aldershot: Avebury.

Vinay, P. (1985) 'Family life cycle and the informal economy.' *International Journal of Urban and Regional Research 9*, 1, 82–98.

Wadsworth, J. (1995) *The Making of the British Underclass. Aggregate Demand and the Declining Economic Performance of Low Skilled Workers*. Working Paper No. 425. London: Centre for Economic Performance.

Walby, S. (1984) 'Spatial variations in women's employment and unemployment.' In The Lancaster Regionalism Group (ed) *Localities, Class and Gender*. London: Pion.

Walby, S. (1990) *Theorizing Patriarchy*. Oxford: Blackwell.

Walby, S. (1994) 'Methodological and theoretical issues in the comparative analysis of gender relations in Western Europe'. *Environment and Planning A 26*, 9, 1339–1354.

Walker, A. (1990) 'Blaming the victims.' In C. Murray (ed) *The Emerging British Underclass*. London: IEA.

Warde, A. (1990) 'Household work strategies and forms of labour conceptual and empirical issues.' *Work, Employment and Society 4*, 4, 495–515.

Warren, M.R. (1994) 'Exploitation or cooperation? The political basis of regional variation in the Italian informal economy.' *Politics and Society 22*, 1, 89–115.

Weber, F. (1989) *Le travail a cote: etude d'ethnographie ouvriere*. Paris: Institut natinal de la recherche agronomique.

Wells, J. (1995) 'The missing million.' In K. Coates (ed) *The Right to Work*, pp.7–28. Nottingham: Spokesman.

Wenig, A. (1990) 'The shadow economy in the Federal Repulic of Germany.' In *Underground Economy and Irregular Forms of Employment*. Final Synthesis Report. Brussels: Office for Official Publications of the European Communities.

White, M. (1983) 'The measurement of spatial segregation.' *American Journal of Sociology 88*, 1008–1018.

White, M. and Lakey, J. (1992) *The Restart Effect*. London: Policy Studies Institute.

Whitehouse, G. (1992) 'Legislation and labour market gender inequality: an analysis of OECD countries.' *Work, Employment and Society 6*, 1, 6586.

Williams, C.C. and Windebank, J. (1993) 'Social and spatial inequalities in informal economic activity: some evidence from the European community.' *Area 25*, 4, 358–364.

Williams, C.C. and Windebank, J. (1995) 'Black market work in the European community: peripheral work for peripheral areas.' *International Journal of Urban and Regional Research 19*, 1, 23–39.

Wilson, W.J. (1987) *The Truly Disadvantaged: The Inner City, the Underclass and Public Policy.* Chicago, IL: University of Chicago Press.

Winchester, H.P.M. and White, P.E. (1988) 'The location of marginalised groups in the inner city.' *Environment and Planning D: Society and Space 6*, 37–54.

Witt, S. (1990) *When the Pit Closes.* Barnsley: Coalfield Communities Campaign.

Wong, D.W.S. (1993) 'Spatial indices of segregation.' *Urban Studies 30*, 559–572.

Wood, A. (1994) *North–South Trade, Employment and Inequality.* Oxford: Clarendon.

Woods, N. (1995) 'Powerhouse gears up.' *The Scotsman*, 27 February, p.29.

Woolford, C. and Denman, J. (1993) 'Measures of unemployment: the claimant count and the LFS compared.' *Employment Gazette 101*, 455–464.

York City Council (1990) *Housing Annual Service Monitor.* York: City of York Housing Services.

York City Council (1995) *The York Data File.* York: Area Economic Development Unit, York City Council.

The Contributors

Christina Beatty, Centre for Regional Economic and Social Research, Sheffield Hallam University.

Mike Danson, Department of Accounting, Economics and Languages, University of Paisley.

Stephen Fothergill, Centre for Regional Economic and Social Research, Sheffield Hallam University.

Anne E. Green, Institute of Employment Research, University of Warwick.

Paul Gregg, Centre for Economic Performance, London School of Economics.

Sally Hardy is Director of the Regional Studies Association.

Susan Harkness, Centre for Economic Performance, London School of Economics.

Paul Lawless is Professor of Urban and Regional Studies at Sheffield Hallam University and Director of its Centre for Regional, Economic and Social Research.

Stephen Machin, Centre for Economic Performance, London School of Economics.

R. Ross MacKay, School of Accounting, Banking and Economics, University of Wales, Bangor.

Ron Martin is the Director of the Graduate School of Geography and a lecturer in Economic Geography at the University of Cambridge, and Fellow of St. Catharine's College, Cambridge.

Gerry Mooney, Department of Applied Social Studies, University of Paisley.

Diane Perrons, Department of Geography, London School of Economics.

Yvonne Smith, Centre for Regional Economic and Social Research, Sheffield Hallam University.

Jonathan Wadsworth, Centre for Economic Performance, London School of Economics.

Jane Waldfogel, School of Social Work, Columbia University, New York.

Colin C. Williams, Senior Lecturer in Economic Geography, Department of Geography, University of Leicester.

Jan Windebank, Department of French, University of Sheffield.

Subject Index

*References in italic indicate figures
or tables*

9 780117 023758

For Product Safety Concerns and Information please contact our EU representative GPSR@taylorandfrancis.com Taylor & Francis Verlag GmbH, Kaufingerstraße 24, 80331 München, Germany

Printed and bound by CPI Group (UK) Ltd, Croydon, CR0 4YY

08/05/2025

01864452-0001